API Design

3 in 1 - "From Beginner to Pro:
Advanced Techniques and
Strategies for Modern API
Development"

Kevin Bates

Table of Contents

BOOK 1 - API Design:*"A Beginner's Guide to Understanding, Building, and Using APIs "*

Introduction 9

Chapter One: The Basics of APIs............................18

Chapter Two: Design Principles for APIs.................29

Chapter Three: Setting Up Your API Development Environment..39

Chapter Four: Building Your First API 46

Chapter Five: Authentication and Authorization 59

Chapter Six: Documentation and User Support.......72

Chapter Seven: API Consumption 84

Chapter Eight: Debugging and Troubleshooting APIs 96

Chapter Nine: Advanced Features in API Design ...109

Chapter Ten: Testing APIs.....................................121

Chapter Eleven: Deploying APIs 134

Chapter Twelve: Consuming Third-Party APIs 148

Chapter Thirteen: Case Studies 159

Conclusion **168**

BOOK 2 - API Design: *"A Middle-Level Guide to Customizing APIs for Scalability and Efficiency"*

Introduction 183

Chapter One: Design Patterns for Scalable APIs 194

Chapter Two: Enhancing API Performance 202

Chapter Three: Security at Scale........................... 210

Chapter Four: Efficient Data Management 218

Chapter Five: Rate Limiting and Throttling 226

Chapter Six: API Gateway Optimization 234

Chapter Seven: Load Balancing Techniques 242

Chapter Eight: Asynchronous APIs and Event-Driven Design 251

Chapter Nine: API Caching Strategies 258

Chapter Ten: Versioning for Continuous Improvement 265

Chapter Eleven: Advanced Testing for Robust APIs 273

Chapter Twelve: Deployment Strategies for High Availability 281

Chapter Thirteen: Monitoring and Analytics 291

Chapter Fourteen: Case Studies of Scalable API Implementations.. 299

Conclusion **308**

BOOK 3 - QA Testing Book:*"A Pro-Level Guide to Advanced Risk Management and Quality Strategies"*

Introduction 320

Chapter One: Advanced Architectural Patterns 331

Chapter Two: Domain-Driven Design (DDD) in APIs 339

Chapter Three: System Modularity and Decomposition......................................347

Chapter Four: Optimizing Data Architecture for APIs 355

Chapter Five: Advanced Security Practices............363

Chapter Six: Fault Tolerance and Resilience..........372

Chapter Seven: Scalable API Gateway Architectures 380

Chapter Eight: State Management in Distributed Systems..388

Chapter Nine: API Composition and Aggregation ..396

Chapter Ten: Real-time Data Handling................. 404

Chapter Eleven: Advanced Versioning Techniques.412

Chapter Twelve: Performance Optimization and Caching 420

Chapter Thirteen: Advanced Deployment Patterns 428

Chapter Fourteen: Monitoring, Logging, and Telemetry..436

Chapter Fifteen: Case Studies and Lessons Learned 446

Conclusion 454

Introduction

Purpose of the Book: Introduce the objective and the target audience of the book

"API Design: A Beginner's Guide to Understanding, Building, and Using APIs" serves as a foundational resource for those new to API development, equipping them with the essential skills to construct scalable, effective, and secure digital solutions. Targeted at novices, this guide systematically unfolds the core concepts and methodologies necessary for mastering API development, providing a well-rounded introduction that transitions readers from beginners to adept practitioners.

In today's technological landscape, APIs are indispensable in software development, enhancing system interactions and enabling shared functionalities in a streamlined manner. These tools are essential for facilitating communication and data exchange between applications, making understanding their design, implementation, and maintenance critical. This book caters to aspiring developers, IT students, early-career software engineers, and tech professionals from other fields who are eager to understand API dynamics and applications.

The narrative begins with an introduction to basic API types such as REST, SOAP, and GraphQL. Each type is thoroughly examined, detailing its structure, benefits, and typical applications, complemented by practical examples that reinforce the use of each API type in real-world scenarios. For example, the book guides readers through establishing a REST API using Python and Flask, illustrated by straightforward code snippets:

```python
# Importing Flask module
from flask import Flask, jsonify

# Creating a new Flask application
app = Flask(__name__)

# Defining a route for a GET request
@app.route('/api/data', methods=['GET'])
def get_data():
    # Sample data returned as JSON
    return jsonify({'name': 'Example', 'type': 'REST API'})
```

```python
# Running the Flask application
if __name__ == '__main__':
    app.run(debug=True)
```

This initial foray into API development showcases how simple setups can effectively return JSON data. As readers progress, they encounter more intricate aspects such as API authentication, version management, and the utilization of third-party APIs.

Significant focus is placed on the best practices in API design. The guide emphasizes the importance of a consistent design ethos to ensure APIs are durable and functional. Extensive discussions on managing requests and responses, error handling, and advanced security measures are included. Techniques such as OAuth 2.0 and JWT (JSON Web Tokens) are covered in depth to enhance security in API communications.

Documentation and user support are also key topics addressed in the book. Effective documentation is vital for making APIs accessible and understandable. The use of tools like Swagger or OpenAPI for creating interactive, maintainable documentation is recommended.

Testing and debugging APIs form another crucial chapter, introducing tools and frameworks that help ensure APIs operate correctly under various conditions. Automated testing platforms such as Postman for endpoint testing and PyTest for extensive testing are introduced:

```python
# Sample PyTest code to test an API endpoint
import requests

def test_api_endpoint():
    response = requests.get('http://localhost:5000/api/data')
    assert response.status_code == 200
    assert response.json() == {'name': 'Example', 'type': 'REST API'}
```

Towards the end of the book, the discussion extends to more sophisticated topics appropriate for beginners, including API integration with different software layers, managing CORS, and exploring asynchronous API communications. These sections expand the reader's understanding of how APIs are integrated within larger software projects and their interaction with various system components.

Ultimately, this guide is designed not only to instruct but also to motivate readers to further explore the field of API development. It provides the tools and insights necessary to comprehend, utilize, and innovate with APIs, preparing readers for advanced studies or professional endeavors in the tech industry, thus cultivating a diverse and valuable skill set.

11

What is an API? Basic definitions and significance in modern software development

An Application Programming Interface, or API, serves as a blueprint and communication protocol for building software applications. It specifies the methods and data formats that developers should employ when constructing software components that interact with one another. APIs function as conduits allowing disparate programs to exchange data and functionalities seamlessly, serving as the unseen framework supporting the smooth operation of our digital devices and services.

The value of APIs in the realm of contemporary software development has grown significantly with the increasing demand for innovative applications that need to operate across varied platforms and environments seamlessly. APIs are instrumental in facilitating this level of interoperability, which is essential for the functionality and adaptability of modern software solutions.

The core advantage of using APIs lies in their ability to promote reusable application functionalities that can be employed across different parts of a single application or even among various applications. This reusability accelerates development workflows, enhances consistency across services, and improves overall efficiency. For example, rather than building every function from scratch, developers can leverage APIs for common tasks like sending emails, processing payments, or integrating social media features, streamlining the development process significantly.

APIs are categorized into several types, including web APIs, operating system APIs, database APIs, and remote APIs, each serving distinct roles. Web APIs, for instance, are crucial for linking web-based applications with server-side functions, facilitating the server's ability to process client-side actions and return appropriate responses. These interactions are typically managed through standard protocols like HTTP and formats such as JSON to ensure that the data exchanged is universally understandable and manageable.

To illustrate, here is a basic example of a web API implemented using Python with the Flask framework, demonstrating how an API facilitates data retrieval:

```python
from flask import Flask, jsonify

app = Flask(__name__)

@app.route('/api/users', methods=['GET'])
def get_users():
    # Placeholder for database query
    users = [{"id": 1, "name": "John"}, {"id": 2, "name": "Jane"}]
    return jsonify(users)

if __name__ == '__main__':
    app.run(debug=True)
```

This code creates an API endpoint that handles HTTP GET requests at the URL path **/api/users**, returning a JSON array of user data. This type of API is fundamental for backend development, linking the frontend of an application with the backend systems that manage the data.

Beyond facilitating application connectivity, APIs are vital for enabling business expansion and strategic integrations with external platforms. They allow businesses to extend their

13

functionalities and reach wider markets by enabling integrations with external platforms and devices. For example, by using platform-specific APIs, mobile app developers can access device-specific features like GPS and cameras, thereby enriching the app's functionality without needing direct control over the platform's core code.

APIs also play a crucial role in nurturing ecosystems of innovation. By exposing certain functionalities through APIs, companies empower external developers to build applications that enhance or complement their services. This not only broadens the capabilities of the original platform but also opens up new avenues for third-party innovation and value creation.

In today's digital economy, APIs act as the essential "glue" that integrates diverse software applications and services, enabling them to interact and share data securely and efficiently. This interoperability is vital for crafting enriched user experiences and driving digital transformation efforts that keep businesses competitive.

In summary, APIs are a strategic component in software development, embodying essential principles such as modularity, scalability, and flexibility, essential for building adaptable systems. As the digital landscape evolves, the importance of APIs in crafting advanced, responsive software architectures continues to increase, making them a cornerstone of modern development practices.

Overview of the Book Structure: Brief overview of what each chapter will cover

"API Design: A Beginner's Guide to Understanding, Building, and Using APIs" meticulously constructs a pathway for novices entering the world of API development, layering information from basic concepts to more sophisticated practices. This book is deliberately structured to provide a progressive learning curve in API mastery, blending foundational knowledge with practical applications to ensure a thorough understanding of each element involved in API design and deployment.

The book begins by setting the stage with an introduction to APIs, explaining their role and significance in modern software development. This section helps clarify the fundamental purpose of APIs and how they facilitate interactions between different software platforms and applications, enabling systems to efficiently share functionalities and data.

Following the introductory groundwork, the book ventures into the principles of API design. In this chapter, readers gain insights into designing APIs that are user-friendly and robust, ensuring longevity and scalability. Essential topics covered include endpoint naming conventions, the handling of errors, and the best practices in employing HTTP methods. This provides a clear guide for beginners on how to create intuitive and durable APIs.

Moving forward, the book discusses the technical setup necessary for API development. It guides through the selection of appropriate development tools and environments, giving practical advice on utilizing integrated development environments (IDEs), version control systems, and API documentation tools like Postman and Swagger. This chapter is supplemented with step-by-step instructions and examples, helping readers configure their first API projects effectively.

The narrative then transitions to hands-on coding, where the readers are walked through the construction of a basic API, starting with simple functions and progressively integrating more complex features such as authentication and data management.

Example code might look like this:

```python
from flask import Flask, request, jsonify

app = Flask(__name__)

@app.route('/api/items', methods=['POST'])
def add_item():
    item = request.get_json()
    # Instructions for saving the item
    return jsonify(item), 201

if __name__ == '__main__':
    app.run(debug=True)
```

This snippet demonstrates how to create a basic POST endpoint using Flask, offering a practical template for readers to develop their capabilities further.

The book also delves deep into API security, detailing necessary protocols, encryption practices, and secure coding guidelines. This chapter is critical as it covers how to safeguard data and ensure API interactions are protected, a vital aspect of software development in the digital age.

Documentation practices are extensively covered, emphasizing the importance of clear, thorough, and accessible API documentation. This section explores effective documentation techniques and tools that help maintain and manage API documentation, ensuring usability for both internal and external stakeholders.

Testing and debugging are addressed in subsequent chapters, outlining the essential tools and techniques for verifying that APIs function as expected. The discussion spans various testing approaches, including unit testing, integration testing, and scenario-based testing, illustrated with examples in popular frameworks.

As the book approaches its conclusion, it explores advanced topics like integrating third-party APIs, handling API dependencies, and strategies for effective API versioning and deprecation. These sections prepare readers to manage real-world challenges they may encounter as they advance in their development careers.

The final chapter serves as a comprehensive review of the concepts discussed throughout the book. It reinforces the material covered, offering additional resources and encouraging readers to continue their journey in API development.

Overall, "API Design: A Beginner's Guide to Understanding, Building, and Using APIs" offers a structured approach to learning API development, from basic principles to advanced practices. It equips beginners with the necessary tools and knowledge to start their journey in API design and prepares them for more complex challenges ahead.

Chapter One

The Basics of APIs

Understanding APIs: What APIs are and how they work

APIs, or Application Programming Interfaces, are vital in enabling seamless interactions between different software systems. They establish protocols and rules that allow diverse software components to communicate, functioning as intermediaries that facilitate essential operations across various applications, enhancing their interoperability and functionality.

Defining APIs

APIs act as conduits between applications and the web servers they interact with, simplifying complex processes by managing data transfers and user requests transparently. They empower applications to perform functions like sending and retrieving data without exposing the user to the underlying complex operations. For instance, when someone books a flight online, it's the API that transmits their details to the airline's booking system and retrieves the flight options without the user accessing the airline's database directly.

How APIs Operate

APIs function through a cycle known as the request-response model. A client (such as a web browser or a mobile app) sends a request to the API that specifies an operation to be performed. The API processes this request at the server level, carries out the necessary actions, and then delivers a response back to the client. This interchange typically uses HTTP (HyperText Transfer Protocol), with the data being formatted in either JSON (JavaScript Object Notation) or XML (eXtensible Markup Language) to ensure clarity and compatibility. Here's a straightforward example of an API in action:

```
# Defining the API endpoint
url = 'http://example.com/api/users/1234'

# Making a GET request to the API
response = requests.get(url)
```

```
# Example of the JSON response containing user information
{
    "id": 1234,
    "name": "John Doe",
    "email": "john.doe@example.com"
}
```

In this example, a client sends an HTTP GET request to retrieve information about a user. The API fetches the necessary data from the server and returns it formatted as JSON, illustrating a typical API interaction.

Types of APIs

Based on their access and use cases, APIs are categorized into:

- **Public APIs** which are open for wider developer use and may require simple registration or an API key.

- **Private APIs** which are used internally within organizations to improve operational efficiencies without external exposure.

- **Partner APIs** which are exposed to strategic business partners under specific terms, facilitating deeper technological integration and cooperation.

The Role of APIs in Modern Software Development

APIs are instrumental in several facets of software development:

- **Efficiency**: They automate routine tasks, allowing systems to function more effectively and with less manual intervention.

- **Integration**: APIs make it possible to introduce new features into existing applications seamlessly, enhancing their capabilities without substantial changes to the core system.

- **Modularity**: APIs help separate the frontend from the backend, which allows for independent updates and modifications without affecting other system components.

- **Scalability**: They enable systems to handle increasing volumes of requests and greater loads, facilitating growth and expansion.

APIs are foundational to digital infrastructure, bridging gaps between different technological platforms and extending system capabilities through third-party applications. As technologies evolve, APIs are continually adapted to support more complex services and drive forward digital strategies, proving their essential role in the ongoing evolution of software development.

Types of APIs: REST, SOAP, GraphQL, and more

Application Programming Interfaces (APIs) are pivotal in enabling different software applications to communicate effectively, serving as a bridge between disparate systems. The landscape of APIs includes various types tailored to different requirements and use cases. The most prevalent among these are REST, SOAP, and GraphQL, each offering unique features and operational advantages.

REST (Representational State Transfer)

REST is an architectural style that leverages standard HTTP methods, making it one of the most adopted types of APIs due to its straightforwardness, flexibility, and efficient performance. It operates using methods like GET, POST, PUT, DELETE, and PATCH.

REST APIs are designed to be stateless, meaning each request from a client contains all the information necessary to execute it without relying on stored context on the server. This statelessness helps REST services manage large volumes of requests from numerous clients efficiently.

Data within REST APIs is typically formatted in JSON or XML, providing versatility in how data is handled and presented. Here is an example of how a simple REST API call looks using Python's **requests** library:

```python
import requests

# Sending a GET request
response = requests.get('https://api.example.com/data')
data = response.json()  # Assuming the server responds with JSON-formatted data

print(data)
```

This snippet demonstrates fetching data from a RESTful service, where the API endpoint returns data in JSON format.

SOAP (Simple Object Access Protocol)

SOAP stands as a protocol, enforcing stricter standards in the data exchange process, primarily using XML for all communications. It can function over various transport protocols including HTTP and SMTP, and is noted for its high security and successful error handling capabilities.

SOAP is highly favored in enterprise environments where security and precise compliance with communication standards are mandatory. However, the verbose nature of SOAP messages often makes them heavier and potentially slower compared to REST. Below is an example of a typical SOAP message structure:

```xml
<soapenv:Envelope xmlns:soapenv="http://schemas.xmlsoap.org/soap/envelope/">
    <soapenv:Header/>
    <soapenv:Body>
        <m:GetInfo xmlns:m="http://www.example.org/stock">
            <m:ID>12345</m:ID>
        </m:GetInfo>
    </soapenv:Body>
</soapenv:Envelope>
```

This example illustrates a SOAP request enveloping the required data in a structured XML format.

GraphQL

Introduced by Facebook in 2015, GraphQL represents a modern approach to APIs by allowing clients to specify exactly what data they need. Unlike REST, where the server dictates the structure of the response, GraphQL queries enable requesting specific fields, thus minimizing the data transmitted and enhancing performance.

GraphQL operates through a single endpoint and provides considerable flexibility in querying data, as shown in the following query example:

```graphql
{
  user(id: "1") {
    name
    age
    email
  }
}
```

This query specifies that only the **name**, **age**, and **email** of a user with ID **1** should be returned, illustrating GraphQL's efficient data-fetching capabilities.

Additional API Styles

Besides REST, SOAP, and GraphQL, there are other noteworthy API styles:

- **gRPC**: Developed by Google, this style uses HTTP/2 and Protocol Buffers, offering a robust framework for inter-service communication, particularly useful in microservices architectures.

- **OData (Open Data Protocol)**: Enhances REST by focusing more on standardizing interactions with data objects.

Each type of API serves distinct purposes; REST is typically utilized for general web-based services, SOAP is ideal for enterprise applications requiring strict security measures, and GraphQL is best suited for applications where precise data fetching is necessary. The choice among these depends on the specific needs of the project, considering factors like scalability, security, and developer efficiency. As technologies evolve, the selection of an API style becomes a critical decision point in many development projects, balancing performance and functionality requirements.

Common Protocols and Standards: HTTP, HTTPS, JSON, XML

In our digitally-driven world, the effective and secure transmission of data is vital. This is facilitated by foundational protocols and standards such as HTTP, HTTPS, JSON, and XML, each playing an essential role in enabling smooth and secure interactions within software and across the internet. These protocols and data formats are critical for modern API communications and efficient data handling, serving as the cornerstone for interoperability and functionality in digital applications.

HTTP and HTTPS

HTTP (HyperText Transfer Protocol) is essential for the transmission of data on the internet, primarily used for loading web pages and associated resources. It operates on a client-server model, with the client (typically a web browser) sending requests to which the server responds. The protocol is designed to be stateless, meaning it doesn't retain any data between transactions, which aids in handling multiple simultaneous requests.

HTTPS (HyperText Transfer Protocol Secure) enhances HTTP by encrypting the transmitted data, thus providing an additional layer of security. This encryption is critical for sensitive interactions, such as personal information submissions or online transactions, ensuring that the data remains private and integral. Browsers indicate HTTPS connections with a padlock icon in the address bar, signaling a secure link.

Here's a basic example of making an HTTP GET request using Python's **requests** library:

```python
import requests

# Initiating an HTTP GET request to a server
response = requests.get('http://example.com')

# Displaying the HTTP response code from the server
print(response.status_code)
```

Changing 'http://' to 'https://' in the URL would signify a secure HTTPS request.

JSON and XML

JSON (JavaScript Object Notation) and XML (eXtensible Markup Language) are the principal formats for structuring and exchanging data between systems. Each format is both human-readable and machine-parseable, although they are utilized under different circumstances and feature different syntaxes.

JSON is streamlined and effective, making it a popular choice for web applications that require frequent server-client interactions. It structures data in key/value pairs or as arrays, which simplifies both reading and processing compared to more verbose formats. Here is an example of JSON:

```json
{
  "firstName": "Jane",
  "lastName": "Smith",
  "age": 25,
  "isEmployed": false,
  "address": {
    "street": "789 Pine St",
    "city": "Anywhere",
    "zipCode": "10112"
  }
}
```

XML, on the other hand, is often used for its capability to represent complex data structures and to be extensively used in systems where document markup and metadata are necessary. XML is more verbose than JSON and is typically used in environments where this complexity is required. For example:

```xml
<person>
  <firstName>Jane</firstName>
  <lastName>Smith</lastName>
  <age>25</age>
  <isEmployed>false</isEmployed>
  <address>
    <street>789 Pine St</street>
    <city>Anywhere</city>
    <zipCode>10112</zipCode>
  </address>
</person>
```

The Role of Protocols and Standards

These protocols and standards are indispensable in setting the framework for consistent and secure data exchange. HTTP and HTTPS dictate the way data is transmitted over the web, ensuring reliable communication, while JSON and XML provide robust and flexible structures for data representation.

27

As the technological landscape evolves, these components become ever more crucial in the design and implementation of scalable, secure, and efficient solutions, underpinning much of the functionality we rely on daily in the digital domain.

Chapter Two

Design Principles for APIs

API Design Best Practices: Consistency, naming conventions, error handling

Implementing best practices in API design is crucial for building interfaces that are not only robust and efficient but also intuitive and easy to manage. Such practices include maintaining design consistency, employing clear and meaningful naming conventions, and deploying effective error handling mechanisms. These elements are foundational in making APIs straightforward and dependable for developers to integrate and operate.

Consistency

Consistency in API design ensures that the API behaves predictably across its various components. This uniformity is critical for developers as it simplifies understanding and interaction with the API. For example, in RESTful API implementations, it is standard to consistently use HTTP methods: GET for data retrieval, POST for creating new entries, PUT for updates, and DELETE for deletions. The structure of endpoint paths should also follow a logical pattern, such as **/items** for accessing a list of items and **/items/{id}** for retrieving a specific item based on its ID.

Naming Conventions

The use of clear and intuitive naming conventions in API design enhances usability and readability. Properly named endpoints give developers a clear indication of what each part of the API does, reducing reliance on detailed documentation.

It is advisable to use nouns for resources (e.g., **/users**, **/orders**) and to reserve the use of HTTP methods to describe actions. When actions do not clearly map to CRUD (Create, Retrieve, Update, Delete) operations, descriptive verb phrases can be employed (e.g., **/submitOrder**). Collections should typically be referred to in plural form (e.g., **/users** for a list of users), and singular forms should be used for individual resource access (e.g., **/users/{id}** for details on a specific user), adhering to common RESTful architecture practices.

Error Handling

Effective error handling is essential for the durability and reliability of APIs. It ensures that when errors occur, they are communicated back to the client with informative messages and appropriate HTTP status codes, facilitating quick and effective troubleshooting.

Error handling within an API should consistently involve:

- Utilizing standard HTTP status codes such as **200 OK** for successful requests, **400 Bad Request** for client errors, **404 Not Found** for unavailable resources, and **500 Internal Server Error** for server failures.

- Providing detailed and actionable error messages that aid developers in understanding and resolving issues.

For instance, a well-structured error response might look like this:

```
{
    "status": 400,
    "error": "Bad Request",
    "message": "Parameter 'xyz' is missing or invalid."
}
```

This example clearly outlines the error with a standard HTTP status code and provides a specific message detailing the nature of the problem.

Implementing Best Practices

Effective implementation of these best practices in API design involves careful planning and attention to detail. Essential strategies include:

- **Documentation**: Ensuring that all aspects of the API are well-documented and that the documentation accurately reflects the designed best practices.

- **Versioning**: Implementing version control to manage updates and modifications, thus ensuring continuity and support for existing API users.

- **Testing**: Conducting thorough testing to ensure that the API functions correctly across all intended scenarios and that error handling is robust under various stress conditions.

By focusing on consistency, clarity in naming conventions, and comprehensive error handling, API designers can craft sophisticated, user-friendly interfaces. These practices not only improve the developer experience but also bolster the

API's reliability, contributing significantly to the effectiveness of the digital platforms they support.

Client-Server Interaction: Request and response models

Client-server interaction underpins the architecture of most modern networked applications, where tasks are distributed between service providers (servers) and service requesters (clients). This model is crucial for efficient communication across the web, allowing for a structured exchange of requests and responses that support a variety of online activities, from web browsing to complex data transactions.

Understanding Client-Server Interaction

In the client-server model, the client initiates contact by sending a request to the server—a system that manages and delivers services. This can happen over a network or within the same system. The server then processes this request, performs the necessary actions, and returns a response to the client. This response could be the requested data, an acknowledgment of receipt, or an error message if the request cannot be fulfilled.

Request and Response Model

The interaction starts when a client sends a request to the server using one of several methods defined by HTTP (HyperText Transfer Protocol), the standard protocol for web communication. The primary HTTP methods are:

- **GET**: Retrieves data from a server at the specified resource.

- **POST**: Sends data to a server to create a new resource.

- **PUT**: Updates existing data on a server.

- **DELETE**: Removes existing data from a server.

- **PATCH**: Makes partial updates to existing data on a server.

These methods help the server understand the desired action by the client. Depending on the operation's success or failure, the server sends back a status code as part of the response, which helps the client determine the next steps.

Common HTTP Status Codes

- **200 OK**: The request was successful, and the server's response contains the requested data.

- **404 Not Found**: The server can't find the requested resource, but it may be available in the future.

- **500 Internal Server Error**: The server encountered an unexpected condition that prevented it from fulfilling the request.

Example of a Simple Client-Server Interaction

Consider a basic scenario where a Python script uses the **requests** library to make an HTTP GET request:

```
import requests

# Specifying the URL for the request
url = 'http://api.example.com/data'

# Making the GET request
response = requests.get(url)

# Outputting the status code and any response data
print(f'Status Code: {response.status_code}')
print('Response Data:', response.json())
```

This example demonstrates how a client can request data from a server. The server processes this request and returns a status code along with any appropriate data.

Best Practices for Client-Server Interaction

1. **Statelessness**: HTTP is designed to be stateless, meaning each request from a client to server must contain all the information needed to understand and complete the request without relying on any stored context.

2. **Session Management**: To manage user sessions, especially in stateless HTTP communications, session identifiers are typically stored in cookies or are carried in each request and response.

3. **Secure Communication**: Ensuring data integrity and confidentiality is crucial, often achieved through HTTPS, which encrypts all transmitted data.

4. **Comprehensive Error Handling**: Implementing robust error handling and providing detailed yet secure error messages ensure that users and developers can understand and resolve issues efficiently.

In essence, the client-server model is a foundational framework in network computing, characterized by an exchange of requests and responses. Mastery of this model involves implementing secure, efficient, and stateless communications, underpinned by effective session and error management, which are vital for developing scalable and reliable networked applications.

Versioning Strategies: How to handle changes and upgrades in APIs

API versioning is an indispensable strategy for managing the natural evolution of software while safeguarding existing user interfaces from disruptions caused by updates and enhancements. Effective versioning ensures that APIs can accommodate new features and fixes without undermining their existing functionality.

The Significance of API Versioning

The process of versioning is key to maintaining stability for applications that depend on APIs, allowing for the seamless introduction of new capabilities and corrections. Without structured versioning, changes to APIs can lead to compatibility issues, potentially resulting in operational failures and negatively impacting user experiences and maintenance overhead.

Various API Versioning Techniques

Several methodologies exist for managing API versions, each offering different benefits depending on the specific requirements:

1. **URI Versioning**: This straightforward approach incorporates the version number directly within the API's URL path, such as **https://api.example.com/v1/** for the first version and **https://api.example.com/v2/** for the subsequent version. Although clear, this method can lead to an accumulation of URLs, which might complicate the API landscape.

2. **Parameter Versioning**: By appending a version query parameter to the API's endpoint, like **https://api.example.com/items?version=1**, this method maintains a consistent base URI. However, the version detail is less prominent as it's embedded within the query string.

3. **Header Versioning**: Placing the version information within HTTP request headers keeps the URL structure clean and utilizes the header fields for managing versions, for example through **Accept-Version: v1**.

4. **Media Type Versioning**: Also known as content negotiation, this advanced method specifies versions within the HTTP Accept header, such as **Accept: application/vnd.example.v1+json**. This approach aligns closely with HTTP specifications and allows detailed control but requires clients to be proficient with HTTP header configurations.

Best Practices in API Versioning

- **Documentation Clarity**: Maintaining comprehensive documentation for each API version is crucial, helping users understand their options, the changes in each version, and how to transition between versions.

- **Smooth Deprecation**: When older versions are retired, users should be given plenty of notice, alongside detailed migration instructions and sufficient time to adjust their applications.

- **Semantic Versioning**: Adopting a versioning scheme that reflects the nature of changes—major versions for significant changes, minor versions for backward-compatible improvements, and patches for minor bug fixes—helps users manage updates more predictively.

Example Implementation of API Versioning

Consider a Flask API designed to serve both plain text and JSON outputs, depending on the version specified:

```python
from flask import Flask, request, jsonify, Response

app = Flask(__name__)

@app.route('/api/data')
def get_data():
    # Fetching the version from headers
    api_version = request.headers.get('Accept-Version')

    data = {"message": "Hello, world!"}

    if api_version == 'v2':
        # Version 2 users receive JSON
        return jsonify(data)
```

```
    else:
        # Version 1 users receive plain text
        return Response(data['message'], mimetype='text/plain')

if __name__ == '__main__':
    app.run()
```

This code snippet showcases how different response formats can be effectively managed under different API versions, facilitating backward compatibility and accommodating new functionalities.

Conclusion

API versioning is a critical component of modern software development, enabling APIs to evolve in response to new requirements and technological advancements without disrupting existing services. By selecting an appropriate versioning strategy and adhering to best practices, developers can ensure that their APIs remain both functional and forward-compatible, supporting a broad range of users and applications.

Chapter Three

Setting Up Your API Development Environment

Tools and Technologies: Overview of necessary tools (e.g., Postman, Swagger)

In API development, the choice of tools is crucial for ensuring that efficiency, functionality, and scalability are maintained throughout an API's lifecycle. From initial design and documentation to testing and ongoing monitoring, the correct tools can substantially elevate the development process. This overview highlights essential tools such as Postman and Swagger, which are foundational in the industry for robust API management.

Postman

Postman stands out as a favorite among developers for API testing and development tasks. It enables the easy construction, testing, documentation, and sharing of APIs within a user-friendly interface. Postman supports various HTTP methods crucial for RESTful API testing, including GET, POST, PUT, and DELETE, allowing developers to send requests and analyze responses efficiently.

A notable feature of Postman is its ability to save requests in collections that can be reused and shared across teams, enhancing collaboration. It also accommodates multiple environments, such as development and production, enabling developers to switch contexts effortlessly without altering request parameters.

Practical Usage of Postman:

Developers can leverage Postman to quickly test API endpoints by specifying the URL, selecting the method, and executing the request. The immediate response from Postman facilitates quick debugging and validation of API behavior.

Swagger (OpenAPI)

Swagger, synonymous with the OpenAPI Specification, focuses on API design and documentation. It offers a comprehensive framework for detailing APIs in a format that is interpretable by both humans and machines, streamlining the process of understanding an API without direct access to its source code.

Swagger includes several key tools:

- **Swagger Editor**: This browser-based editor is used for writing and validating OpenAPI specifications.

- **Swagger UI**: It dynamically generates beautiful, interactive API documentation that allows users to visualize and interact with the API's endpoints without any implementation.

- **Swagger Codegen**: Generates server stubs, client libraries, and API documentation directly from an OpenAPI Specification, facilitating consistent and streamlined builds.

Swagger enhances API visibility and simplifies integration, making it easier for developers to understand, interact with, and test APIs. It also supports automated testing by ensuring that the actual API conforms to its documented specifications.

Swagger UI Example:

Swagger UI enables interactive documentation, where developers can make real API calls in the browser. This tool is invaluable for real-time feedback during the API development phase and helps new users integrate with the API more effectively.

Choosing the Right Tools

When selecting tools for API development and management, important considerations include:

- **Integration Capabilities**: The tool should integrate well with existing systems and workflows, such as Postman's ability to interface seamlessly across various development stages.

- **Ease of Use**: Tools should be intuitive, enabling quick onboarding and usability without extensive training.

- **Collaboration Features**: Tools should facilitate easy sharing and management of API resources, especially in team settings.

- **Automation Support**: Automation features are essential for integrating with continuous integration/continuous delivery (CI/CD) pipelines.

- **Community and Support**: A strong user community and good support channels are invaluable for troubleshooting and enhancing developer skills.

Conclusion

Tools like Postman and Swagger are integral to the API development ecosystem, helping to design, test, document, and manage APIs more effectively. By utilizing these tools, developers can ensure that their APIs are not only functional but also scalable and maintainable. Proper tool selection can lead to significant improvements in API lifecycle management, enhancing the overall quality and reliability of the end products.

Setting Up a Basic Development Environment: Step-by-step setup guide

Establishing a basic development environment is essential for any software development project, as it provides developers with the necessary tools and infrastructure to efficiently code, test, and deploy their applications. This guide outlines a step-by-step process for setting up a straightforward yet functional development environment, with a focus on web development.

1. Select an Operating System

The foundational step in creating a development environment is choosing an operating system (OS). Popular options include Windows, macOS, and various Linux distributions. The choice may depend on personal preferences, project-specific requirements, or compatibility with essential development tools. Linux and macOS are often favored in web development for their strong command-line utilities and broad support for numerous programming languages and databases.

2. Install a Code Editor or IDE

A good code editor or Integrated Development Environment (IDE) is crucial. Lightweight text editors like Visual Studio Code (VS Code), Sublime Text, or Atom are suitable for those who appreciate simplicity and support for multiple languages through extensive plugins.

For more complex projects or specific languages like Java or C#, robust IDEs such as IntelliJ IDEA, Eclipse, or Visual Studio offer advanced features like integrated debugging, code suggestions, and built-in build tools.

Installing Visual Studio Code:

- **Windows and macOS**: Download from the Visual Studio Code website and follow the setup guide.

- **Linux**: Install via your distribution's package manager (e.g., for Ubuntu: **sudo apt install code**).

3. Implement Version Control

Effective version control is indispensable for tracking code changes, collaborating on projects, and maintaining historical versions. Git is the most commonly used system. Download and install Git from its official site, and set it up on your machine.

Configuring Git:

```
git config --global user.name "Your Name"
git config --global user.email "your.email@example.com"
```

Start a new repository or clone an existing one to manage your project effectively using Git. For collaborative projects, consider using services like GitHub, GitLab, or Bitbucket, which offer hosted repositories and additional collaboration features.

4. Install Required Languages and Frameworks

Identify and install the programming languages and frameworks that your projects will require. For web development, this typically includes:

- **HTML/CSS/JavaScript**: Fundamental web technologies that need no installation but might require frameworks like React or Angular.

- **Backend languages**: Such as Python, Ruby, Node.js, or PHP. For instance, to install Node.js and npm, download from Node.js's official website.

Installing Node.js on Ubuntu:

```
curl -fsSL https://deb.nodesource.com/setup_current.x | sudo -E bash -
sudo apt-get install -y nodejs
```

5. Set Up a Database

For applications needing data storage, configure a suitable database:

- **SQL databases**: Like PostgreSQL, MySQL, or SQLite.

44

- **NoSQL databases**: Such as MongoDB or Cassandra.

Installing PostgreSQL on Ubuntu:

```
sudo apt update
sudo apt install postgresql postgresql-contrib
```

Ensure the database server is configured to start with the system and set up a new database and user specifically for your projects.

6. Install Supplementary Tools and Utilities

Depending on the project's needs, you might also require additional tools like Docker for containerization, Postman for API testing, or version managers like nvm (Node Version Manager) or pyenv for Python.

7. Verify Your Environment

After installation, test your environment by creating a basic project, such as a "Hello, World!" program, to ensure that all components—IDE, version control, languages, and tools—are functioning correctly.

Conclusion

Setting up a development environment is a critical first step that directly impacts the productivity and success of your projects. By carefully choosing and configuring your tools and technologies, you can create a dynamic, efficient, and supportive workspace that caters to the demands of your development tasks.

Chapter Four

Building Your First API

Planning Your API: Defining goals and functionalities

Launching an Application Programming Interface (API) starts with rigorous planning, crucial to ensuring the API fulfills its intended purposes and is equipped for future growth and integration. This involves setting precise goals and defining functionalities that act as a roadmap for all following stages of development, deployment, and upkeep.

Clarifying the API's Objectives

Initially, determine the primary goal of the API. Consider what specific issues it aims to resolve and how it will enhance or integrate with existing systems. The API's objectives should align with broader business goals to ensure relevance and focus, helping to define its scope and prevent extraneous features that could complicate its use.

For example, an API built for internal purposes, such as facilitating communication between internal data systems and a CRM system, will differ in structure from one intended for external use, where user-friendliness and ease of integration are paramount.

Recognizing the Intended Users

Identifying who will use your API is essential for tailoring its design, documentation, and support. Whether they are internal developers, partners, or external third-party developers influences the API's complexity and the comprehensiveness of the documentation required. An API intended for a broader external audience should include detailed documentation and robust support to ensure it is accessible and adaptable.

Outlining Essential Functionalities

After pinpointing the API's purpose and audience, it's important to list the functionalities it must provide. Separate these into:

- **Core Functionalities**: The indispensable operations your API must facilitate. For instance, in an e-commerce API, these would include processing payments, managing shopping carts, and conducting transactions.

- **Supplementary Functionalities**: Additional features that enhance the user experience but are not crucial for the API's basic operations, such as product reviews or personalized recommendations.

Data Flow Design

Mapping how data will be managed within the API is crucial. Define how data will be inputted, how it will be processed, and what outputs will be generated. For APIs that involve data retrieval, detail the methods for accessing, filtering, and returning data, ensuring the process is streamlined and secure.

Security Planning

Security is a critical aspect of API design, particularly when sensitive data is handled. In the planning stage, recognize potential security vulnerabilities and how they will be addressed. Implementing security measures such as authentication protocols, encryption, and rate limiting is necessary to safeguard the API from potential threats.

Versioning Considerations

Considering how the API will evolve over time is vital. Implementing a versioning strategy, such as semantic versioning, helps manage updates without disrupting existing implementations, ensuring the API remains compatible with older versions.

Prototyping for Feedback

Developing a prototype allows actual users to test the API's functionalities and provide feedback, which can be invaluable for refining the API's final design to better meet user needs.

Documenting the API

Creating thorough, accessible documentation is critical for a successful API. This should include technical specifications, setup guides, usage examples, and troubleshooting information to assist developers in integrating and using the API effectively.

Illustrative API Function Example

For a booking system, consider a function like this:

```
/**
 * Schedules an appointment for a user.
 * @param {string} userId - The unique identifier for the user.
 * @param {string} appointmentId - The identifier for the appointment slot.
 * @returns {object} - Details of the scheduled appointment, including confirmation.
 */

function scheduleAppointment(userId, appointmentId) {
    // Implementation code here
}
```

This example demonstrates a function that directly supports a primary operation of scheduling within a system and could serve as a part of the API documentation.

Conclusion

Meticulous planning is imperative when developing an API. By systematically defining the API's purpose, target audience, key functionalities, and data handling processes, and by considering security, versioning, and documentation from the outset, you establish a robust foundation. This ensures the API not only meets its initial objectives but is also prepared for future expansion and integration, enhancing its long-term viability and success.

Implementing CRUD Operations: Creating a simple API with Create, Read, Update, Delete operations

Implementing CRUD (Create, Read, Update, Delete) operations is essential for any application that requires data manipulation capabilities, providing fundamental methods to interact with database records. This article will guide you through developing a basic RESTful API that includes these operations using Node.js and the Express framework, demonstrating a practical approach to managing data in web applications.

Foundations of CRUD Operations

CRUD operations are the backbone of data management within many applications, allowing them to perform critical tasks involving data. Each operation corresponds to typical HTTP methods:

- **Create**: Introduces new data into your database, typically through HTTP POST.

- **Read**: Retrieves information, using HTTP GET.

- **Update**: Modifies existing information via HTTP PUT or PATCH.

- **Delete**: Eliminates existing information using HTTP DELETE.

Initializing the Development Setup

Begin by ensuring Node.js and npm (Node Package Manager) are installed in your development environment. Confirm their installations by executing **node -v** and **npm -v** in your terminal to check their versions.

Starting a Node.js Project

Create a directory for your project and initialize it with Node.js:

```
mkdir simple-crud-api
cd simple-crud-api
npm init -y  # Automatically creates a package.json file
```

Installing Required Libraries

Install Express, which is a streamlined and flexible Node.js web application framework that simplifies the API development process:

```
npm install express
```

For this tutorial, data operations will be simulated using an in-memory array, avoiding the complexity of a real database setup.

Crafting the API

Set up your basic server by creating a file named **app.js** and configuring Express:

```
const express = require('express');
const app = express();

app.use(express.json()); // Enables JSON body parsing

const port = process.env.PORT || 3000;
app.listen(port, () => console.log(`Listening on port ${port}`));
```

Structuring Data

Define a rudimentary data model using an array of objects to represent your data storage:

```
let items = [
    { id: 1, name: 'Item 1' },
    { id: 2, name: 'Item 2' }
];
```

Create Operation

Set up a route to handle the creation of items:

```
app.post('/items', (req, res) => {
    const { name } = req.body;
    const newItem = { id: items.length + 1, name };
    items.push(newItem);
    res.status(201).send(newItem);
});
```

Read Operation

Create routes to retrieve all items and a specific item by ID:

```javascript
app.get('/items', (req, res) => {
    res.send(items);
});

app.get('/items/:id', (req, res) => {
    const item = items.find(c => c.id === parseInt(req.params.id));
    if (!item) res.status(404).send('Item not found');
    res.send(item);
});
```

Update Operation

Implement a route to update an existing item:

```javascript
app.put('/items/:id', (req, res) => {
    const item = items.find(c => c.id === parseInt(req.params.id));
    if (!item) res.status(404).send('Item not found');

    item.name = req.body.name;
    res.send(item);
});
```

Delete Operation

Add a route to remove an item:

```javascript
app.delete('/items/:id', (req, res) => {
    const item = items.find(c => c.id === parseInt(req.params.id));
    if (!item) res.status(404).send('Item not found');

    const index = items.indexOf(item);
    items.splice(index, 1);

    res.send(item);
});
```

Testing Your API

Utilize Postman or another similar HTTP client tool to test the API endpoints. Ensure that you can successfully perform GET, POST, PUT, and DELETE requests and that each operation modifies the in-memory array as expected.

Conclusion

Creating an API with CRUD operations is a fundamental skill for backend developers, enabling effective management of application data. Through Node.js and Express, this process is streamlined, allowing developers to build APIs that can efficiently perform these essential operations, forming the basis for dynamic data-driven applications.

Testing Your API: Basic testing methods to ensure functionality

Thorough testing of an API prior to its release is critical to ensure it functions correctly under various conditions. Effective testing can uncover potential issues in functionality, security, and system integration, potentially preventing problems that could impact end-user experiences and system reliability. This guide discusses essential testing strategies for ensuring the operational efficiency of APIs.

Importance of API Testing

APIs act as pivotal links between different software systems, facilitating essential communications. Rigorous testing of these interfaces is crucial because:

- **It confirms adherence to design specifications**: Testing verifies that the API behaves as planned according to its design documents.

- **It ensures proper system integration**: It checks that the API correctly interacts with other parts of the system.

- **It identifies and resolves errors**: Testing helps detect errors that could lead to serious issues such as data corruption, security vulnerabilities, or unexpected downtime.

Types of API Testing

API testing encompasses several approaches, each aimed at assessing different aspects of the API's performance and security:

1. **Unit Testing**: Focuses on individual components of the API to ensure that each one functions independently as expected.

2. **Integration Testing**: Tests the interactions between the API's components and with other parts of the application to verify collective operations.

3. **Functional Testing**: Ensures the API meets all its functional requirements, handling requests and responses correctly under various scenarios.

4. **Load Testing**: Determines the API's capacity to perform under heavy loads, identifying limits and potential performance breakdowns.

5. **Security Testing**: Assesses the API for potential security breaches, ensuring data is securely handled and protected against threats.

6. **Endurance Testing**: Measures the API's ability to handle expected loads over extended periods, useful for spotting issues such as memory leaks or degradation.

Tools for API Testing

Selecting effective tools is vital for comprehensive API testing. Among the tools frequently used are:

- **Postman**: Known for its user-friendly interface, Postman supports both manual and automated testing, ideal for a range of testing scenarios from exploratory to regression testing.

- **SoapUI**: A tool geared towards automated testing, perfect for working with both SOAP and REST APIs. It allows testers to simulate complex testing procedures.

- **JMeter**: Originally designed for load testing, JMeter also supports functional API testing, making it a versatile tool for testing API performance under stress.

Example: Conducting Functional Testing with Postman

Setting up a functional test using Postman involves:

1. **Preparing the Request**: Define the details of the request in Postman, including the method, URL, headers, and body data.

2. **Running the Test**: Send the request and analyze the response to evaluate the API's performance. Ensure the status code, response time, and the response content meet the expected results.

For example, to test a GET method on an endpoint:

```
GET /api/resource
```

Ensure to check:

- The HTTP status code (e.g., 200 OK).

- The format and schema of the response (e.g., JSON).

- The correctness of the returned data.

```
pm.test("Status code is 200", function () {
    pm.response.to.have.status(200);
});

pm.test("Response time is acceptable", function () {
    pm.expect(pm.response.responseTime).to.be.below(200);
});
```

```
pm.test("Verify the data is accurate", function () {
    let responseData = pm.response.json();
    pm.expect(responseData.items.length).to.eql(10);
});
```

This script ensures that the API's response is as expected in terms of status, timing, and content accuracy.

Conclusion

Comprehensive testing of your API before it goes live is indispensable to confirm that it is robust, secure, and performs optimally across different scenarios. By employing a variety of testing types and tools, developers can detect and mitigate potential issues, enhancing the reliability and security of the API. Proper testing not only prevents disruptions but also instills confidence in the API's capabilities among stakeholders and users.

Chapter Five

Authentication and Authorization

Basics of Securing APIs: Understanding the need for security

Implementing robust security measures in APIs is vital to protect the critical data and services they facilitate between software platforms. APIs, by virtue of their access to valuable information, are frequently targeted by cyber threats, emphasizing the need for stringent security practices to prevent unauthorized access and ensure system stability.

The Critical Role of API Security

APIs are integral to enabling seamless data interactions between disparate systems, making them crucial components in any digital architecture. Compromised API security can lead to severe consequences, such as data breaches, operational failures, diminished user trust, and substantial financial and regulatory repercussions, particularly in sensitive industries like healthcare and finance.

Properly secured APIs ensure that only authorized users can access the API, maintain data integrity during interactions, and keep services operational, thereby enhancing the reliability and trustworthiness of the interconnected systems.

Key API Security Threats

Recognizing the variety of threats that APIs face is essential for implementing effective security measures. Common security risks include:

1. **Injection Attacks**: Occur when attackers inject malicious scripts or commands into an API, which are then executed, potentially leading to unauthorized activities or data exposure.

2. **Broken Authentication**: When authentication mechanisms are not robust enough, attackers can gain access by impersonating legitimate users.

3. **Exposure of Sensitive Data**: APIs that do not properly secure sensitive data can inadvertently expose personal, financial, or critical business information.

4. **Mass Assignment**: A risk that arises when APIs allow clients to modify data properties they should not access, leading to unintended data alterations.

5. **Security Misconfiguration**: Inappropriate security settings can accidentally expose sensitive information and functionalities, providing easy access to attackers.

6. **Insufficient Rate Limiting**: Without proper rate limiting, APIs can be overwhelmed by too many requests, leading to Denial of Service (DoS) attacks.

Best Practices for Securing APIs

Implementing a series of best practices can significantly enhance API security:

- **Robust Authentication and Authorization**: Use advanced mechanisms to verify user identities and manage access rights. Protocols such as OAuth are effective for these purposes.

- **Data Encryption**: Encrypt all data in transit using HTTPS to prevent interception, and ensure sensitive data at rest is also encrypted.

- **Rate Limiting**: Set limitations on the number of requests that can be made to the API from a single IP to prevent abuse and potential system overload.

- **Input Validation**: Thoroughly validate all incoming data to protect against vulnerabilities like SQL injections.

- **Regular Security Audits**: Continuously assess the API for vulnerabilities and implement necessary security upgrades or patches.

- **Proper Error Handling**: Craft error responses that do not reveal details about the system's architecture or provide attackers with potential exploit insights.

Example: Securing a Node.js API

Here is how to implement basic security features in a Node.js API using Express:

```javascript
const express = require('express');
const helmet = require('helmet'); // Helmet helps secure your app by setting
    various HTTP headers.
const rateLimit = require('express-rate-limit'); // Helps prevent brute-force
    and DoS attacks.

const app = express();

// Utilize Helmet to enhance HTTP security
app.use(helmet());
```

```javascript
// Set up rate limiting for request management
const limiter = rateLimit({
    windowMs: 15 * 60 * 1000, // Set the window for 15 minutes
    max: 100, // Limit each IP to 100 requests per window
    message: "Rate limit exceeded. Please try again later."
});

app.use(limiter);

// Example of a secure route
app.get('/', (req, res) => {
    res.send('Hello, this is a secure API endpoint!');
});

const port = process.env.PORT || 3000;
app.listen(port, () => console.log(`API server active on port ${port}`));
```

In this setup, **helmet** is used to secure HTTP headers, while **express-rate-limit** controls the rate at which users can make requests, thus safeguarding against potential DoS attacks.

Conclusion

Securing an API is fundamental to maintaining the security and operational integrity of the digital services it enables. By integrating stringent security measures early in API development, you can safeguard sensitive data, ensure service reliability, and establish a secure foundation that promotes trust and confidence in the API-driven functionalities.

Implementing Basic Authentication: How to secure an API using basic authentication methods

Securing an API using basic authentication is a straightforward method that provides a fundamental level of security by requiring users to verify their identity with a username and password. This method is often employed for quick setups and applications where complex security layers are not a primary concern. Here, we'll delve into how to implement basic authentication, its operational mechanics, and the pros and cons associated with this security approach.

Overview of Basic Authentication

Basic authentication is a direct method supported by the HTTP framework, functioning by sending a header with a Base64-encoded username and password. It operates as follows:

1. **Initial Request**: A client requests access to a server's protected resource.

2. **Server Response for Authentication**: If the incoming request lacks authentication credentials, the server responds with a **401 Unauthorized** status and a header indicating the requirement for basic authentication.

3. **Credential Submission**: The client then resubmits the request with an **Authorization** header, which includes the word **Basic** followed by the Base64-encoded string **username:password**.

4. **Credential Verification**: Upon receiving the credentials, the server decodes the Base64 string, verifies the credentials against its database, and either grants or denies access.

5. **Final Access Decision**: Access is granted if the credentials match the server's records; otherwise, access is denied.

Implementation Example in Node.js

Here's a practical example of setting up basic authentication in a Node.js application using the Express framework:

```javascript
const express = require('express');
const app = express();

// Middleware for basic authentication
const authenticateUser = (req, res, next) => {
    const authHeader = req.headers['authorization'];
    if (!authHeader) {
        res.setHeader('WWW-Authenticate', 'Basic');
        return res.status(401).send('Authentication required.');
    }

    const encodedCredentials = authHeader.split(' ')[1];
    const decodedCredentials = Buffer.from(encodedCredentials, 'base64').toString('ascii');
    const [username, password] = decodedCredentials.split(':');
```

```javascript
    // Example credentials check (use database or other secure methods in production)
    if (username === "admin" && password === "password") {
        next(); // Proceed if authenticated
    } else {
        return res.status(403).send('Access Denied');
    }
};

// Apply the authentication middleware to a protected route
app.get('/secure-area', authenticateUser, (req, res) => {
    res.send('Access to this resource is secured.');
});

const port = 3000;
app.listen(port, () => console.log(`Server is active on port ${port}`));
```

Benefits of Basic Authentication

- **Ease of Implementation**: It requires minimal setup and is supported out-of-the-box by most HTTP clients.

65

- **Built-In HTTP Support**: Since basic authentication is inherently supported by HTTP, it integrates smoothly without the need for additional tools or libraries.

Drawbacks of Basic Authentication

- **Security Limitations**: Basic authentication is less secure than other methods as it transmits credentials in plain text (albeit Base64-encoded), making it vulnerable to interception, particularly if not used in conjunction with HTTPS.

- **Lack of Session Control**: It doesn't handle sessions; the client must send credentials with each request, which can lead to increased data overhead and reduced performance.

- **User Experience Issues**: Continuous credential requests can detract from the user experience, making it less suitable for interfaces requiring frequent access.

Conclusion

Basic authentication provides a straightforward solution for securing APIs, suitable for non-critical applications or environments where complex security mechanisms are unnecessary. However, for applications requiring higher security or those handling sensitive data, more robust authentication mechanisms such as OAuth or JWT (JSON Web Tokens) should be considered to provide enhanced security and better user experience. Despite its limitations, basic authentication remains a valid choice for developers seeking simple, quick-to-implement security for their APIs.

OAuth and Token-Based Authentication: Introducing more secure methods

In today's digital landscape, the importance of robust API security cannot be overstated, especially as services become more complex and interconnected. Traditional methods such as basic authentication may provide elementary security, but they are often inadequate for higher-stakes environments. This necessitates the adoption of more sophisticated authentication methods, such as OAuth and token-based authentication, which offer superior security features that align with the demands of modern applications.

OAuth: An Advanced Authorization Protocol

OAuth is a prominent open standard for authorization that enables users to permit websites or applications to access their information on other websites without sharing their passwords. This protocol is particularly useful when an application needs to access resources from another service on behalf of the user without directly handling their login credentials.

How OAuth Functions

OAuth facilitates access delegation via tokens, following a structured process:

1. **Authorization Request**: The client application requests permission from the user to access specific resources.

2. **User Authorization**: The user authorizes the request through a secure interface provided by the OAuth service.

3. **Token Issuance**: Subsequently, the OAuth service issues an access token to the application.

4. **Resource Access**: The application then uses this token to access the user's data, circumventing the need for direct access to user credentials.

Example of OAuth Usage

Consider an application that needs to retrieve user data from a social media platform:

```javascript
// Function to retrieve data using an OAuth token
function retrieveSocialMediaData(accessToken) {
    fetch('https://api.socialplatform.com/userdata', {
        headers: { 'Authorization': `Bearer ${accessToken}` }
    })
    .then(response => response.json())
    .then(profile => console.log(profile))
    .catch(error => console.error('Error retrieving data: ', error));
}
```

This function demonstrates accessing user data securely through OAuth without needing the user's direct credentials.

Token-Based Authentication Using JWT

Unlike OAuth, token-based authentication secures the authentication process itself, often utilizing JSON Web Tokens (JWT) to manage user sessions. This method ensures that the user sessions are secure and stateless, maintaining session integrity across requests.

Process of Token-Based Authentication

Token-based authentication works by following these steps:

1. **User Login**: The user provides credentials which the server verifies.

2. **Token Generation**: On successful authentication, the server issues a token to the client.

3. **Token Use**: The client includes this token in the Authorization header of their requests.

4. **Request Verification**: The server checks the token with each request to verify the user's identity and session validity.

Implementing JWT Authentication

Here's how JWT can be implemented in a simple authentication system:

```javascript
const jwt = require('jsonwebtoken');

// Function to authenticate a user and issue a JWT
function issueToken(req, res) {
    const user = { id: 1, username: 'UserExample' }; // Typically this would
        involve validating against a user database
    const token = jwt.sign(user, 'your_secret_key', { expiresIn: '1 hour' });

    res.json({ token });
}

// Middleware to verify JWT
function authenticateWithToken(req, res, next) {
    const token = req.headers.authorization?.split(' ')[1];

    if (!token) {
        return res.status(401).send('Authentication token is missing.');
    }

    jwt.verify(token, 'your_secret_key', (err, decoded) => {
        if (err) {
            return res.status(403).send('Token is invalid.');
        }
        req.user = decoded;
        next();
    });
}
```

This example shows how a server might generate and verify a JWT, ensuring that each subsequent request by the user is authenticated.

Conclusion

Modern authentication methods such as OAuth and token-based authentication provide robust solutions for securing

70

APIs in today's interconnected digital environment. OAuth is ideal for scenarios that require access to resources without exposing user credentials, while token-based authentication is excellent for maintaining secure and stateless user sessions. Implementing these advanced strategies ensures that digital operations are both secure and efficient, catering to the security demands of contemporary online services.

Chapter Six

Documentation and User Support

The Importance of Documentation: Why good documentation is crucial

Documentation is a fundamental component in software development, serving as a critical guide for developers, users, and stakeholders throughout the lifecycle of a project. Effective documentation can greatly streamline the development process, boost the functionality, and extend the longevity of software applications. As technologies continue to evolve at a brisk pace, robust documentation becomes essential for managing the complexities associated with modern software development.

What Constitutes Good Documentation?

Documentation in the realm of software development includes all written materials that describe, explain, or instruct on the software product's functionalities, architectures, or operational procedures. This typically encompasses:

- **API Documentation**: This details the interfaces of the API, including its endpoints, request formats, and expected responses, enabling developers to integrate and interact with the API effectively.

- **Code Documentation**: Inline comments and notes within the code that help explain the code's purpose, logic, and functionality to developers.

- **User Manuals**: Instructional content for end-users that details how to utilize the software effectively.

- **Architectural Descriptions**: Overviews of the software's architecture and design, offering insights into its structural and behavioral frameworks.

The Significance of Documentation

Streamlines Onboarding and Knowledge Sharing

Documentation is invaluable for acclimating new team members, allowing them to quickly familiarize themselves with the product's architecture and rationale. Well-documented codebases enable developers to understand complex functionalities and dependencies efficiently, facilitating a smoother and faster integration into the team.

Boosts Code Quality and Maintainability

Quality documentation promotes high coding standards and maintainability. When developers take the time to document their code and architectural decisions, it enhances clarity and intentionality in the coding process. This not only helps maintain consistency across the codebase but also simplifies future modifications and debugging efforts.

Enhances User Engagement and Satisfaction

For end-users, comprehensive and clear documentation is crucial for a satisfying product experience. Well-crafted manuals and guides decrease user frustration by providing clear instructions and insights into the software's capabilities, thus fostering greater user engagement and retention.

Ensures Compliance and Enhances Security

In many regulated industries, detailed documentation is not merely beneficial—it's compulsory. Documents that clearly outline data handling, security measures, and compliance protocols help organizations adhere to legal and regulatory standards, avoid legal complications, and build trust among stakeholders.

Supports Effective Collaboration and Scalability

Documentation lays a foundation for scaling projects and teams. It provides a shared knowledge base that ensures all team members, from developers to project managers, understand the project's scope, objectives, and procedures. This is particularly crucial in collaborative environments where precise communication and uniformity are key.

Example of Effective Documentation: API Reference

Consider an API designed to fetch user data. Effective documentation for such an API might look like this:

```
GET /api/users/{id}
Retrieves a user by their unique identifier.

Parameters:
- id (required): The unique ID of the user.

Successful Response:
- Code: 200 OK
- Content: {"id": "123", "name": "Jane Doe", "email": "jane.doe@example.com"}
```

```
Failure Response:
- Code: 404 Not Found
- Content: {"error": "User not found"}

Example Request:
curl -X GET "http://example.com/api/users/123" -H "accept: application/json"

Notes:
- The user ID must be valid and exist within the database.
- Access to this endpoint requires authentication using an API key.
```

This example provides developers with essential details about the endpoint, its parameters, expected responses, and how to make a request, illustrating the API's functionality clearly and concisely.

Conclusion

The importance of thorough documentation in software development is undeniable. It not only facilitates efficient and effective software deployment and use but also ensures that applications are accessible, maintainable, and compliant with necessary standards. As software technology advances, the role of detailed and accurate documentation will remain crucial in linking complex software systems with their intended users. Investing in quality documentation is a strategic move that helps organizations protect their software assets, improve user and developer experiences, and promote ongoing growth and innovation.

Tools for Documentation: Tools that can be used to create effective API documentation

In today's software development landscape, clear and thorough API documentation is crucial for developers to effectively understand and interact with APIs. Optimal documentation tools not only facilitate the documentation process but also enhance the functionality and user-friendliness of the APIs themselves. Various tools have become go-to choices for developers, each offering specific features tailored to different documentation needs and developer preferences.

Essential Tools for Creating API Documentation

Swagger (OpenAPI)

Swagger, now officially known as the OpenAPI Specification, is renowned for its comprehensive approach to documenting RESTful APIs. It provides a universally readable format that both humans and machines can understand without needing access to the source code or extensive documentation.

Features:

- **Swagger UI**: Generates interactive API documentation automatically, allowing developers to perform API requests directly from the browser.

- **Swagger Editor**: A web-based editor designed to write OpenAPI specifications easily.

- **Swagger Codegen**: Enables the generation of client libraries, server stubs, and API documentation from an OpenAPI Specification.

76

Example Usage:

```yaml
openapi: "3.0.0"
info:
  title: Sample API
  description: Example of API documentation
  version: "1.0.0"
servers:
  - url: 'http://api.example.com/v1'
paths:
  /users:
    get:
      summary: Retrieves all users
      responses:
        '200':
          description: A JSON array of user names
          content:
            application/json:
              schema:
                type: array
                items:
                  type: string
```

This YAML example outlines a basic API that lists users, defining the expected response and request format, which Swagger UI can then visualize as interactive documentation.

Postman

Postman is a popular tool among developers for building, testing, and documenting APIs. It allows for easy collaboration and sharing within teams, making it both a development and a documentation tool.

Features:

- **User-Friendly Interface**: Simplifies the creation, testing, and documentation processes for APIs.

- **Postman API Network**: Facilitates the sharing of APIs and collections with others.

- **Automated Testing Capabilities**: Enables scripting tests for APIs to ensure they perform as expected.

Example Usage: Developers can document an API directly within Postman by creating and describing collections of API requests. These collections can be shared or published, providing accessible documentation for teams and users.

Docusaurus

Docusaurus is a static site generator that excels in creating and maintaining open source documentation websites, ideal for more extensive API documentation projects.

Features:

- **Version Control**: Supports documentation versioning naturally.

- **Customizability**: Offers extensive customization options through React.

- **Built-In Search**: Integrates searching capabilities using Algolia.

Example Usage: Developers can set up a Docusaurus project to document APIs by managing JavaScript and Markdown files that outline the site's structure and content, creating a comprehensive documentation website.

MkDocs

MkDocs is a straightforward static site generator focusing on project documentation. It uses Markdown for documentation files, making it easy to edit and manage.

Features:

- **Markdown Support**: Fully supports documentation in Markdown, facilitating easy content creation.

- **Theming Options**: Includes several themes that can be customized to fit specific needs.

- **Plugin Support**: Allows for extensions via plugins to increase its functionality.

Example Usage: To document an API with MkDocs, developers would write Markdown files for different API sections and configure the navigation and appearance with a **mkdocs.yml** file. MkDocs then compiles these into a static website that can be hosted almost anywhere.

Conclusion

The choice of a documentation tool for APIs should be guided by the project's specific requirements, the technical skills of the team, and the desired level of interactivity and accessibility of the documentation. Tools like Swagger and Postman offer excellent capabilities for dynamic and interactive documentation, whereas Docusaurus and MkDocs are better suited for static, detailed documentation sites. Proper documentation is critical for the successful adoption and operation of APIs, making the selection and use of an appropriate documentation tool a vital aspect of API development projects.

Writing Good Documentation: Best practices in writing clear and helpful docs

Creating clear and effective documentation is crucial in software development, serving both as a guide for development teams and a manual for end-users, ensuring the software is accessible and manageable throughout its lifecycle. Good documentation acts as an educational tool for newcomers, a reliable resource during maintenance, and a user-friendly guide for clients. This article outlines best practices for producing documentation that is informative and approachable.

Customize Content to Fit Your Audience

Successful documentation starts with a clear recognition of the intended readers. The content needs to be tailored according to whether it is meant for beginner developers, experienced coders, project managers, or non-technical end-users. This understanding influences the complexity of information, the technicality of terms used, and how in-depth the explanations should be. For instance, developer-focused documentation will likely delve into technical specifics and include code examples, whereas user documentation would prioritize straightforward instructions and usability.

Focus on Clarity and Simplicity

Effective documentation should be straightforward and concise, providing all necessary information without over-complication. Utilize plain language and aim for clear, brief sentences to enhance readability. Avoid unnecessary jargon; if specialized terms are required, make sure to define them clearly to keep the document accessible to all readers.

Employ Examples Effectively

Incorporating examples into documentation can significantly boost comprehension by illustrating abstract concepts or instructions practically. For APIs, detailed examples of requests and responses can clarify functionality. For software documentation, including code snippets or operational screenshots can demonstrate usage and procedures effectively.

Example of an API usage in documentation:

```javascript
// Demonstrating how to create a new user with a POST request
fetch('https://api.example.com/users', {
    method: 'POST',
    headers: {
        'Content-Type': 'application/json',
    },
    body: JSON.stringify({
        name: "Eve Adams",
        email: "eve.adams@example.com"
    })
})
.then(response => response.json())
.then(user => console.log(user))
.catch((error) => console.error('Error:', error));
```

This snippet shows how to execute a POST request to add a new user, detailing the request format and handling responses and errors effectively.

Update Documentation Consistently

Documentation must evolve alongside the software it describes. As new features are developed, or existing features are changed or removed, the documentation needs updates to reflect these changes accurately. Establish a routine for reviewing and revising documentation, possibly linking this process with the software development cycle to maintain continuity and accuracy.

Structure Documentation for Ease of Use

Well-organized documentation is more user-friendly and effective. Organize the material in a logical manner, use clear headings and subheadings, and provide a table of contents for lengthier documents. If the documentation is online, ensure it is navigable, searchable, and responsive to different device screens.

Integrate Visuals Thoughtfully

Visuals like diagrams, flowcharts, and screenshots can significantly enhance the understanding of textual information, especially when explaining complex systems or workflows. Ensure visuals are of high quality, appropriately labeled, and directly relevant to the text they accompany.

Example of integrating visuals:

Use a flowchart to depict the sequence of API calls and how they interact within the software system, providing a visual mapping of processes that complements the written documentation.

Seek and Implement Feedback

Feedback is essential for refining documentation. Encourage feedback from both users and team members on the documentation's clarity, completeness, and ease of use. Monitoring user support queries can also provide insights into areas where the documentation may be lacking, allowing for continuous improvement.

Conclusion

Writing clear, concise, and practical documentation is pivotal to the success of any software project. By effectively addressing the needs of the audience, maintaining clarity, updating regularly, organizing content smartly, using visuals wisely, and incorporating feedback, documentation becomes a valuable asset in the development process. The goal is to make documentation not just informative but also engaging and helpful, facilitating smoother operations and better user engagement with the software.

Chapter Seven

API Consumption

Using APIs: How to consume APIs in applications

In contemporary software ecosystems, APIs (Application Programming Interfaces) are indispensable for enabling inter-application communication. Proper utilization of APIs expands application functionality, integrates external services, and enhances interaction across various systems. This guide discusses the critical aspects of consuming APIs effectively in applications, emphasizing proven practices and incorporating practical code examples.

Essentials of API Consumption

API consumption involves sending requests to a web service and effectively handling the responses. This interaction permits applications to carry out functions such as data retrieval, resource modification, and other operations allowed by the API.

Common API Types

There are several API architectures, each tailored for specific needs:

- **REST (Representational State Transfer)**: Utilizes straightforward HTTP methods like GET, POST, PUT, and DELETE. Known for its simplicity and stateless nature, REST is widely adopted for web services.

- **SOAP (Simple Object Access Protocol)**: Characterized by its structured communication format, SOAP typically uses XML for messaging.

- **GraphQL**: A newer API model that optimizes data retrieval by letting clients specify exactly what data they need, reducing bandwidth and improving performance.

Procedure for Consuming an API

1. Examine the API Documentation

The cornerstone of effective API usage is a deep understanding of its documentation, which should detail:

- Base URL for the API.

- Descriptions of endpoints and their operations.

- Necessary headers and parameters for requests, including authentication.

- Formats for requests and expected responses.

- Error codes and their implications.

2. Establish Authentication

Secure API access typically requires authentication, with common schemes including:

- **API Keys**: Straightforward identifiers that validate a client's requests to the server.

85

- **OAuth**: A robust authorization protocol that allows secure delegated access, commonly used by major platforms.

- **Bearer Tokens**: Frequently used in conjunction with OAuth, these tokens are included in HTTP headers to provide credentials.

3. Perform API Requests

The core activity in API consumption is making requests.

Example of executing a REST API request with JavaScript (Fetch API):

```javascript
fetch('https://api.example.com/data', {
    method: 'GET',
    headers: {
        'Authorization': 'Bearer YOUR_ACCESS_TOKEN',
        'Content-Type': 'application/json'
    }
})
.then(response => response.json())
.then(data => console.log(data))
.catch(error => console.error('Error:', error));
```

This example illustrates a GET request to fetch data, including how to authenticate and specify response format expectations.

4. Process API Responses

Handling API responses effectively is critical for integrating API data into your application.

Example of managing API response statuses:

```javascript
fetch('https://api.example.com/data')
    .then(response => {
        if (!response.ok) {
            throw new Error('Network response was not ok: ' + response.statusText);
        }
        return response.json();
    })
    .then(data => console.log(data))
    .catch(error => console.error('Error fetching data:', error));
```

This snippet demonstrates how to validate response status and handle errors before processing the data.

5. Integrate API Data

The ultimate step involves incorporating the retrieved API data into your application, whether for display, computation, or storage.

Best Practices for API Consumption

- **Observe Rate Limits**: Respect the API's rate limits to maintain access and functionality.

- **Develop Robust Error Handling**: Prepare for possible API downtimes or unexpected responses to maintain application reliability.

- **Implement Caching**: Utilize caching to minimize repeat API calls, enhancing performance and reducing latency.

- **Maintain Secure Practices**: Use HTTPS for secure communications and handle sensitive information like API keys and tokens cautiously.

Conclusion

Efficiently consuming APIs is fundamental in modern software development, enabling developers to enhance application capabilities and user experiences. By meticulously following documentation, setting up proper authentication, executing and handling requests correctly, and seamlessly integrating API data, developers can ensure their applications are both powerful and reliable. Following these best practices in API consumption not only optimizes application performance but also secures application data and user interactions.

Handling API Responses: Working with different data formats

In the diverse landscape of software development, one of the fundamental skills involves adeptly handling API responses, which often come in various data formats. Knowing how to efficiently process these responses is critical for integrating API capabilities into applications effectively. This discussion offers insights into working with different data formats when handling API responses, providing practical advice and examples for developers.

Overview of Common Data Formats

APIs can deliver responses in multiple formats, but JSON (JavaScript Object Notation) and XML (eXtensible Markup Language) are among the most prevalent. Mastery of these formats is vital for developers to manage data within their applications successfully.

JSON

JSON is favored for its straightforward, text-based format that is both human-readable and machine-parsable. It aligns well with the needs of modern web applications and is the default response format for many REST APIs.

Example of processing a JSON response:

```javascript
fetch('https://api.example.com/data')
.then(response => response.json()) // Convert JSON string into JavaScript object
.then(data => {
    console.log(data);  // Output data to the console
})
.catch(error => console.error('Error:', error));
```

Here, the **fetch** API is utilized to make a GET request. The JSON response is transformed into a JavaScript object with the **.json()** method, making it easy to access and manipulate the data.

XML

Despite being more verbose and complex than JSON, XML is extensively used in many enterprise-level applications. It allows for structured and hierarchical data representation.

Example of processing an XML response:

```javascript
fetch('https://api.example.com/data')
.then(response => response.text()) // Get the response as raw text
.then(str => (new window.DOMParser()).parseFromString(str, "text/xml")) // Parse
    the text into an XML document
.then(data => {
    console.log(data);  // Display the XML document
})
.catch(error => console.error('Error:', error));
```

In this example, the XML text is parsed into an XML document using **DOMParser**, facilitating access to its elements and attributes.

Handling Less Common Data Formats

Apart from JSON and XML, APIs may return data in other formats such as CSV (Comma-Separated Values) or YAML (YAML Ain't Markup Language), each serving specific purposes.

CSV

CSV is a simple format used primarily for spreadsheet data. It can be challenging to parse without a dedicated library but is highly effective for tabular data.

Example of processing a CSV response:

```javascript
fetch('https://api.example.com/data.csv')
.then(response => response.text())
.then(text => {
    const lines = text.split('\n'); // Divide text into lines
    lines.forEach(line => {
        const values = line.split(','); // Split each line by comma
        console.log(values); // Log array of values
    });
})
.catch(error => console.error('Error:', error));
```

This snippet demonstrates how to parse CSV data manually, splitting each line into separate values based on commas.

Best Practices for API Response Management

1. **Robust Error Handling**: Ensure to check the API's response status and handle different scenarios

appropriately to prevent errors from disrupting the application flow.

2. **Data Validation**: Always validate API response data to confirm it conforms to expected formats and contains all required fields before using it.

3. **Security Measures**: Exercise caution with data from external APIs to protect against security threats such as XSS attacks or SQL injections.

4. **Utilize Libraries**: Employ well-supported libraries and frameworks for data parsing to simplify development and reduce errors.

Conclusion

Effectively handling various data formats from API responses is crucial for building functional and robust applications. Developers should be proficient in interpreting different data structures and applying appropriate parsing techniques to integrate API services seamlessly. Implementing sound practices in error handling, data validation, and secure data processing ensures applications are secure and performant, enhancing overall functionality and user experience.

Error Handling in API Consumption: How to gracefully handle possible errors

In software development, handling API responses accurately, especially when errors occur, is crucial for maintaining the stability and usability of applications. Effective error handling ensures that an application can cope with unexpected situations gracefully, thereby enhancing both its reliability and the overall user experience. This article discusses practical strategies for managing errors in API consumption, underlining best practices along with illustrative code examples.

Key Concepts in Error Handling for API Consumption

When consuming APIs, several types of errors can arise due to various reasons—issues from the client's end, problems on the server side, or network-related interruptions. Recognizing and accurately responding to these errors is paramount.

Typical Types of API Errors

1. **Client Errors (4xx status codes)**: Occur when there are issues such as incorrect input or authentication failures. For instance, **400 Bad Request** for incorrect data or **401 Unauthorized** when authentication credentials are invalid.

2. **Server Errors (5xx status codes)**: These errors indicate problems on the server-side, like **500 Internal Server Error** for unexpected conditions encountered by the server or **503 Service Unavailable**, which generally indicates temporary unavailability.

3. **Network Errors**: Include problems like timeouts or DNS issues which prevent the API from being reachable.

Strategies for Robust Error Handling

1. Differentiate Between Client and Server Errors

Identifying whether an error originates from the client or the server is crucial for determining how to handle it. Modifications to the request are often needed for client-side errors, whereas server-side errors may require retry strategies or simply informing the user to attempt the action later.

2. Utilize HTTP Status Codes

HTTP status codes are invaluable for identifying the type of error encountered. They help streamline the process of handling errors by providing standardized indications of what went wrong.

Example of using HTTP status codes:

```javascript
fetch('https://api.example.com/resource')
  .then(response => {
    if (!response.ok) {
      throw new Error(`HTTP error! Status: ${response.status}`);
    }
    return response.json();
  })
  .catch(error => {
    console.error('Request failed:', error);
  });
```

This snippet demonstrates checking the response status and throwing an error if the response indicates a failure (status codes outside the 200-299 range).

3. Implement Retry Mechanisms

For transient server-side errors (like **503 Service Unavailable**), setting up a retry mechanism might allow the

93

application to recover from temporary issues without user intervention.

Example of implementing retries:

```javascript
function fetchWithRetry(url, retries = 3) {
  return fetch(url).then(response => {
    if (!response.ok && retries > 0) {
      console.log(`Retrying... ${retries} retries left.`);
      return fetchWithRetry(url, retries - 1);
    }
    if (!response.ok) {
      throw new Error(`HTTP error! Status: ${response.status}`);
    }
    return response.json();
  });
}

fetchWithRetry('https://api.example.com/resource')
  .then(data => console.log('Data:', data))
  .catch(error => console.error('Error fetching data:', error));
```

This function recursively retries the fetch operation up to three times in case of non-successful HTTP responses.

4. Craft Informative Error Messages

Providing clear, informative error messages that guide users or developers on what went wrong and potential next steps is beneficial for troubleshooting and user satisfaction.

5. Maintain Security in Error Handling

When handling errors, ensure that no sensitive information is exposed to the user or logged inappropriately. Only provide information necessary to understand and resolve the issue, adhering to security best practices.

Best Practices for Error Handling

- **Consistency**: Employ a consistent strategy across your application for managing errors to simplify maintenance and debugging.

- **Detailed Logging**: Implement logs that provide enough detail to understand and trace back errors when they occur.

- **User Guidance**: Offer users constructive feedback on errors, preferably with suggestions on how to proceed.

Conclusion

Handling errors effectively in API consumption is essential for building resilient and user-friendly applications. By differentiating error sources, using HTTP status codes, implementing retry logic, providing detailed messages, and ensuring secure error processing, developers can create robust systems that withstand operational hiccups and enhance the overall user experience.

Chapter Eight

Debugging and Troubleshooting APIs

Common API Issues: Identifying frequent problems

In contemporary software development, effective API integration is pivotal, yet developers often encounter challenges that can impede functionality if not appropriately addressed. Understanding these common issues is vital for developers to ensure smooth interactions between applications and APIs. This article provides an overview of typical problems associated with API consumption and offers solutions to mitigate these issues effectively.

Common API Issues and Strategic Solutions

1. Rate Limiting and Throttling

Issue: APIs enforce rate limits to prevent abuse and manage load, which, when exceeded, can lead to **429 Too Many Requests** errors. This rate limiting can disrupt service access and degrade application performance.

Solution: Implement client-side rate limiting, retry mechanisms with exponential backoff, and closely monitor API usage to stay within established limits. Additionally, optimize the efficiency of API interactions by fetching only necessary data and improving caching techniques.

Code Example:

```javascript
function retryFetch(url, retries = 3) {
  return fetch(url)
    .then(response => {
      if (response.status === 429 && retries > 0) {
        // Wait and retry if rate limit is exceeded
        setTimeout(() => {
          console.log('Rate limit exceeded, retrying...');
          return retryFetch(url, retries - 1);
        }, 1000); // Delay retry by 1 second
      }

      if (!response.ok) {
        throw new Error(`HTTP error, status: ${response.status}`);
      }
      return response.json();
    });
}
```

2. Authentication and Authorization Errors

Issue: Common errors such as **401 Unauthorized** and **403 Forbidden** occur due to issues with authentication tokens, expired credentials, or incorrect access permissions.

Solution: Regularly verify and refresh authentication tokens before they expire, ensure credentials are correctly implemented, and handle errors by prompting for re-authentication or clearly communicating access limitations to users.

Code Example:

```javascript
function authenticatedFetch(url, token) {
  return fetch(url, {
    headers: { 'Authorization': `Bearer ${token}` }
  })
  .then(response => {
    if (response.status === 401) {
      throw new Error('Unauthorized: Check your API token.');
    }
    if (response.status === 403) {
      throw new Error('Forbidden: Access denied.');
    }
    return response.json();
  });
}
```

3. Data Integrity and Format Issues

Issue: Inconsistencies or unexpected data formats in API responses can cause application errors or system crashes.

Solution: Rigorously validate API responses to confirm data consistency and structure. Employ schema validation tools or robust data parsing techniques to safeguard against data-related errors.

Code Example:

```javascript
function checkApiResponse(data) {
  if (!data || typeof data !== 'object' || !data.requiredField) {
    throw new Error('Invalid API response: Essential data missing.');
  }
  // Implement further checks as necessary
  return data;
}

fetch('https://api.example.com/data')
  .then(response => response.json())
  .then(checkApiResponse)
  .then(data => console.log('Data check successful:', data))
  .catch(error => console.error('API data issue:', error));
```

4. Network Connectivity Problems

Issue: Network issues like timeouts or failures can prevent successful API requests.

Solution: Enhance error handling for network failures, establish retry strategies with incremental backoffs, and ensure robust network configurations.

Code Example:

```javascript
function resilientFetch(url, retries = 5) {
  return fetch(url)
    .catch(error => {
      if (retries > 0) {
        console.log('Experiencing network issues, attempting retry...');
        return new Promise(resolve =>
          setTimeout(() => resolve(resilientFetch(url, retries - 1)), 2000)
        );
      }
      throw new Error('Network error: Unable to reach API.');
    });
}
```

Conclusion

Navigating common API issues effectively is essential for developers to maintain application reliability and performance. By recognizing and addressing issues related to rate limits, authentication, data integrity, and network connectivity, developers can ensure that their API integrations are both robust and user-friendly. Adopting these strategies helps in mitigating potential disruptions and enhancing the overall effectiveness of API interactions.

Tools for Debugging: Tools and strategies to debug APIs

Debugging APIs is an integral part of software development that ensures seamless communication between applications and their interfacing services. Effective tools and methodologies for debugging can significantly aid developers in identifying and resolving issues that may arise during API interaction. This guide details the essential tools and effective strategies for debugging APIs, enhancing the stability and efficiency of software integrations.

Critical Tools for Debugging APIs

The choice of debugging tools can profoundly impact a developer's ability to efficiently diagnose and resolve issues. Here are several key tools that are widely recognized and utilized in the field of API debugging:

1. Postman

Postman is a favored tool among developers for its comprehensive features that facilitate API testing and debugging. It enables users to send requests to APIs and scrutinize the responses, helping to pinpoint issues such as incorrect header configurations or malformed requests.

Capabilities:

- Management of collections of API requests for systematic testing.

- Configuration of different environments to mirror various deployment conditions.

- Automation of tests which can be integrated into CI/CD workflows.

Practical Application: Using Postman, developers can set up a request by entering the API URL, choosing the appropriate method (e.g., GET, POST), and configuring headers before sending the request to observe the detailed response.

2. cURL

cURL is a versatile command-line tool used to transfer data using various protocols, ideal for quick API tests and automating script-based interactions.

Usage Example:

```
curl -X POST https://api.example.com/data -H "Content-Type: application/json" -d
    '{"key1":"value1", "key2":"value2"}'
```

This example illustrates how to execute a POST request with JSON data, allowing for rapid endpoint testing directly from the command line.

3. Fiddler

Fiddler is a robust web debugging proxy that tracks all HTTP(S) traffic between the internet and your computer, providing granular insights essential for debugging API communications.

Features:

- Detailed examination of incoming and outgoing data.

- Modification capabilities for testing different request and response behaviors.

- Performance analysis tools for evaluating API response timings and data size.

4. Wireshark

Wireshark is a network protocol analyzer that excels in providing detailed visibility into network traffic, including HTTP and HTTPS used in API calls.

Usage Tip: Deploying Wireshark can help visualize the flow of API communications, identifying issues like delays and packet losses that might affect API functionality.

Strategies for Efficient API Debugging

Alongside utilizing powerful tools, implementing structured debugging strategies is vital for resolving API issues effectively.

1. Logging and Monitoring

Establishing comprehensive logging and consistent monitoring for API activity is critical for spotting unusual behavior or errors in real time.

Recommended Tools:

- **ELK Stack (Elasticsearch, Logstash, Kibana)**: Enables powerful logging, real-time data analysis, and visualization.

- **Prometheus and Grafana**: Ideal for tracking API metrics and visualizing data through detailed dashboards.

2. Automated Testing

Incorporating automated tests into the development process helps identify and address potential API issues early, reducing the impact on production systems.

Useful Tools:

- **JMeter**: Offers extensive capabilities for load testing and performance benchmarking.

- **Swagger Tools**: Assists in creating accurate client libraries and API documentation that facilitate comprehensive testing.

3. Interactive Debugging Techniques

Employing interactive debugging through IDEs that support step-through execution and breakpoints can significantly help in understanding API data handling and resolving issues.

Effective Tools:

- **Visual Studio Code**

- **IntelliJ IDEA**

Conclusion

Mastering API debugging involves a blend of utilizing sophisticated tools and adopting strategic debugging practices. Tools such as Postman, cURL, Fiddler, and Wireshark provide essential capabilities for sending requests, examining responses, and monitoring traffic. Techniques like detailed logging, automated testing, and interactive debugging ensure robust API interactions, ultimately leading to more reliable applications and enhanced user experiences. By equipping themselves with these tools and strategies, developers can effectively tackle API-related challenges, ensuring their software integrations perform optimally.

Best Practices in Troubleshooting: Efficient problem-solving techniques

Troubleshooting is a critical capability in technical disciplines, especially in software development and IT, where complex environments can spawn intricate problems. Effective troubleshooting is more than quick fixes; it involves strategic prevention and minimizing the operational impact of issues. This article discusses best practices in troubleshooting, focusing on systematic and effective resolution methods.

Understanding the Issue

A fundamental step in troubleshooting is gaining a thorough understanding of the problem. This involves collecting detailed data about how and when the issue occurs, its symptoms, and its broader effects.

Core Steps Include:

- **Issue Reproduction**: Strive to replicate the problem under controlled conditions to observe its behavior and identify possible triggers.

- **Log Analysis**: Scrutinize log files and error messages coinciding with the time the issue was reported to uncover useful clues.

- **User Feedback**: Obtain precise descriptions of the problem from users, including the steps they followed before encountering the issue and any screenshots they can provide.

Prioritizing the Issue

Properly understanding the issue allows for its effective prioritization, which is critical in directing resource allocation and timing for resolutions, especially when multiple issues are present.

Considerations for Prioritization:

- **Impact on Business Operations**: Evaluate how essential the affected system or function is to the continuity of business operations.

- **Scope of Impact**: Determine the extent of the user base that is or might be affected.

- **Resource Assessment**: Gauge the available technical resources and expertise that are necessary to effectively tackle the issue.

Systematic Troubleshooting Approach

A methodical approach to troubleshooting ensures comprehensive coverage and enhances effectiveness by focusing efforts on the most probable sources of the problem.

Methodical Techniques:

- **Root Cause Analysis**: Implement investigative techniques like the "Five Whys" to trace back to the root cause of the problem.

- **Segmentation Strategy**: Break down the issue into smaller, manageable segments, testing each individually to isolate the problem.

- **Single-Variable Changes**: When exploring potential fixes, adjust only one variable at a time to clearly identify which change solves the problem.

Selecting the Right Tools

The efficacy of troubleshooting can be significantly amplified by employing the right tools, from software diagnostics to debugging tools, which streamline the identification and resolution of issues.

Essential Tools:

- **Debugging Software and IDEs**: Utilize integrated development environments and debuggers to navigate through code and pinpoint where errors occur.

- **Network Diagnostics**: Use tools like Wireshark to analyze network traffic, which is crucial for diagnosing issues related to data transmission.

- **Performance Monitoring**: Deploy monitoring tools to track system performance metrics such as CPU and memory usage to identify potential bottlenecks.

Documentation and Communication

Keeping detailed documentation and maintaining open lines of communication are crucial aspects of effective troubleshooting. They ensure that solutions are well-documented for future reference and that the troubleshooting process is transparent.

Documentation Practices:

- **Comprehensive Records**: Keep detailed records of all diagnostics, observations, and actions taken during the troubleshooting process.

- **Knowledge Base Contributions**: Add to a shared knowledge base to assist others in solving similar problems in the future.

- **Regular Updates**: Keep all stakeholders informed about the troubleshooting progress, especially if the issue impacts critical operations.

Continuous Improvement

After resolving an issue, it's important to take steps to prevent similar problems in the future. Reviewing and analyzing the incident to implement preventative measures can enhance the robustness of systems and troubleshooting protocols.

Follow-Up Actions:

- **Address Root Causes**: Implement solutions that address and eliminate the root causes of issues to prevent recurrence.

- **Refine Troubleshooting Methods**: Regularly review and improve troubleshooting procedures to keep pace with new technological challenges.

- **Skill Enhancement**: Encourage continuous learning and development to keep team skills sharp and in line with the latest troubleshooting methodologies.

Conclusion

Efficient troubleshooting combines analytical thinking, structured methods, appropriate tools, thorough documentation, and ongoing improvements. By adhering to these best practices, technical professionals can resolve issues more effectively, ensuring that systems are robust and perform optimally. These practices prepare teams to adeptly handle technical challenges, ensuring high performance and user satisfaction.

Chapter Nine

Advanced Features in API Design

Rate Limiting: How to implement and why it's important

Rate limiting is a crucial mechanism in API management and network operations, playing a vital role in controlling how users and applications access services. It is fundamental for managing service load, preventing abuse, maintaining service quality, and ensuring fair usage among consumers. This article delves into the significance of rate limiting, explores various implementation methods, and highlights best practices for optimal setup.

Importance of Rate Limiting

1. **Protection Against Abuse**: APIs without rate limits can be susceptible to misuse, such as data scraping, brute force attacks, or denial-of-service (DoS) attacks, potentially leading to service degradation or outages.

2. **Load Management**: Rate limiting is critical to prevent servers from being overwhelmed by too many requests at once, which helps in maintaining stable and reliable service performance.

3. **Fair Resource Distribution**: It ensures that no single user or service can monopolize access, promoting equitable resource sharing among all users.

4. Cost Control: For businesses that incur costs per API call, implementing rate limits helps in managing operational expenses by curbing excessive use.

Implementing Rate Limiting

Rate limiting can be implemented using different algorithms, each suited to specific needs and scenarios of the application or service.

1. **Token Bucket Algorithm**: This common approach allows requests at a steady rate, with allowances for bursts up to a configured maximum.

Example Code:

```python
import time

class TokenBucket:
    def __init__(self, capacity, rate):
        self.capacity = capacity
        self.tokens = capacity
        self.rate = rate
        self.last_checked = time.time()

    def allow_request(self, num_tokens=1):
        now = time.time()
        elapsed = now - self.last_checked
        self.tokens += elapsed * self.rate
        self.tokens = min(self.tokens, self.capacity)
        self.last_checked = now

        if num_tokens <= self.tokens:
            self.tokens -= num_tokens
            return True
        return False

# Initialize bucket with capacity of 10 tokens and rate of 1 token per second
bucket = TokenBucket(10, 1)
print(bucket.allow_request())  # Outputs True if request can proceed, otherwise False
```

2. **Leaky Bucket Algorithm**: Ensures a consistent output rate regardless of bursty incoming requests, ideal for scenarios where consistency is required.

3. **Fixed Window Counter**: Involves tracking the number of requests over a set period of time (e.g., minute or hour) and blocking requests that exceed the limit.

4. **Sliding Log Algorithm**: More complex, this method logs each request's timestamp, allowing precise control over request counts in a sliding window fashion.

Best Practices in Rate Limiting

1. **Define and Communicate Policies**: Establish and clearly articulate rate limiting policies tailored to the technical and business objectives of your service.

2. **Adaptability and User Control**: Provide users some flexibility in rate limits, particularly useful in multi-tenant environments where usage needs can vary significantly.

3. **Transparent Feedback**: Utilize HTTP headers to inform clients about their current rate limit status, remaining quota, and reset timing.

4. **Regular Monitoring and Adjustment**: Continuously monitor the impact of rate limiting on user experience and system performance, adjusting thresholds and rules as necessary to align with changing usage patterns and system capabilities.

Conclusion

Rate limiting is an indispensable strategy for safeguarding the stability and availability of APIs and services. By understanding various rate limiting techniques and adhering to established best practices, organizations can effectively manage user access, prevent abuse, and maintain optimal service conditions. Properly implemented rate limiting not only enhances system resilience but also improves user satisfaction by ensuring consistent and reliable service performance.

Caching Strategies: Enhancing API performance with caching

Caching is a pivotal practice in software development, especially critical for enhancing API performance and scalability. By temporarily storing frequently requested data, caching minimizes the need to repeatedly retrieve or compute the same information, thus reducing latency and improving response times. This article explores various caching strategies that significantly augment API performance, delineates their advantages, and provides implementation examples.

The Significance of Caching for APIs

Caching plays a vital role in optimizing API functionality due to several key benefits:

- **Lowered Latency**: By caching data close to the user, either on local servers or within the network, the time to retrieve data is drastically reduced.

- **Reduced Backend Load**: Caching decreases direct hits on the backend servers by serving data from the cache, thus preserving backend resources.

- **Enhanced User Experience**: Quick data access speeds result in faster response times, leading to a smoother user interaction.

- **Cost Reduction**: Fewer requests to backend services and databases can lower operational costs, especially where API usage fees apply.

Strategies for Effective Caching

1. In-Memory Caching

This strategy stores data within the server's RAM, providing ultra-fast data retrieval but is constrained by the server's memory capacity.

Implementation Example: Using Python's **cachetools**, set up an in-memory cache:

```python
from cachetools import cached, TTLCache

# Cache setup with a maximum of 100 items and a TTL of 180 seconds
cache = TTLCache(maxsize=100, ttl=180)

@cached(cache)
def fetch_data(key):
    # This mimics fetching data from a primary data source
    print("Accessing data source...")
    return f"Data for {key}"

# Usage
print(fetch_data("key1"))
# Subsequent access within TTL from cache
print(fetch_data("key1"))
```

2. Distributed Caching

Utilized in environments spread across multiple servers or geographical locations, this method involves a network of cache servers to reduce latency and balance loads.

Common Tools:

- **Redis**: A robust, open-source, in-memory data structure store used as a distributed cache.

- **Memcached**: Designed for simplicity and efficiency in networked cache storage.

3. Database Caching

Caching at the database level involves storing the results of costly fetch operations, which can be particularly effective for complex queries.

Example Code:

```python
def fetch_from_database(query):
    print("Querying database...")
    return f"Results for {query}"

def cache_query_results(func):
    cache = {}
    def wrapper(query):
        if query not in cache:
            cache[query] = func(query)
        else:
            print("Delivering from cache...")
        return cache[query]
    return wrapper

cached_query = cache_query_results(fetch_from_database)
```

```
# First fetch will query the database
print(cached_query("SELECT * FROM users"))
# Second fetch will utilize the cache
print(cached_query("SELECT * FROM users"))
```

4. CDN Caching

CDNs are primarily used for caching static resources across a globally distributed network, minimizing distances to users and accelerating delivery.

Caching Best Practices

- **Optimal TTL Settings**: Configure appropriate Time-to-Live values based on how frequently the data updates. Static information can have longer TTLs while dynamic content may require frequent refreshes.

- **Effective Cache Invalidation**: Establish robust mechanisms to invalidate outdated data, ensuring the cache reflects recent changes.

- **Ensure Data Consistency**: Pay attention to maintaining consistency across cached and actual data, particularly in distributed environments.

- **Monitoring and Adjustments**: Regularly monitor caching efficiency and make necessary adjustments based on performance analytics and user feedback.

Conclusion

Implementing strategic caching is crucial for optimizing API performance, reducing resource load, and improving user experience. By selecting suitable caching strategies and adhering to best practices, developers can ensure efficient and scalable API operations. Effective caching not only speeds up data access but also contributes to a more resilient and economical infrastructure.

Asynchronous Operations: Handling long-running API operations

Asynchronous operations are crucial in enhancing API performance, particularly valuable for managing long-running tasks that might otherwise block server responsiveness. By enabling certain operations to run in the background, asynchronous programming allows a system to continue functioning efficiently, improving scalability and user experience. This article explores why asynchronous operations are vital for APIs, the various methods of implementation, and offers practical examples for incorporating these strategies.

The Role of Asynchronous Operations in APIs

Asynchronous operations are integral in situations where processes might take more time than a typical synchronous request-response cycle would permit. Here's why they're important:

1. **Increased Throughput**: Asynchronous operations do not block the server while processing. This means that a server can handle other requests while waiting for a task to complete, significantly increasing throughput and handling more requests simultaneously.

2. **Optimized Resource Use**: Asynchronous operations allow for more effective use of computational resources

116

by preventing servers from idling while waiting for tasks to finish. This optimization is critical in environments with high resource demands.

3. **Improved User Interaction**: In client-facing applications, asynchronous operations prevent the user interface from becoming unresponsive, which is often critical for maintaining a smooth user experience.

Implementing Asynchronous Operations

There are several effective methods to implement asynchronous operations within APIs, each suitable for different scenarios and technologies.

1. Callbacks

One of the earliest methods to handle asynchronous operations, callbacks are functions passed as arguments to other functions that get called to continue execution after the initial function completes.

Example with Node.js:

```javascript
const fs = require('fs');

// Asynchronously reading a file
fs.readFile('example.txt', (err, data) => {
    if (err) throw err;
    console.log(data.toString());
});

console.log('Reading file asynchronously...');
```

This Node.js example uses a callback to handle the file reading operation asynchronously, allowing the program to continue running other tasks.

117

2. Promises

Promises represent a proxy for a value not necessarily known when the promise is created. It allows you to associate handlers with an asynchronous action's eventual success or failure.

Example with JavaScript:

```javascript
function fetchApiData(url) {
    return new Promise((resolve, reject) => {
        fetch(url)
            .then(response => response.json())
            .then(data => resolve(data))
            .catch(error => reject(error));
    });
}

fetchApiData('https://api.example.com/data')
    .then(data => console.log(data))
    .catch(error => console.error(error));
```

This script wraps a network request in a promise, simplifying the management of the asynchronous operation.

3. Async/Await

Async/await is syntactic sugar built on promises, introduced to simplify asynchronous programming, making it more readable and easier to understand.

Example in JavaScript:

```javascript
async function loadApiData(url) {
    try {
        const response = await fetch(url);
        const data = await response.json();
        console.log(data);
    } catch (error) {
        console.error('Error fetching data:', error);
    }
}

loadApiData('https://api.example.com/data');
```

Using **async** and **await** makes the code cleaner and more intuitive compared to handling promises with **.then()** and **.catch()**.

Best Practices for Asynchronous Operations in APIs

- **Comprehensive Error Handling**: It's crucial to manage errors effectively in asynchronous code to prevent them from causing unhandled exceptions or crashes.

- **Task Cancellation**: Provide the ability to cancel ongoing tasks if they are no longer needed, improving resource management and responsiveness.

- **Debugging Asynchronous Code**: Utilize tools that support asynchronous debugging to trace and diagnose issues that may not be evident in synchronous code.

- **Implement Throttling**: Apply throttling techniques to limit how often a function can execute, preventing overuse of resources under high load conditions.

Conclusion

Asynchronous operations provide a robust solution for enhancing API performance by managing long-running tasks efficiently. By implementing modern asynchronous programming techniques, developers can ensure that their APIs are performant, responsive, and capable of handling extensive operations without sacrificing user experience. Effective asynchronous programming, coupled with good error handling and system design, ensures that applications remain efficient and robust.

Chapter Ten

Testing APIs

Unit Testing: Testing individual parts of an API

Unit testing stands as a cornerstone of software development, particularly critical in API contexts, where it serves to verify the functionality of individual segments of the API independently. This meticulous approach to testing ensures that each component of an API performs correctly, facilitating bug detection early in the development cycle, easing integration processes, and mitigating the costs associated with later error remediation. This discussion outlines the principles of unit testing within API frameworks, details various execution methods, and illustrates these points with practical examples.

Why Unit Testing is Crucial for APIs

Unit testing plays several key roles in the development of APIs:

- **Guaranteed Functionality**: It certifies that each segment of the API conforms to its specified design.

- **Early Issue Identification**: It enables the detection of issues at the earliest stages, simplifying fixes and integration.

- **Documenting Behavior**: It serves as a detailed documentation source, illustrating how different parts of the API should function.

- **Confidence in Code Changes**: It allows developers to refactor or update parts of the API with the assurance that changes do not negatively impact existing functionality.

- **Efficient Problem Resolution**: By isolating each component, it simplifies identifying and fixing errors.

Effective Unit Testing Methods for APIs

Proper implementation of unit testing involves strategic preparation, focusing on crafting tests for individual units, managing test environments, and controlling external interactions.

1. Component Isolation

Unit tests should focus on individual functions or components, assessing them in isolation to ensure no external processes affect the outcome.

JavaScript Testing Example with Jest and Supertest:

```javascript
const request = require('supertest');
const app = require('../app'); // Importing the Express app

describe('GET /users', () => {
    it('should return a JSON array containing user data', done => {
        request(app)
            .get('/users')
            .set('Accept', 'application/json')
            .expect('Content-Type', /json/)
            .expect(200, done);
    });
});
```

This example demonstrates a unit test for an API route, verifying that the **/users** endpoint correctly returns a JSON array of user data.

2. Mocking Dependencies

Given that APIs often rely on external systems or components, such as databases or other services, it is crucial to mock these dependencies during testing to ensure true component isolation.

JavaScript Mocking Example:

```javascript
jest.mock('../models/user');
const { getUser } = require('../services/userService');

test('fetches user data correctly', async () => {
    require('../models/user').__mockImplementation(() => {
        return { id: 1, name: 'John Doe' };
    });
    const user = await getUser(1);
    expect(user.name).toEqual('John Doe');
});
```

In this code snippet, the **User** model is mocked to test the **getUser** function independently of the database interactions.

3. Management of Test Data

Maintaining control over test data ensures that each test can be executed consistently and independently.

Python Test Data Management Example:

```python
import unittest
from myapp import query_user

class TestUserData(unittest.TestCase):
    def setUp(self):
        self.expected_data = {'id': 123, 'name': 'Alice'}

    def test_user_query_functionality(self):
        result = query_user(123)
        self.assertEqual(result, self.expected_data)

if __name__ == '__main__':
    unittest.main()
```

This Python example uses the **setUp** method to prepare expected results for a test, ensuring each test run is predictable and isolated.

Unit Testing Best Practices

- **Simplicity and Clarity**: Each test should be straightforward and focused on a single functionality.

- **Automated Test Runs**: Incorporating tests into a continuous integration/continuous deployment (CI/CD) framework ensures they are executed automatically and frequently.

- **Broad Coverage**: Aim for comprehensive test coverage but prioritize testing the most crucial and error-prone areas of the API.

- **Frequent Testing**: Regular test execution helps quickly identify and correct regressions or newly introduced errors.

Conclusion

Unit testing is an invaluable methodology in API development, ensuring that each component functions correctly and efficiently. By employing rigorous unit testing strategies and adhering to best practices, developers can maintain high-quality APIs that are robust, maintainable, and ready to meet the demands of production environments.

Integration Testing: Testing the integration of API components

Integration testing plays an essential role in the software development lifecycle, emphasizing the need to verify the collective functionality of multiple components or systems working together. Distinct from unit testing, which assesses individual units independently, integration testing ensures that all components of a system, such as an API, operate in unison effectively. This kind of testing is particularly crucial for APIs, as it ensures that various API components interact properly with each other and with external systems, maintaining system integrity and user experience.

The Value of Integration Testing for APIs

Integration testing is pivotal for API development for multiple reasons:

- **Detection of Interaction Issues**: It helps uncover issues that surface when individual units interact, such as data format inconsistencies, workflow errors, or interface conflicts.

- **Verification of System Specifications**: Confirms that the integrated API meets all specified functional, performance, and reliability requirements.

- **Consistency Assurance**: Ensures that data remains consistent across subsystems and that the API behaves predictably across all operations.

- **Cost Efficiency in Maintenance**: Identifying and resolving problems early through integration testing can significantly reduce the cost of later fixes, especially if issues are discovered post-deployment.

Techniques for Implementing Integration Testing in API Development

Various strategies can be adopted for integration testing, each suitable for different project needs and complexities:

1. Big Bang Approach

This approach involves integrating all components at once and testing them collectively. This strategy works well for smaller, less complex APIs.

Pros:

- Simplifies testing by focusing on a single integration event.

- Suitable for smaller systems with minimal interdependencies.

Cons:

- More challenging to isolate specific faults.

- Not ideal for larger, more complex systems.

2. Incremental Testing Approach

This method tests components one at a time and can follow a Top-Down or Bottom-Up approach.

- **Top-Down**: Testing begins from the top layer of the application and progresses downwards, often requiring stubs to simulate lower-layer functionality until those layers are ready for testing.

- **Bottom-Up**: Starts at the bottom layer and works upwards, utilizing drivers to simulate upper-layer functionality not yet developed.

Top-Down Testing Example: If testing an API responsible for user management, you might start by testing the user interface layer with a stub to represent the data storage layer.

```
// Example of a stub for database operations in Top-Down Integration Testing
function UserDBStub() {
  return {
    getUser: function(id) {
      return { id: id, name: "Test User", email: "test@example.com" };
    }
  };
}
```

3. Hybrid Approach

This strategy merges both top-down and bottom-up methods, optimizing the advantages of each approach. It's particularly beneficial for complex systems where components are developed asynchronously.

Best Practices for Integration Testing

- **Comprehensive Test Scenarios**: Develop detailed test cases that encompass all potential interactions between system components.

- **Leverage Test Automation**: Where applicable, automate tests to efficiently handle extensive and detailed test cases.

- **Maintain Environment Consistency**: Align the test environment closely with the production environment to avoid discrepancies that can lead to unexpected behaviors.

- **Effective Monitoring**: Implement monitoring tools during testing to track API performance and identify bottlenecks or other issues.

Conclusion

Integration testing is indispensable for building robust and reliable APIs. By ensuring that all parts of an API work together seamlessly, developers can deliver a stable and functional product. Thorough integration testing not only boosts the quality of the API but also optimizes maintenance costs and ensures that the final product is well-prepared for real-world deployment. Strategic implementation of integration testing, supported by thoughtful planning and execution, is foundational for delivering superior software solutions.

Automated Testing: Tools and strategies for automating tests

Automated testing is a crucial element of contemporary software development, enhancing the testing process by automating both test execution and the handling of outcomes. This method proves invaluable amid rapid development cycles and the requirements of continuous integration and deployment practices. This article will explore the range of tools and strategies integral to automated testing, providing detailed insights into their application and utility, supported by practical examples.

Role of Automated Testing in Software Development

Automated testing is essential within the software development lifecycle for several reasons, notably enabling continuous and thorough quality assessments before deployment. It automates the execution of tests, ensuring that any new updates do not disrupt existing functionalities, facilitates early detection of defects, reduces the burden of manual testing, and quickens the feedback loop to developers.

- **Efficiency**: Automated tests can be executed swiftly and on a regular basis, offering a cost-effective alternative to manual regression testing.

- **Consistency**: It guarantees that tests are performed uniformly every time, eliminating the possibility of human error.

- **Comprehensive Coverage**: Automation enables broader and deeper test coverage, enhancing the software's overall quality.

- **Speed**: With the ability to run tests overnight or simultaneously, feedback is accelerated.

Leading Tools for Automated Testing

The automated testing landscape features a variety of tools tailored to different testing requirements, from unit testing to broader integration testing, each equipped with features suited to specific environments or programming languages.

1. Selenium

Selenium is a prominent open-source tool for automated web application testing, supporting multiple languages such as Java, Python, and Ruby. It integrates well with frameworks like TestNG and JUnit to manage test cases and generate reports effectively.

Example Usage:

```python
from selenium import webdriver

driver = webdriver.Chrome()
driver.get("http://www.example.com")
assert "Example Domain" in driver.title
elem = driver.find_element_by_name("q")
elem.clear()
elem.send_keys("domain")
elem.submit()
assert "No results found." not in driver.page_source
driver.quit()
```

This script showcases how Selenium can automate browser interactions to perform tasks like navigating pages and validating content.

2. Jenkins

Jenkins is a robust CI/CD tool that facilitates the automation of various stages of a development pipeline, including test execution. It can configure automatic code pulls from repositories, execute testing scripts, and handle responses based on the outcomes.

Example Workflow:

- Jenkins retrieves code updates from a Git repository.

- It runs a script to execute automated tests.

- Depending on the test results, Jenkins either advances the build or triggers alerts if tests fail.

3. JUnit (for Java)

JUnit is a preferred framework for executing repeatable tests in Java, fundamental in test-driven development and unit testing scenarios.

Example Usage:

```java
import static org.junit.Assert.assertEquals;
import org.junit.Test;

public class TestSimpleCalculator {
    @Test
    public void testAddition() {
        SimpleCalculator calc = new SimpleCalculator();
        assertEquals(4, calc.add(2, 2));
    }
}
```

This code snippet uses JUnit to test a simple calculator's addition functionality, ensuring the method operates as expected.

Strategies for Effective Automated Testing

- **Tool Selection**: Opt for tools that best match the project's technology stack and the specific nature of the tests required.

- **Maintain Testing Scripts**: Regularly update testing scripts to accommodate changes in the application's functionality.

- **CI/CD Integration**: Integrate testing within the CI/CD pipeline to guarantee immediate feedback on code modifications.

- **Analyze Test Results**: Implement tools to systematically track and analyze test outcomes to improve testing strategies over time.

Conclusion

Automated testing is vital for upholding high standards in software development, facilitating streamlined and effective testing processes that enhance team productivity. By employing advanced tools and adhering to strategic testing practices, organizations can consistently produce software that is both robust and reliable. Automated testing not only optimizes the testing procedures but also fosters a culture of continuous enhancement and accuracy in software development.

Chapter Eleven

Deploying APIs

Deployment Strategies: Different ways to deploy APIs

In the dynamic world of software development, deploying APIs effectively is crucial for the success of applications. The deployment strategy selected greatly affects the API's scalability, reliability, and overall manageability. Given that APIs facilitate crucial interactions between different software applications and services, choosing and implementing the right deployment strategy is key. This article examines various API deployment strategies, each with its distinct benefits and challenges.

Key Deployment Strategies for APIs

Deploying an API involves making it accessible to its end users or client applications, necessitating strategic considerations about version control, environment setup, and load management, among others. The choice of strategy typically hinges on factors like the API's complexity, anticipated traffic, environmental constraints, and specific organizational needs.

1. Monolithic Deployment

A monolithic deployment strategy involves deploying all components of an application as a single unit, typically on one server or node. This approach, while straightforward, may pose scalability challenges as traffic increases.

Advantages:

- Simplified development and deployment.

- Easier management due to the singular nature of the application.

Disadvantages:

- Limited scalability.

- Updates cause downtime.

- Failures impact the entire application.

2. Microservices Deployment

In a microservices architecture, each feature or service is developed and deployed independently, enhancing flexibility and scalability. This method allows for individual components to be updated without disrupting the entire system.

Advantages:

- Greater scalability and flexibility.

- Minimized risk of widespread failures.

- Facilitates continuous deployment and integration.

Disadvantages:

- Increased complexity in management.

- Requires advanced tools for coordination and monitoring.

3. Serverless Deployment

Serverless architecture offers a way to deploy applications and services without managing underlying servers. Platforms like AWS Lambda, Azure Functions, and Google Cloud Functions support running code in response to events, handling server management automatically.

Advantages:

- Highly scalable and cost-effective.

- Focuses developer efforts on code rather than infrastructure.

- Automatically handles scaling and load balancing.

Disadvantages:

- Possible vendor lock-in.

- Latency issues due to cold starts.

4. Containerized Deployment

Containers allow APIs and their dependencies to be packaged into isolated environments. Technologies like Docker package these containers, which can then be managed using orchestrators like Kubernetes or Docker Swarm.

Advantages:

- Consistent deployment environments from development through to production.

- High portability and efficient resource use.

- Reduced overhead compared to virtual machines.

Disadvantages:

- Complexities in orchestrating containers.

- Learning curve associated with container technology.

5. Blue-Green Deployment

Blue-green deployment minimizes downtime by maintaining two identical production environments, only one of which is live at any time. This setup allows quick rollback if issues arise after deployment.

Advantages:

- Immediate rollback capabilities.

- Zero downtime during transitions.

Disadvantages:

- High costs due to duplicated environments.

- Challenges in synchronizing data across environments.

6. Canary Deployment

Canary deployment strategy introduces a new version to a small segment of users initially, expanding to the broader user base gradually. This controlled approach helps mitigate risks by gauging the new version's stability on live traffic.

Advantages:

- Lowers risk by limiting exposure to new versions.

- Provides real feedback from users.

Disadvantages:

- Implementation complexity.

- Requires sophisticated traffic routing and monitoring.

Best Practices for API Deployment

- **Automate Deployments**: Use automation to minimize human errors and streamline processes.

- **Implement Monitoring and Logging**: Establish robust monitoring and logging to quickly identify and rectify issues.

- **Prioritize Security**: Focus on security measures, including authentication, authorization, and encryption throughout the deployment.

- **Keep Detailed Documentation**: Maintain comprehensive documentation to ensure consistency and facilitate knowledge transfer within the team.

Conclusion

Selecting an appropriate deployment strategy for APIs is essential to ensure they perform optimally under various conditions. Whether opting for a traditional monolithic approach or a more contemporary serverless or microservices architecture, the strategy should align with the organization's specific requirements. By understanding the pros and cons of each method and following best deployment practices, organizations can effectively manage their APIs to meet operational goals and enhance user experiences.

Continuous Integration/Continuous Deployment (CI/CD): How CI/CD fits into API development

Continuous Integration and Continuous Deployment (CI/CD) are critical practices in modern software development, designed to minimize the time gap between code development and deployment. This framework is particularly essential in API development, where updates are frequent and swift iterations are necessary. CI/CD not only accelerates development cycles but also maintains high standards of quality through automated, systematic updates. This article examines how CI/CD integrates into API development, detailing its processes, advantages, and implementation tips.

Role of CI/CD in API Development

CI/CD combines continuous integration, continuous deployment, and continuous delivery into an integrated process that streamlines coding, testing, and deployment tasks. Continuous integration involves merging all developers' changes into a shared mainline multiple times a day. Continuous deployment automates the delivery of applications to specified infrastructure environments. These methodologies aim to improve collaboration, enhance code quality, and decrease the time it takes to deliver changes.

Advantages of CI/CD for API Development

1. **Quick Integration and Testing**: CI/CD enables developers to frequently merge their code into a shared repository where builds and tests are conducted automatically. This is particularly useful for APIs as it allows for early detection and rectification of integration issues.

2. **Accelerated Release Cycles**: CI/CD facilitates quicker and more frequent updates to APIs, speeding up the release cycle without sacrificing stability or quality.

3. **Increased Productivity and Efficiency**: By automating build, test, and deployment processes, CI/CD reduces manual overhead and minimizes errors, freeing developers to concentrate on creating features.

4. **Improved Quality Assurance**: Continuous testing ensures that defects are discovered and addressed sooner in the development cycle, boosting the overall quality of the API.

5. **Optimized Resource Management**: CI/CD pipelines are designed for efficient resource utilization, ensuring that infrastructure is only used as needed, which helps in reducing operational costs.

Critical Components of CI/CD in API Development

Continuous Integration

Continuous integration mandates developers to integrate their code changes into a central repository frequently, where builds and preliminary tests are run. Tools like Jenkins, Travis CI, and CircleCI automate these steps by executing predefined test suites and integration scripts, confirming the new code integrates seamlessly with the existing codebase.

Example CI Workflow:

```
# Example Jenkins pipeline configuration for building a Node.js API
pipeline {
    agent any
    stages {
        stage('Build') {
            steps {
                sh 'npm install'
            }
        }
        stage('Test') {
            steps {
                sh 'npm test'
            }
        }
        stage('Deploy') {
            steps {
                sh 'deploy-script.sh'
            }
        }
    }
}
```

This Jenkins pipeline script automatically handles building, testing, and deploying the API upon any new commits to the repository.

Continuous Deployment

Continuous deployment extends automation by ensuring any code change that passes all set tests is automatically deployed to production environments. This is essential for APIs to ensure prompt updates to end-users without manual interference.

Deployment Tools: Technologies like Docker and Kubernetes facilitate scalable and manageable deployments of containerized APIs. Kubernetes, for example, can handle the seamless rollout and rollback of API deployments.

Implementing CI/CD in API Development

1. **Implement Version Control**: Utilize tools like Git for managing and tracking code changes.

2. **Configure CI Tools**: Select a CI tool compatible with your stack and establish pipelines that automatically build and test code upon commits.

3. **Automate Testing**: Develop exhaustive automated tests that encompass various aspects of API functionality, including unit, integration, and end-to-end tests.

4. **Establish Deployment Protocols**: Set up automated deployment processes capable of deploying the API across different environments based on the stage of the pipeline.

5. **Monitor and Enhance**: Continuously monitor the performance of the CI/CD pipelines and adjust for improved speed, efficiency, and reliability. Incorporate

feedback to enhance the development process continually.

Conclusion

CI/CD is transformative in API development, offering substantial benefits in speed, efficiency, and quality. By automating integration, testing, and deployment processes, CI/CD not only simplifies development workflows but also ensures that teams can deliver high-quality APIs more consistently and predictably. Effective implementation of CI/CD requires thoughtful planning and commitment but results in a more agile and responsive development environment, well-suited to the demands of contemporary software deployment.

Monitoring and Maintenance: Keeping an API healthy post-deployment

Post-deployment monitoring and maintenance are pivotal to ensuring that an API remains operational, secure, and meets performance benchmarks, which in turn promotes a seamless user experience and continuous service availability. This article discusses key methodologies, tools, and practices for effective post-deployment monitoring and maintenance of APIs, aimed at preventing failures and improving service quality over time.

Necessity of Monitoring and Maintenance

Continuous monitoring and timely updates are crucial for sustaining an API's performance post-deployment. These practices are fundamental for:

- **Reliable Availability**: Monitoring verifies that the API is constantly available and functioning as intended.

- **Security Upgrades**: Maintenance routines help detect and address security threats promptly.

- **Performance Optimization**: Regular monitoring identifies slowdowns or other performance issues that may affect user experience.

- **Future-Proofing the Service**: Updating the API in accordance with evolving business needs or technological advancements ensures it remains relevant and effective.

Monitoring Techniques for APIs

Monitoring an API involves the systematic collection and analysis of data to assess its health and efficiency. Important strategies include:

1. Real-Time Monitoring

This strategy involves observing the API's operations continuously to quickly identify and rectify any operational issues. Popular tools for real-time monitoring include Prometheus, New Relic, and Datadog due to their powerful monitoring capabilities.

Example: Setting up Prometheus for API monitoring:

```
# Prometheus configuration example for API monitoring
scrape_configs:
  - job_name: 'api-monitoring'
    scrape_interval: 5s
    static_configs:
      - targets: ['your_api_server.com:9090']
```

This configuration directs Prometheus to collect metrics from the API server every five seconds, providing continuous performance data.

2. Log Management

Effective log management captures and analyzes API logs, offering insights into the API's operational trends and user interactions. Tools such as the ELK Stack or Splunk are crucial for logging data aggregation and analysis.

Example: Using Logstash to manage API logs:

```
input {
  file {
    path => "/var/api_logs/api_activity.log"
    start_position => "beginning"
  }
}
```

```
filter {
  grok {
    match => { "message" => "%{TIMESTAMP_ISO8601:time} %{LOGLEVEL:severity}
      %{DATA:log_message}" }
  }
}
output {
  elasticsearch {
    hosts => ["http://your_elasticsearch_server:9200"]
    index => "api-logs-%{+YYYY.MM.dd}"
  }
}
```

This setup configures Logstash to parse API logs, extracting critical information for storage and analysis in Elasticsearch.

3. Automated Health Checks

Health checks are critical for routinely verifying that all components of the API are operational and interact correctly.

Example: Creating a health check route in a Node.js API:

```
app.get('/health-check', (req, res) => {
  res.status(200).send('API is fully operational');
});
```

This endpoint provides a quick method to verify the API's health and ensure it is functioning properly.

Maintenance Practices

To effectively maintain an API:

- **Regularly Update and Patch**: Consistently update the API to repair bugs, apply security fixes, and introduce new features.

- **Conduct Performance Reviews**: Regularly analyze performance data to identify and resolve any issues that could degrade the API's effectiveness.

- **Manage Dependencies**: Ensure all connected libraries and services are up-to-date to mitigate security risks.

- **Keep Documentation Current**: Continuously update the API documentation to accurately reflect any changes or enhancements.

Conclusion

Thorough monitoring and meticulous maintenance are essential for maintaining the health and effectiveness of APIs after deployment. By employing sophisticated monitoring tools and following robust maintenance practices, organizations can ensure their APIs remain secure, dependable, and high-performing. These efforts not only enhance the user experience but also extend the life and relevance of the API, adapting smoothly to changing business requirements and technological shifts. Engaging proactively in these activities establishes a foundation for sustained API success and operational excellence.

Chapter Twelve

Consuming Third-Party APIs

Finding and Evaluating APIs: How to find and assess third-party APIs

In the landscape of modern software development, third-party APIs are indispensable tools that allow developers to integrate complex functionalities into applications efficiently. From enhancing features to streamlining operations, third-party APIs can significantly speed up development timelines and expand capabilities. This article provides insights on how to locate and critically evaluate third-party APIs to ensure they align with specific project needs concerning functionality, reliability, and security.

Locating Third-Party APIs

The search for the right third-party API begins with knowing where to look. Here are several effective methods for discovering APIs that may suit your project requirements:

1. API Directories and Marketplaces

Platforms such as ProgrammableWeb, RapidAPI, and GitHub are treasure troves of APIs categorized by function and industry. These sites provide extensive resources including documentation, developer reviews, and sometimes, sandbox environments for testing APIs.

2. Utilizing Search Engines

A straightforward search through Google or other search engines with specific keywords related to your needs, like "payment processing API" or "geolocation services API," can lead to a variety of options.

3. Engaging with Developer Communities

Online forums and communities such as Stack Overflow, Reddit's r/programming, and various coding groups on platforms like Discord and Slack are excellent for obtaining unbiased opinions and reviews from peers who have firsthand experiences with specific APIs.

4. Analyzing Competitor Tools

Reviewing the tools and APIs implemented by competitors can provide insight into which APIs are proven in your field and potentially suitable for your needs.

Assessing Third-Party APIs

Finding a potential API is only the first step; assessing its suitability is next. Important factors to consider include:

1. Documentation Quality

Well-documented APIs save time and reduce integration headaches. Effective documentation should be comprehensive, clear, and complete with setup instructions, endpoint details, sample calls, and troubleshooting tips.

2. Ease of Integration

Assessing the API firsthand, preferably through a trial or a free usage tier, helps determine its compatibility and ease of integration with your existing systems.

3. Performance Metrics

Essential for core functionalities, the API's performance metrics like response times and uptime records are critical. Tools like Pingdom can provide performance insights.

4. Security Protocols

Security is paramount. Ensure the API adheres to the best security practices including data encryption (HTTPS/SSL) and robust authentication methods (e.g., OAuth).

5. Cost Efficiency

Understand the API's cost structure. Many APIs offer different tiers based on usage, and it's crucial to choose one that offers the best balance between cost and functionality.

6. Developer Support and Community

Availability of developer support and an active community can be invaluable for resolving potential issues. Check the kind of support offered—whether through forums, direct support, or extensive documentation.

7. Regulatory Compliance

Make sure the API complies with all relevant legal and regulatory requirements, especially those related to data privacy and protection, such as GDPR for services operating within or targeting the EU.

Conclusion

Choosing the right third-party API involves a thorough analysis of potential options against a set of criteria crucial to your project's success. By diligently searching for and evaluating APIs based on documentation, usability, performance, security, cost, support, and compliance, developers can effectively harness the power of third-party APIs to enhance their applications. This careful selection process ensures that integrated APIs not only meet but exceed functionality expectations, driving value and innovation in software development projects.

Integrating Third-Party APIs: Strategies for integration

Incorporating third-party APIs effectively is essential for adding sophisticated features to applications and enhancing user interactions by leveraging external services. However, the integration of these APIs can bring about challenges such as ensuring system compatibility, securing communications, and maintaining optimal performance. This guide discusses a structured approach for integrating third-party APIs into software projects effectively.

Strategic Planning Stage

The integration process begins with a detailed planning stage. Understanding the API's features and how it aligns with your project goals ensures a seamless integration and optimal functionality within your software architecture.

Essential steps in the planning phase include:

- **Requirement Analysis**: Clearly identify what you expect from the API. Evaluate the kinds of data it will retrieve, forecast the load it will handle, and understand how it will enhance your application.

- **Documentation Scrutiny**: Carefully review the API's documentation to grasp request and response formats, error handling, and rate limits. This helps in understanding how to effectively communicate with the API.

- **Security Assessment**: Determine the necessary security measures to ensure data exchanged with the API is protected. Confirm the API's authentication protocols, such as OAuth tokens or API keys.

Implementation Phase

After thorough planning, you can move forward with the actual integration, employing best practices to ensure robustness and effectiveness.

1. Building an API Client

Develop a specialized API client within your application to manage interactions with the third-party API. This client should be responsible for making requests, processing responses, and handling errors efficiently.

Example: Implementing an API client in Python using the requests library:

```python
import requests

class APIClient:
    def __init__(self, base_url, api_key):
        self.base_url = base_url
        self.headers = {'Authorization': f'Bearer {api_key}'}

    def get(self, endpoint, params=None):
        try:
            response = requests.get(f'{self.base_url}/{endpoint}', headers=self
                .headers, params=params)
            response.raise_for_status()  # Ensures handling of HTTP errors
            return response.json()
        except requests.RequestException as e:
            print(f'An error occurred: {e}')
            return None

api_client = APIClient('https://api.example.com', 'your_api_key')
data = api_client.get('data_endpoint', params={'param1': 'value1'})
```

This snippet illustrates a simple API client that conducts authenticated GET requests and incorporates basic error handling.

2. Error Handling Strategies

Integrate advanced error handling to effectively manage potential disruptions:

- **Retry Logic**: Develop retry mechanisms for transient errors, ideally incorporating exponential backoff to mitigate server load.

- **Alternative Measures**: Set up backup procedures for situations when the API is inaccessible, like using cached data or an alternative API.

- **User Feedback**: Implement mechanisms to inform users effectively if their experience is impacted by API performance issues.

3. Thorough Testing

Extensive testing is vital to ensure that the API integration functions correctly under various scenarios:

- **Unit Testing**: Perform tests on individual functions within your API client to verify their accuracy.

- **Integration Testing**: Assess the entire integration setup to ensure that interactions and error handling are working as planned.

- **Stress Testing**: Utilize load testing tools to simulate high usage and examine API stability under pressure.

4. Continuous Monitoring

After integrating the API, continuously monitor its performance to adjust and optimize as necessary. Keep track of critical metrics like response times, failure rates, and throughput to ensure ongoing efficiency and effectiveness.

Conclusion

Effectively integrating third-party APIs can substantially broaden the functionalities of your applications and elevate the user experience. By engaging in careful planning, implementing strategic integration practices, and maintaining vigilant oversight, developers can maximize the benefits of these external services. This proactive approach helps ensure that APIs are integrated smoothly and continue to deliver significant value, enhancing the application's overall effectiveness and user satisfaction.

Handling Third-Party API Limitations: Dealing with limitations and issues

Utilizing third-party APIs effectively enriches software applications, adding advanced functionality without extensive in-house development. However, integration of these APIs often introduces challenges related to system constraints and limitations which, if not properly managed, can impact overall application performance and user experience. Recognizing how to manage these limitations adeptly is essential for maintaining optimal application functionality and reliability. This article describes the common challenges associated with third-party APIs and provides techniques for effectively addressing these issues.

Prevalent Third-Party API Challenges

1. Rate Limits and Quotas: To safeguard their systems and maintain stability, many APIs set limits on the number of requests that can be made within a specified period. Surpassing these limits can lead to throttled requests or temporary blocks, disrupting application functionality.

2. Limited Data and Features: Third-party APIs might not always offer the specific data or functionality required, or the data available may lack the necessary detail or scope.

3. Response Delays: Slow API response times can significantly degrade user experience, particularly in applications dependent on real-time data.

4. API Evolution: Providers may update or modify APIs, deprecating features or changing specifications, which can adversely affect pre-existing integrations.

5. Security and Compliance Risks: Integrating external APIs involves data exchanges that could introduce security vulnerabilities. It is also vital to ensure that the integration complies with legal standards like GDPR or HIPAA.

Strategies to Address API Limitations

Managing Rate Limits and Quotas

Strategies to effectively handle rate limits include:

- **Caching**: Reduce the frequency of API calls by caching responses, particularly for data that does not change often.

Python Example with requests-cache:

```python
import requests
import requests_cache

requests_cache.install_cache('api_cache', backend='sqlite', expire_after=180)

def fetch_data(url):
    response = requests.get(url)
    if response.ok:
        return response.json()
    else:
        return "API Error: " + str(response.status_code)

data = fetch_data('https://api.example.com/data')
```

- **Adaptive Request Rate**: Implement adaptive mechanisms to monitor and adjust the request rate to the API based on current usage and known limits.

- **Scheduling**: Organize API calls by prioritizing essential requests and scheduling less critical ones during periods of lower demand.

Overcoming Data and Feature Shortcomings

- **Supplementing Data**: Where necessary, complement API data by sourcing additional data from other APIs or services.

- **Negotiating with Providers**: Maintain a dialogue with API providers to request new features or data enhancements that meet your application's needs.

Mitigating Latency Issues

- **Asynchronous Processing**: Manage API requests asynchronously to keep the user interface responsive and prevent delays in application operations.

JavaScript Example Using Async/Await:

```javascript
async function fetchData(url) {
    try {
        const response = await fetch(url);
        return await response.json();
    } catch (error) {
        console.error('API request error:', error);
    }
}

fetchData('https://api.example.com/data').then(data => console.log(data));
```

- **API Request Optimization**: Reduce the volume and frequency of requests. Employ batching techniques if the API allows, or refine requests to limit the scope of data retrieved.

Adapting to Changes in APIs

- **Stay Updated**: Regularly update your API client libraries and routinely test the application to quickly identify and remedy issues arising from changes in the API.

- **Version Management**: Specify API versions in your requests to ensure stability and prevent disruptions from unexpected changes in the API.

Securing Integration and Compliance

- **Implement Strong Security Protocols**: Use HTTPS for secure data transmission and follow best security practices as recommended by the API provider.

- **Regulatory Adherence**: Ensure that API integration aligns with all applicable legal and regulatory standards to mitigate risks related to data privacy and security.

Conclusion

Third-party APIs offer powerful capabilities for enhancing applications but come with inherent challenges that need strategic management. By understanding these limitations and employing effective strategies, developers can ensure robust API integration. Proper management of these aspects not only enhances the application's functionality but also ensures a reliable and secure user experience.

Chapter Thirteen

Case Studies

Real-World Examples: Analysis of successful API implementations

In the current technological landscape, APIs are integral to expanding application functionalities and optimizing user experience. This analysis of successful real-world API implementations offers insights into how companies strategically employ APIs to promote growth, streamline services, and enhance interactions. Here, we explore case studies of effective API usage across various sectors.

1. Stripe: Transforming Payment Solutions

Stripe's API has become a standard in the fintech industry for seamlessly incorporating payment processing capabilities into applications. This API facilitates easy integration of online payment services, democratizing access to financial transactions for businesses of all sizes.

Key Success Factors:

- **Developer-Centric Design**: Stripe's comprehensive documentation, complete with interactive examples, makes integration straightforward for developers.

- **Robust Security Protocols**: The API prioritizes security, simplifying the complexity of data compliance and encryption for developers.

- **Adaptable Architecture**: Designed to support businesses from small startups to large corporations, Stripe's API scales effectively to handle a broad range of transaction volumes.

Example Python Code (Creating a Stripe Charge):

```python
import stripe
stripe.api_key = 'your_secret_key'

# Execute a payment charge
charge = stripe.charge.create(
    amount=2000,  # amount in cents
    currency='usd',

    source='tok_visa',  # obtained through Stripe.js
    description='Charge for example.email@example.com'
)
print(charge)
```

This snippet demonstrates creating a payment charge with Stripe, emphasizing the API's ease of use and effectiveness.

2. Twilio: Streamlining Communications

Twilio's API has revolutionized business communications, allowing developers to embed phone calls, messaging, and other communication functionalities directly into applications. This enhances direct customer engagement without extensive infrastructure investments.

Key Success Factors:

- **Rich Documentation and Testing Environment**: Twilio's detailed documentation and accessible sandbox environment facilitate easy testing and integration by developers.

- **Flexible Application**: The API supports a wide array of communication needs, making it versatile across different industries.

- **Extensive Reach**: Twilio's capability to connect with global phone networks enables businesses to engage with a worldwide audience.

Example Python Code (Sending an SMS with Twilio):

```python
from twilio.rest import Client

account_sid = 'ACXXXXXXXXXXXXXXXXXXXXXXXX'
auth_token = 'your_auth_token'
client = Client(account_sid, auth_token)

message = client.messages.create(
    body="Hello from Twilio!",
    from_='+1234567890',
    to='+0987654321'
)
print(message.sid)
```

This example shows how to send an SMS using Twilio, highlighting how the API facilitates straightforward communication integrations.

3. Google Maps: Innovating Location-Based Services

The Google Maps API is widely utilized by apps requiring mapping, directions, and location data. It provides rich, detailed geographic information that enhances apps with dynamic and interactive mapping capabilities.

Key Success Factors:

- **Comprehensive Features**: The API offers extensive functionalities including real-time traffic updates,

161

panoramic street views, and detailed location data, enriching the user interface.

- **Dependable Performance**: Google ensures consistent API performance and reliability, crucial for apps depending on real-time data.

- **Developer Support**: Google backs its API with detailed documentation, active forums, and direct support channels.

Example HTML Code (Embedding Google Maps):

```
<!DOCTYPE html>
<html>
<head>
    <title>Simple Map</title>
    <script src="https://maps.googleapis.com/maps/api/js?key
        =YOUR_API_KEY&callback=initMap" async defer></script>
    <script>
    function initMap() {
        var map = new google.maps.Map(document.getElementById('map'), {
            center: {lat: -34.397, lng: 150.644},
            zoom: 8
        });
    }
    </script>
</head>
<body>
    <div id="map" style="height: 400px; width: 100%;"></div>
</body>
</html>
```

This code embeds Google Maps into a webpage, showcasing how the API can be integrated to offer advanced mapping solutions to users.

Conclusion

The API implementations of Stripe, Twilio, and Google Maps illustrate how thoughtfully applied APIs can be transformative, fostering innovation and improving user experiences across applications. These examples underscore the importance of easy-to-use documentation, reliable functionality, and flexible integration options in the success of API implementations. By drawing on these examples, developers can understand how to harness APIs effectively to create robust, efficient, and user-focused digital solutions.

Learning from Failures: Common pitfalls in API design and how to avoid them

Developing an API involves more than just coding skills—it requires careful planning and foresight to avoid common design errors that could undermine the functionality and usability of the application. This article outlines frequent pitfalls in API design and suggests practical strategies to sidestep these issues, thereby enhancing the efficiency and security of APIs.

1. Inconsistency in Design

Challenge: A lack of uniformity in API design can lead to confusion, errors, and a steeper learning curve for users. Inconsistent naming conventions for endpoints, parameters, and data fields, or varying behaviors across similar functions, are common inconsistencies.

Solution: Adopt consistent design principles from the beginning. Establish and adhere to a uniform naming convention for all parts of the API. Ensure that similar operations are handled in similar ways throughout the API. Tools like Swagger or API Blueprint can aid in documenting these conventions and ensuring consistency is maintained.

2. Inadequate Documentation

Challenge: Poorly documented APIs are difficult to use and integrate, potentially leading to improper usage and integration failures.

Solution: Dedicate ample resources to develop comprehensive, understandable, and accessible documentation. Good documentation should include:

- Exhaustive details on every endpoint, including parameters and expected data types.

- Examples of requests and responses.

- Clear definitions of error codes and associated messages.

- Guides on authentication and security protocols.

Interactive documentation platforms like Swagger UI can significantly improve usability by allowing developers to test API calls directly from the documentation.

3. Misuse of HTTP Status Codes

Challenge: Not using HTTP status codes effectively or using them incorrectly can create ambiguous responses, complicating troubleshooting and debugging.

164

Solution: Implement a wide range of HTTP status codes to provide clear, context-specific feedback on API requests. For instance:

- **201 Created** when a new resource has been successfully created.

- **400 Bad Request** for malformed requests.

- **404 Not Found** when a requested resource is unavailable.

- **503 Service Unavailable** for temporary server issues.

Appropriate use of status codes clarifies the API's responses, aiding in client-side error handling.

4. Neglecting Security

Challenge: Security oversights such as exposing sensitive information, weak authentication, or lack of data encryption can lead to significant vulnerabilities.

Solution: Prioritize security in API design:

- Enforce HTTPS to secure data in transit.

- Utilize strong authentication mechanisms, like OAuth2, to manage access controls.

- Sanitize all incoming data to prevent SQL injection and other attacks.

- Continuously update and refine security measures to address new threats.

5. Rigid Versioning Strategy

Challenge: APIs evolve over time, and without a flexible versioning approach, updates can disrupt existing clients.

Solution: Design your API with future changes in mind, allowing multiple versions of the API to coexist without disruption. Implement versioning through:

- URL paths (e.g., **/api/v1/** vs. **/api/v2/**).

- Custom headers.

- Media type versioning in the Accept header.

Example of URL path versioning in Python with Flask:

```python
from flask import Flask
app = Flask(__name__)

@app.route('/api/v1/items')
def get_items_v1():
    return "Item list version 1"

@app.route('/api/v2/items')
def get_items_v2():
    return "Item list version 2 with additional data"
```

This example shows how different API versions can operate simultaneously, facilitating smoother transitions for users.

6. Ineffective Error Handling

Challenge: Vague or unhelpful error messages can leave users uncertain about what went wrong or how to resolve issues.

Solution: Develop error responses that are as informative as possible. Include an appropriate HTTP status code, a concise error message, and a link to more detailed information or documentation where necessary.

Conclusion

Steering clear of these common API design pitfalls is crucial for building robust and user-friendly APIs. By emphasizing consistent design, thorough documentation, proper use of HTTP status codes, stringent security practices, flexible versioning, and detailed error handling, developers can create more reliable and secure APIs. Learning from these typical mistakes and adopting best practices will lead to smoother integrations and a better overall user experience.

Conclusion

Recap of Key Learnings: Summarize the most important lessons from the book

This summary synthesizes the critical insights derived from the book, centered around the strategic development and efficient management of APIs—key components in contemporary digital ecosystems. It highlights foundational practices, identifies typical setbacks, and discusses proactive strategies in API design and deployment, providing a rounded view that is essential for developers and IT professionals.

1. Core Design Principles

Central teachings emphasize strict adherence to fundamental design principles ensuring APIs are user-friendly, maintainable, and scalable. Significant principles include:

- **Consistency**: Achieve consistency across API interfaces in naming conventions, data formats, and procedural operations to aid user comprehension and predictability.

- **Simplicity**: Strive for simplicity to prevent unnecessary complexity that could confound users and hinder maintenance.

- **Comprehensive Documentation**: Documentation is crucial and should be thorough and articulate, enabling developers to quickly understand and effectively employ the API.

168

- **Effective Versioning**: Implement meticulous version control to manage evolutionary changes without impacting existing users, clearly communicating any deprecations.

2. Security Strategies

Security within API design is emphasized as a paramount concern. The book underscores the importance of:

- **Strong Authentication Systems**: Utilize advanced authentication protocols such as OAuth2 to ensure secure access control.

- **Encryption Practices**: Enforce HTTPS for all communications to protect data in transit and consider encrypting sensitive stored data.

- **Regular Security Reviews**: Conduct consistent security audits to discover and remedy security vulnerabilities.

3. Performance Enhancement Techniques

API performance significantly affects the user experience and operational efficacy. The book covers several optimization strategies:

- **Strategic Caching**: Use caching to reduce server query frequency, particularly for static data, which can significantly quicken response times.

- **Implementing Rate Limiting**: Apply rate limiting to prevent service abuse and maintain performance under high load conditions.

- **Selective Data Retrieval**: Facilitate mechanisms that allow users to specify exactly which data fields they need, minimizing data transfer volumes and speeding up interactions.

4. Robust Error Management and Feedback Mechanisms

Effective error management is vital for operational clarity and user support. Highlighted practices include:

- **Detailed Error Responses**: Utilize appropriate HTTP status codes and provide extensive error messages to aid in troubleshooting.

- **Graceful Failure Handling**: Design APIs to function in a degraded state during downtime, providing essential services and clear user notifications.

- **Advanced Monitoring**: Implement thorough monitoring and logging to evaluate API usage and identify issues proactively.

5. Scalability and System Flexibility

Ensuring APIs can accommodate growth in user numbers and data demands is crucial for long-term viability. Notable strategies involve:

- **Utilizing Load Balancers**: Employ load balancing to evenly distribute traffic across multiple servers.

- **Microservices Architecture**: Leverage a microservices architecture for greater scalability and flexibility, allowing components to be scaled independently according to demand.

6. Lifecycle Management and API Evolution

Sustaining API reliability and adapting to technological advancements require ongoing dedication. Points of focus include:

- **Gathering User Feedback**: Establish robust channels for receiving and analyzing user feedback to continuously improve the API.

- **Transparent Deprecation Strategies**: Develop clear policies for retiring older API versions, providing users with sufficient notification and detailed migration guidance.

Conclusion

The book offers a comprehensive blueprint for designing APIs that are not just functional and secure but also robust and prepared for future advancements. Each chapter consolidates this knowledge, offering actionable advice for developing APIs that proficiently meet current demands while being adaptable to future changes. By integrating these principles, developers can ensure their APIs remain valuable and promote ongoing innovation.

Next Steps in API Mastery: Guiding readers on where to go next in their API journey

As you near the end of this foundational exploration into API design and management, it's pivotal to look ahead and plan your next steps toward advancing your API expertise. Whether you're a developer, a software architect, or a project manager, enhancing your proficiency in API development will prove invaluable. This guide provides directions for further learning, applying your skills more broadly, and delving into more complex aspects of API technology.

1. Enhance Theoretical Understanding

A robust theoretical foundation is essential for mastering technical subjects, including APIs. To deepen your knowledge:

- **Advanced Reading**: Expand your learning with books that delve into niche topics such as API security or sophisticated design principles. Titles like "API Security in Action" by Neil Madden offer insights into specific areas crucial for advanced developers.

- **Educational Courses**: Pursue higher education in subjects related to software architecture or network communication. Many educational institutions and online platforms offer courses that can provide deeper insights into the technical aspects of APIs.

2. Practical Application

Hands-on experience is crucial for skill enhancement. Continue to refine your abilities through active participation in projects and professional tasks:

- **Personal Projects**: Develop APIs for personal use or to solve problems you encounter in daily activities, such as a personal project management tool that integrates various software.

- **Open Source Contributions**: Get involved with the open source community. This is an excellent way to learn from seasoned developers, improve your skills, and contribute to meaningful projects.

3. Stay Current with Emerging Technologies

As API technologies evolve, new protocols and methodologies emerge. Keeping up with these trends is vital:

- **GraphQL**: If you're seasoned in RESTful APIs, consider learning GraphQL—a powerful query language that enables clients to extract precisely what they need.

- **Serverless Computing**: Explore how APIs operate within serverless architectures, an area offered by cloud services like AWS Lambda and Azure Functions, which allows for scaling API logic without extensive infrastructure management.

4. Community Engagement and Networking

Building a network within the tech community can lead to new insights, project ideas, and career opportunities:

- **Conferences and Meetups**: Engage in industry conferences or local meetups focused on API development to stay informed about the latest trends and network with peers.

- **Professional Groups**: Participate in online forums and professional groups on platforms such as LinkedIn or Stack Overflow, which can be excellent resources for advice, sharing knowledge, and making professional connections.

5. Certifications and Further Specialization

Pursuing certifications can validate your expertise and open up further career opportunities:

- **API-Specific Certifications**: Seek out certifications that specifically enhance API skills, such as those offered by tech companies like Google or through tools like Postman.

- **Comprehensive IT Certifications**: Broad IT certifications that cover software development, cybersecurity, and system architecture can also bolster your API skills and resume.

Conclusion

Advancing your API mastery is a multifaceted journey that involves expanding both theoretical knowledge and practical skills, exploring new technologies, engaging with the community, and obtaining relevant certifications. As you continue to navigate your professional development, remember that mastery is an ongoing process—staying curious, proactive, and connected with the latest industry developments will be key to your growth and success in the field of API development.

Further Resources: Books, websites, courses, and more to continue learning

Advancing your API development skills involves continuous education and keeping up with the fast-paced changes in technology. As the areas of API design and implementation are perpetually evolving, it's critical to utilize a variety of educational tools and resources to deepen your expertise. This guide details a comprehensive selection of books, websites, courses, and other educational media essential for anyone looking to enhance their knowledge in API development.

Books

Adding specialized books to your repertoire can greatly expand your technical understanding and proficiency:

1. **"Designing APIs with Swagger and OpenAPI" by Josh Ponelat and Lukas Rosenstock** - This book is invaluable for developers looking to excel in API specification formats to improve design, construction, and documentation skills.

2. **"APIs: A Strategy Guide" by Daniel Jacobson, Greg Brail, and Dan Woods** - Offers a strategic perspective on how to develop APIs that mesh well with business objectives and drive technological success.

3. **"RESTful Web APIs" by Leonard Richardson, Sam Ruby, and Mike Amundsen** - A critical resource for those wanting a comprehensive understanding of RESTful architecture.

175

4. **"API Security in Action" by Neil Madden** - Concentrates on API security, providing strategies for designing secure APIs from the start.

Websites

Online platforms provide the latest tutorials, articles, and discussions about API technologies and trends:

1. **API Evangelist (apievangelist.com)** - Led by Kin Lane, this site explores a wide range of topics on API technology and business implications.

2. **Swagger.io** - A central resource for those using Swagger tools, it supports developers in building and documenting RESTful web services.

3. **ProgrammableWeb (programmableweb.com)** - Hosts a rich directory of APIs, along with current news and tutorials to keep developers informed.

4. **REST API Tutorial (restapitutorial.com)** - Dedicated to educating on REST APIs, this site offers detailed guidance on best practices in API development.

Online Courses

Structured courses are an excellent way to stay updated with current knowledge and practices:

1. **"Building RESTful APIs with Flask" by Treehouse** - A tutorial-driven course that teaches creating scalable and maintainable APIs using the Flask framework.

2. **"API Design and Fundamentals of Google Cloud's Apigee API Platform" by Coursera** - Introduces learners to sophisticated API design and management techniques using Google's Apigee platform.

3. **"Developing APIs with Google Cloud's Apigee API Platform" by Pluralsight** - Provides deeper insights into API development strategies using Apigee.

4. **"Restful API with Express.js" by Codecademy** - An extensive program on crafting RESTful APIs with Express.js, encompassing both foundational and advanced topics.

Workshops and Webinars

Hands-on workshops and webinars allow for practical experience and direct interaction with leading experts:

1. **API World Conference** - Hosts numerous workshops and sessions where experts discuss the newest API innovations and strategies.

2. **Postman Webinars** - Features regular webinars on a variety of topics from API basics to sophisticated techniques and updates.

3. **O'Reilly Media Webinars** - Provides lectures and discussions by knowledgeable authors on several API-related subjects.

Podcasts

For those who prefer auditory learning, podcasts are a great way to absorb information on the go:

1. **APIs You Won't Hate (APIs You Won't Hate podcast)** - Hosts discussions with experts sharing their API development experiences and advice.

2. **The RESTful Web (The RESTful Web podcast)** - Focuses on RESTful API design and development, addressing common challenges and innovative solutions.

3. **Software Engineering Daily (Software Engineering Daily podcast)** - Features interviews with industry leaders on a wide range of topics, including API development.

Conclusion

Enhancing your proficiency in API development requires a multi-faceted approach to learning, incorporating books, online resources, structured courses, interactive workshops, and even podcasts. Each of these resources offers unique insights and knowledge, providing a solid foundation for becoming proficient in modern API technologies and practices. As you continue to explore these resources, you'll gain a deeper understanding of how to design, secure, and manage APIs effectively, keeping you at the forefront of technological advancements.

API Design

"A Middle-Level Guide to Customizing APIs for Scalability and Efficiency"

Kevin Bates

or indirect, which are incurred as a result of the use of information contained within this document.

Table of Contents

Introduction 4

Chapter One: Design Patterns for Scalable APIs 15

Chapter Two: Enhancing API Performance 23

Chapter Three: Security at Scale 31

Chapter Four: Efficient Data Management 39

Chapter Five: Rate Limiting and Throttling............47

Chapter Six: API Gateway Optimization 55

Chapter Seven: Load Balancing Techniques 63

Chapter Eight: Asynchronous APIs and Event-Driven Design..72

Chapter Nine: API Caching Strategies 79

Chapter Ten: Versioning for Continuous Improvement...86

Chapter Eleven: Advanced Testing for Robust APIs.94

Chapter Twelve: Deployment Strategies for High Availability...102

Chapter Thirteen: Monitoring and Analytics 112

Chapter Fourteen: Case Studies of Scalable API Implementations 120

Conclusion 129

Introduction

Purpose of the Book: Outline the focus on scalability and efficiency

"API Design: A Middle-Level Guide to Customizing APIs for Scalability and Efficiency" is crafted to advance the knowledge of developers familiar with basic API concepts towards mastering sophisticated techniques that enhance API scalability and efficiency. This book targets professionals eager to optimize their APIs to support increased loads and complex interactions without sacrificing performance.

Objective of the Book

This manual is designed to act as a bridge connecting intermediate API knowledge to advanced methodologies focused on improving an API's ability to scale and operate efficiently under various demands. It is intended for developers who understand fundamental API structures and are seeking to apply more complex practices that ensure APIs can handle growth in users, data, and traffic seamlessly.

Enhancing Scalability

Scalability is a crucial focus of this book, ensuring that APIs can accommodate growth efficiently. The text explores different architectural approaches and patterns that are pivotal for building scalable APIs, such as:

- **Microservices Architecture**: Breaking down large systems into smaller, independently scalable services that interact via APIs. This segment explains how microservices can be deployed and scaled independently to enhance system manageability and responsiveness.

- **Load Balancing Techniques**: Discussing the distribution of traffic across multiple servers to prevent any single server from becoming a bottleneck. The book reviews practical implementations using tools like DNS round-robin and cloud-based solutions such as AWS Elastic Load Balancing.

- **Advanced Caching Mechanisms**: Implementing caching to minimize backend loads by storing and reusing frequently accessed data. Different caching techniques, including client-side, server-side, and distributed caching systems like Redis, are thoroughly examined to facilitate quick data retrieval.

Focusing on Efficiency

Efficiency in API design involves optimizing resource usage to ensure swift and effective task performance. This book addresses crucial efficiency strategies, including:

- **Data Handling Techniques**: Employing data compression and selective data queries to minimize data transfer over networks, thus enhancing the speed and efficiency of API responses.

- **Asynchronous Processing**: Leveraging asynchronous operations to handle multiple tasks concurrently, thereby keeping the API responsive and quick even under heavy loads.

- **Optimized Connection Management**: Managing connections intelligently to reduce latency and resource consumption, with insights into connection pooling and maintaining persistent HTTP connections.

Practical Examples and Code Snippets

To ground the theoretical knowledge in practical reality, the book is peppered with real-world examples and detailed code demonstrations. For instance, it includes a tutorial on setting up an Nginx-based load balancer:

```
http {
    upstream myapp1 {
        server srv1.example.com weight=3;
        server srv2.example.com;
        server srv3.example.com;
    }

    server {
        listen 80;

        location / {
            proxy_pass http://myapp1;
        }
    }
}
```

This code snippet shows how to distribute incoming requests across servers, using Nginx to balance the load effectively, illustrating a direct application of one of the scalability strategies discussed.

Conclusion

"API Design: A Middle-Level Guide to Customizing APIs for Scalability and Efficiency" equips developers with advanced strategies to build APIs that are not just functional but also robust enough to withstand and adapt to increasing demands. By focusing on these sophisticated elements, the book prepares developers to craft APIs that meet current requirements and are ready to evolve, ensuring long-term performance and scalability. This guide is an invaluable asset for any developer aiming to refine their API design skills and build systems that effectively manage future growth.

Prerequisites: Review of what knowledge and skills are expected from the reader

To fully benefit from "API Design: A Middle-Level Guide to Customizing APIs for Scalability and Efficiency," it is crucial for readers to possess certain foundational knowledge and skills. This ensures that the advanced concepts discussed throughout the book can be effectively understood and applied in real-world API development scenarios.

Essential Programming Knowledge

Proficiency in at least one high-level programming language commonly used in back-end development, such as Python, JavaScript (Node.js), or Java, is essential. Readers should be comfortable with basic programming concepts including syntax, control structures such as loops and conditionals, functions, and data structures like lists and dictionaries.

Example Code (Python):

```python
# Python function demonstrating basic programming concepts
def find_even_numbers(numbers):
    return [num for num in numbers if num % 2 == 0]

sample_numbers = [1, 2, 3, 4, 5, 6]
print(find_even_numbers(sample_numbers))  # Output: [2, 4, 6]
```

Web Technologies and HTTP Protocol

A basic understanding of web technologies, especially the HTTP protocol, is crucial. This includes familiarity with HTTP requests and responses, common methods (GET, POST, PUT, DELETE), status codes, and the use of headers and cookies. This foundational knowledge is key to grasping how APIs function and communicate over the web.

Example HTTP Request:

```
PUT /api/users/123 HTTP/1.1
Host: example.com
Content-Type: application/json
Authorization: Bearer youraccesstoken

{
    "name": "John Doe",
    "email": "john.doe@example.com"
}
```

Introductory API Design Experience

Readers are expected to have basic experience with API usage and design, including making calls to external APIs and designing simple APIs. Knowledge of RESTful principles and familiarity with API styles such as GraphQL, particularly how endpoints are structured and resources managed, will be beneficial.

Database Knowledge

Understanding how to interact with databases is important for API development. Readers should know how to execute basic CRUD operations via SQL or through an ORM. This helps in effectively linking databases with APIs to manage data flow.

Example SQL Query:

```sql
SELECT name, age FROM users WHERE age >= 18;
```

Proficiency with Development Tools

An acquaintance with common development tools and environments is necessary. This includes the use of integrated development environments (IDEs), familiarity with version control systems like Git, and basic command-line skills. These tools are fundamental for effective software development and management.

Debugging and Testing Skills

Competence in debugging and testing is also required. Readers should know how to conduct unit testing and use debugging tools to navigate through code. This skill set is crucial for identifying and resolving issues within software applications.

Example of a simple unit test in Python using unittest:

```python
import unittest

def multiply(a, b):
    return a * b

class TestMultiplyFunction(unittest.TestCase):
    def test_multiply(self):
        self.assertEqual(multiply(3, 4), 12)

if __name__ == '__main__':
    unittest.main()
```

Conclusion

Having these skills ensures that readers can seamlessly engage with the more complex subjects covered in the book, such as enhancing API architectures for better scalability, optimizing efficiency, and implementing advanced security measures. "API Design: A Middle-Level Guide to Customizing APIs for Scalability and Efficiency" builds on this existing knowledge, guiding readers toward mastering sophisticated API design techniques.

Structure of the Book: Brief introduction to the content of each chapter

"API Design: A Middle-Level Guide to Customizing APIs for Scalability and Efficiency" is strategically structured to help developers who already understand basic API principles delve into more complex aspects of API design, with a specific focus on scalability and efficiency. The book progressively builds on topics, allowing readers to expand upon their existing knowledge and acquire new skills methodically.

Chapter 1: Foundations of Scalable and Efficient API Design

The first chapter reintroduces essential API concepts, with a special focus on scalability and efficiency. It discusses common challenges developers face as applications scale and previews the solutions that will be explored in subsequent chapters.

Chapter 2: Architectural Patterns for Scalability

This chapter delves into the various architectural frameworks and design strategies that enhance API scalability. It discusses the use of microservices, serverless computing, and load balancers, providing insights into how to select the best architecture to meet specific project needs.

Example Code:

```
# Basic Nginx load balancing configuration
upstream api_servers {
    server server1.example.com;
    server server2.example.com;
}
server {
    location /api/ {
        proxy_pass http://api_servers;
    }
}
```

Chapter 3: Maximizing API Performance

Focusing on optimizing performance, this chapter introduces techniques to enhance API speed and resource efficiency, such as effective caching, connection pooling, and data handling optimization. Practical implementations of these concepts are provided to aid comprehension.

Chapter 4: Techniques for Advanced Data Management

Critical for handling large data volumes, this chapter covers pagination, data compression, and query optimization, alongside asynchronous processing methods to bolster API throughput and efficiency.

Example Code:

```python
# Asynchronous data retrieval in Python using asyncio
import asyncio

async def retrieve_data(api_url):
    await asyncio.sleep(1)  # Simulate a network call
    return f"Data retrieved from {api_url}"

async def main():
    data = await retrieve_data('https://example.com/api')
    print(data)

asyncio.run(main())
```

Chapter 5: Securing High-Scale APIs

As APIs grow, security needs become more complex. This chapter explores advanced security challenges, focusing on authentication management and secure data handling across distributed systems, with an emphasis on OAuth and JWT protocols.

Chapter 6: Testing and Monitoring for Scalable APIs

This chapter discusses the essential tools and practices for testing APIs under high loads and monitoring them to ensure they maintain expected performance standards. It includes guidance on utilizing logs, metrics, and real-time monitoring tools.

Chapter 7: Effective Deployment Methods

Exploring strategies for deploying scalable and efficient APIs, this chapter covers the use of containers, Kubernetes, and outlines CI/CD methodologies to enhance deployment processes and maintainability.

Chapter 8: Case Studies from the Field

Providing real-world insights, this chapter presents case studies from companies that have successfully scaled their APIs. It examines the strategies employed and the outcomes achieved, offering practical perspectives and lessons learned.

Chapter 9: Looking Ahead: Emerging API Technologies

The concluding chapter projects future trends in API development, such as the integration of artificial intelligence and the impacts of advancing network technologies like 5G. This forward-looking perspective prepares readers for upcoming innovations in API technology.

Conclusion

The book wraps up by summarizing essential takeaways from each chapter, reinforcing the importance of creating APIs that are both powerful and efficient. Readers are encouraged to further explore advanced API design topics and apply their newfound knowledge in their projects.

This structured approach not only introduces advanced concepts but also connects them in a coherent educational journey, guiding readers through a holistic learning experience that enhances their abilities to design, implement, and maintain sophisticated APIs.

Chapter One

Design Patterns for Scalable APIs

Overview of Scalable Architectures: Discussing microservices, serverless, and event-driven architectures

In today's dynamic software development landscape, scalability is a cornerstone of successful application architecture. This discussion delves into three advanced architectural strategies pivotal for building scalable applications: microservices, serverless computing, and event-driven architectures. Each of these frameworks is tailored to enhance the system's ability to efficiently handle growth in user demand and data processing without a compromise in performance.

Microservices Architecture

Microservices architecture structures an application as a collection of small, autonomous services, each performing a specific business function and communicating via well-defined APIs. Unlike traditional monolithic architectures where components are interdependent, microservices are developed, deployed, and scaled independently. This modularity allows for focused updates and scaling of individual components without impacting the entire system, facilitating agile development and deployment practices.

Example Code: Consider a Docker setup for a microservice:

```
# Start with a lightweight Python base image
FROM python:3.8-alpine

# Set the working directory
WORKDIR /app

# Install dependencies
COPY requirements.txt .
RUN pip install --trusted-host pypi.python.org -r requirements.txt
```

```
# Copy the local code to the container
COPY . .

# Make port 80 available
EXPOSE 80

# Command to run the application
CMD ["python", "app.py"]
```

This Dockerfile configures a minimal Python environment suited for running a microservice, illustrating how Docker can encapsulate a service's runtime environment.

Serverless Computing

Serverless computing abstracts server management and infrastructure decisions away from the developers, allowing them to focus solely on writing code. In this model, the execution environment is fully managed by a cloud provider, which dynamically allocates resources to match the current demand precisely. This not only ensures efficient resource use but also optimizes costs, as resources are consumed only when the code is executed.

Example Scenario: In a serverless setup using AWS Lambda, functions are executed in response to events, automatically triggered by various sources such as HTTP requests via Amazon API Gateway. This allows the application to efficiently handle varying loads with minimal management overhead.

Event-Driven Architecture

Event-driven architecture (EDA) is predicated on the detection, production, and reaction to events, which signal changes in state within a system. This architecture is designed to be highly reactive, processing events as they occur, which ensures high responsiveness and efficient resource utilization. EDA is especially useful when combined with microservices, as it helps maintain loose coupling and promotes scalability.

Example Implementation: Using a message broker like RabbitMQ in an EDA setup:

```python
import pika

# Setup connection to RabbitMQ
connection = pika.BlockingConnection(pika.ConnectionParameters(host='localhost'))
channel = connection.channel()
```

```python
# Declare a queue
channel.queue_declare(queue='task_queue')

# Define a callback function for processing messages
def callback(ch, method, properties, body):
    print(" [x] Received %r" % body)

# Consume messages from the queue
channel.basic_consume(queue='task_queue', on_message_callback=callback, auto_ack=True)

print(' [*] Waiting for messages. To exit press CTRL+C')
channel.start_consuming()
```

This Python script demonstrates setting up a consumer with RabbitMQ that listens for and processes messages asynchronously, typical of an event-driven approach.

Conclusion

Selecting an appropriate architecture for application development is crucial for ensuring scalability and efficiency. Microservices provide flexibility, serverless computing offers cost efficiency, and event-driven architectures deliver responsiveness. Understanding these options and their optimal use cases is vital for developers aiming to build robust, scalable systems. Often, leveraging a combination of these architectural styles will yield the best results, adapting fluidly to the demands of complex applications.

Design Patterns Specific to APIs: Discuss patterns like CQRS, BFF (Backend for Frontend), and others that help in scalability

In contemporary software architecture, leveraging design patterns tailored for APIs is crucial when addressing scalability and performance challenges. Design patterns such as Command Query Responsibility Segregation (CQRS), Backend for Frontend (BFF), and others are pivotal in managing increased service demands efficiently. This overview explains how these patterns facilitate scalability and detail how they can be strategically implemented in API development.

Command Query Responsibility Segregation (CQRS)

CQRS is a design pattern that divides operations into two distinct types: commands, which modify data, and queries, which retrieve data. This division allows each operation type to be optimized independently, enhancing performance and scalability. Particularly useful in systems with disparate read and write demands, CQRS facilitates focused scaling efforts where they are most needed, either on the read side or the write side.

Example Code:

```csharp
// C# Example for Command in CQRS
public class UpdateUserCommandHandler : ICommandHandler<UpdateUserCommand>
{
    private readonly ApplicationContext _context;

    public UpdateUserCommandHandler(ApplicationContext context)
    {
        _context = context;
    }

    public void Handle(UpdateUserCommand command)
    {
        var user = _context.Users.Find(command.UserId);
        user.Name = command.Name;
        _context.SaveChanges();
    }
}
```

```
// C# Example for Query in CQRS
public class UserQueryService
{
    private readonly ApplicationContext _context;

    public UserQueryService(ApplicationContext context)
    {
        _context = context;
    }

    public UserDto GetUser(int id)
    {
        var user = _context.Users.Find(id);
        return new UserDto { Name = user.Name, Email = user.Email };
    }
}
```

In this C#

-implementation, **UpdateUserCommandHandler** and **UserQueryService** demonstrate how commands and queries are handled separately, aligning with the CQRS methodology.

Backend for Frontend (BFF)

The BFF pattern is designed to create specialized API endpoints tailored to the unique requirements of different client types, such as mobile, web, or desktop applications. This approach allows for customization of the backend services for each specific frontend, optimizing data delivery and enhancing overall user experience.

Example Scenario: Imagine a scenario where a mobile app and a web application require different data sets and structures. BFF enables the creation of distinct backend services for each, ensuring optimal data delivery that is customized for the constraints and needs of each frontend platform.

Other Scalable API Patterns

API Gateway: Employing an API gateway provides a unified entry point for all client interactions, directing requests to the appropriate backend services. This pattern simplifies client interactions, manages cross-cutting concerns like security and monitoring, and enhances the management of complex API ecosystems.

Rate Limiting: Integrating rate limiting ensures that no single user or service overloads the system, maintaining equitable resource distribution and system reliability even under high load. This is especially critical for public APIs to prevent misuse and ensure service availability.

Asynchronous Messaging: Asynchronous messaging through queues allows services to communicate without direct connections, supporting independent scaling. This method reduces dependencies among services, fostering a more resilient and scalable architecture.

Conclusion

Implementing specific design patterns such as CQRS, BFF, API Gateway, Rate Limiting, and Asynchronous Messaging profoundly impacts API scalability and efficiency. These patterns provide robust solutions for managing load distribution, optimizing data flow, and ensuring responsive service architectures. By adopting these design strategies, developers can craft sophisticated APIs that are well-equipped to handle growth and dynamic user demands, ensuring high performance and scalability in large-scale applications.

Chapter Two

Enhancing API Performance

Performance Metrics: Understanding what makes an API fast

In API development, enhancing performance is crucial to ensure optimal user experiences and efficient backend operations. A swift and reliable API can significantly boost user engagement and streamline various processes. This discussion focuses on essential metrics that impact API speed and outlines effective strategies for improving these metrics.

Core Metrics for Evaluating API Performance

Several critical performance metrics are vital for maintaining and improving the efficiency of an API. These metrics include:

1. Latency

Latency represents the time it takes for a request to be sent from the client to the server and for the server to respond. This metric is crucial as it directly affects user perception of the application's responsiveness. Reducing latency is especially important in applications where quick feedback is essential.

2. Throughput

Throughput is the measure of how many requests an API can handle within a specific period. This metric indicates the API's capacity to manage varying traffic levels, ensuring steady performance during high-demand periods.

3. Error Rate

Error rate measures the percentage of requests that result in errors, including client-side (4xx) and server-side (5xx) errors. Keeping the error rate low is vital for ensuring the reliability of the API.

4. Utilization

Utilization assesses the consumption of system resources like CPU, memory, and bandwidth by the API. Efficient utilization is essential for ensuring the API operates smoothly under different load conditions without straining the system.

Strategies for Optimizing API Performance

Implementing specific strategies can significantly enhance these key performance metrics:

Improving Latency

- **Content Delivery Networks (CDN):** Utilizing CDNs can substantially reduce latency by caching content in multiple geographic locations, thus shortening the distance data travels to the user.

- **Connection Reuse:** Employing persistent connection techniques such as HTTP Keep-Alive or HTTP/2 reduces the need to establish new connections for subsequent requests, decreasing overall latency.

Increasing Throughput

- **Load Balancing:** Applying load balancing techniques allows incoming API requests to be distributed across several servers, preventing any single server from becoming overwhelmed and enhancing overall throughput.

- **Asynchronous Processing:** Using asynchronous methods enables the API to handle several requests simultaneously, greatly improving throughput.

Reducing Error Rate

- **Robust Error Handling:** Developing comprehensive error management and validation protocols can prevent many common errors, ensuring operations are more likely to succeed.

- **Continuous Monitoring:** Regular monitoring and logging enable quick detection and correction of issues, maintaining a low error rate.

Optimizing Resource Usage

- **Regular Profiling:** Conducting routine assessments of the API helps identify operations that consume excessive resources, allowing for targeted optimizations.

- **Dynamic Scaling:** Implementing auto-scaling techniques ensures that resources are allocated based on real-time demands, optimizing usage without underutilizing or overloading the system.

Example: Implementing HTTP Keep-Alive in Python

Here is a practical demonstration of using HTTP Keep-Alive in Python to maintain a persistent connection, which aids in reducing latency:

```python
import requests

# Initialize a session to maintain persistent settings
session = requests.Session()

# Use the session to send multiple requests
initial_response = session.get('https://example.com/api')
print(initial_response.status_code)

subsequent_response = session.get('https://example.com/api')
print(subsequent_response.status_code)
```

Conclusion

Optimizing critical performance metrics such as latency, throughput, error rate, and resource utilization is fundamental to developing high-performing APIs. Techniques like leveraging CDNs, managing persistent connections, and asynchronous processing are crucial in improving these metrics. By focusing on these strategies, developers can ensure their APIs are equipped to handle diverse and demanding operational requirements effectively, providing a seamless experience for users and reliable performance for backend systems.

Profiling and Benchmarking: Tools and techniques for measuring API performance

Profiling and benchmarking are critical methodologies in API development, pivotal for measuring and enhancing performance. These practices allow developers to deeply understand the operational characteristics of an API, helping to pinpoint inefficiencies, manage resource utilization more effectively, and optimize overall system performance. This discussion outlines the essential tools and methods involved in profiling and benchmarking APIs, with practical implementations highlighted.

Key Concepts in Profiling and Benchmarking

Profiling involves analyzing an application while it runs to collect vital data such as function call times, memory usage, and CPU load. This is key for identifying resource-intensive operations within an API that could be optimized for better performance.

Benchmarking measures the performance of an API against defined standards or previous performance levels. This is crucial for validating the impact of code or infrastructure changes on API performance.

Tools for Profiling and Benchmarking

A variety of tools are available that aid in the effective profiling and benchmarking of APIs. These range from broad monitoring solutions to specific utilities tailored to certain programming languages or environments:

1. **Application Performance Management (APM) Tools**: Platforms such as New Relic, Dynatrace, and Datadog offer robust monitoring capabilities that include profiling features and real-time performance tracking, making them invaluable for ongoing performance assessment.

2. **Dedicated Profiling Tools**:

- o **VisualVM**: Offers comprehensive diagnostics for Java applications, enabling detailed CPU and memory profiling in real-time.

- o **Py-Spy**: A profiler for Python applications that operates without interrupting the application, ideal for live performance diagnostics.

- o **MiniProfiler**: Targets .NET and Ruby environments, providing a streamlined tool for profiling SQL queries and HTTP requests during development and QA phases.

3. **Benchmarking Utilities**:

- o **JMeter**: Useful for load testing and performance measurement of web applications, including APIs.

- o **Apache Bench (ab)**: A straightforward command-line tool for benchmarking HTTP services.

- o **Postman and SoapUI**: Primarily testing tools for API interfaces, they also offer capabilities to simulate load scenarios and measure response under stress.

Effective Profiling and Benchmarking Techniques

Adopting certain techniques can maximize the effectiveness of profiling and benchmarking efforts:

- **Simulate Realistic Usage**: Employ data and access patterns that closely mirror real-world user behavior to ensure relevancy of performance data.

- **Isolated Testing Environments**: Conduct tests in environments that replicate the production settings without affecting live operations.

- **Automated Testing**: Automate benchmark tests to run routinely or as part of the build and deployment process to detect performance regressions promptly.

- **Regular Monitoring**: Continuous profiling helps in early detection and resolution of performance bottlenecks.

Example: Benchmarking with Apache Bench

Here's an example of using Apache Bench to perform a benchmark test on an API endpoint. This example measures how the API handles 100 concurrent requests:

```
ab -n 100 -c 10 http://example.com/api/resource
```

The output from Apache Bench provides numerous metrics, such as:

- Total test duration

- Requests per second

- Average time per request

- Distribution of request completion times

These metrics offer insights into the API's capacity to handle concurrent loads and serve as a basis for further optimization.

Conclusion

Profiling and benchmarking are indispensable in the lifecycle of API development, providing the insights necessary for continual performance enhancement. Utilizing the right tools and adhering to best practices in profiling and benchmarking not only ensures APIs operate at optimal efficiency but also supports scalability and reliability. Regular implementation of these practices is vital for maintaining superior performance and ensuring a robust user experience.

Chapter Three

Security at Scale

Challenges of Securing Scalable APIs: Common security pitfalls in scalable environments

Securing APIs within scalable environments poses distinct challenges that escalate as the network and its components expand. As APIs underpin a vast array of digital services, safeguarding them against potential vulnerabilities and threats becomes crucial. This article delves into prevalent security pitfalls associated with scalable APIs and suggests methods to address these risks effectively.

Exploring Security Challenges in Scalable API Settings

Expanding Attack Surface: The more an API scales, the more services it typically connects with and the more endpoints it exposes. Each new endpoint potentially introduces vulnerabilities, thereby broadening the attack surface and making APIs more attractive to attackers.

Complexity of Security Management: In scalable environments, where deployments may stretch across multiple servers and cloud platforms, maintaining uniform security measures becomes difficult. Disparities in configurations or inconsistent application of security policies can introduce weaknesses.

Vulnerability to DoS Attacks: Without adequate rate limiting, APIs are vulnerable to Denial of Service (DoS) attacks, where attackers overload the system with excessive requests, rendering the service unavailable to legitimate users.

Risk of Data Breaches: Scalable APIs often process and store large volumes of potentially sensitive data. Protecting this data from unauthorized access and breaches is essential.

Frequent Security Oversights in Scalable Environments

Weak Authentication and Authorization Practices: Neglecting to implement strong authentication and authorization can lead to unauthorized access to critical API functions. Secure authentication mechanisms like OAuth 2.0 should be in place, along with strict role-based access controls.

Inadequate Data Encryption: Transmitting or storing data without adequate encryption exposes it to potential interception and misuse. It's critical to implement robust encryption protocols such as TLS for data in transit and ensure strong encryption for stored data.

Deficient Monitoring and Logging: Insufficient monitoring and logging capabilities can delay the detection of security breaches or suspicious activities. Scalable APIs require extensive logging and real-time monitoring systems to identify and address security incidents promptly.

Security Flaws in API Gateways: API gateways consolidate various security and management functions but can become a focal point for attacks. Protecting the gateway is essential, as any compromise could endanger all connected services.

Mitigating Security Risks in Scalable APIs

Enhance Authentication and Authorization Mechanisms: Adopt standard protocols and frameworks that support robust authentication and strict authorization checks for each API access point.

Example Code: Secure Authentication Using JWT in Node.js:

```javascript
const jwt = require('jsonwebtoken');

function verifyToken(req, res, next) {
    const token = req.headers['authorization']?.split(' ')[1];
    if (!token) return res.sendStatus(401);

    jwt.verify(token, process.env.TOKEN_SECRET, (err, decoded) => {
        if (err) return res.sendStatus(403);
        req.user = decoded;
        next();
    });
}
```

Implement Rate Limiting: Apply rate limiting to prevent abuse and protect against DoS attacks. Use cloud services or third-party tools to set flexible rate limits that adjust based on traffic patterns.

Ensure Comprehensive Data Protection: Encrypt all data in transit using TLS and secure data at rest with effective encryption solutions. Regularly review and update encryption practices to tackle emerging threats.

Intensive Logging and Monitoring: Establish a thorough logging framework to document access and activities. Utilize advanced monitoring tools to analyze these logs and spot unusual patterns that might indicate potential security threats.

Fortify API Gateways: Keep your API gateways updated with the latest security patches and consider integrating advanced security features such as threat intelligence and anomaly detection to enhance protection.

Conclusion

Addressing the security challenges of scalable APIs requires a thorough understanding of the risks posed by their extensive and complex nature. By employing strong authentication protocols, enforcing rate limiting, securing data vigorously, and implementing robust monitoring practices, organizations can shield their APIs from common security pitfalls. As the reliance on APIs grows, ensuring their security in scalable deployments is imperative to safeguard sensitive data and maintain user trust.

Advanced Authentication and Authorization: Implementing more robust security mechanisms like JWT, OAuth2 scopes

In the contemporary digital ecosystem, ensuring robust security protocols for APIs is crucial, particularly in systems where sensitive data is exchanged. Advanced authentication and authorization technologies like JSON Web Tokens (JWT) and OAuth 2.0 scopes are instrumental in crafting these secure environments. This discussion provides insights into leveraging these tools to fortify API security.

An Overview of JWT and OAuth2 Scopes

JSON Web Tokens (JWT) offer a method for securely transmitting information between parties as a JSON object. Because they are digitally signed, their authenticity can be verified. JWTs can be encrypted using a private secret or a public/private key pair, ensuring that the tokens are both secure and verifiable.

OAuth 2.0 is a protocol that facilitates authorized access to resources without exposing user credentials. It allows third-party services to perform actions on behalf of a user by obtaining limited access via authorization tokens.

Utilizing JWT for Enhanced Authentication

JWTs streamline the authentication process by encapsulating user identities and permissions in a secure token. This token is then used by the server to validate user requests and grant access to resources.

Example of JWT Implementation in Node.js:

```javascript
const jwt = require('jsonwebtoken');
const secretKey = 'your_private_secret';

// Function to generate JWT
function generateJWT(user) {
    const claims = { sub: user.id, email: user.email };
    return jwt.sign(claims, secretKey, { expiresIn: '2h' });
}

// Function to verify JWT
function verifyJWT(token) {
    try {
        return jwt.verify(token, secretKey);
    } catch (error) {
        console.error('Error verifying token:', error);
        return null;
    }
}
```

Managing Authorization with OAuth2 Scopes

OAuth 2.0 scopes restrict the API's access to user data, specifying what actions are permissible by third-party applications. These scopes ensure that applications do not overreach their user-given permissions.

Typical OAuth2 Workflow:

1. **Client Registration**: Clients specify needed permissions during registration with an OAuth provider.

2. **Authorization Request**: The client requests permission from the user for specific actions.

3. **Consent by User**: The user grants the requested permissions on the provider's interface.

215

4. **Token Issuance**: The OAuth provider issues a token to the application, scoped to the user's permissions.

Secure API Implementation Strategies

Integrating JWT and OAuth2 can significantly enhance API security by providing robust mechanisms for authentication and granular access control.

- **Secure API endpoints with JWT**: Use JWTs to validate that all incoming requests have a valid token, thereby ensuring that calls to the API are authorized.

- **Control access with OAuth2 Scopes**: Define and enforce scopes that correspond to different levels of user permissions within your API.

Example of JWT Authentication Middleware in Express.js:

```javascript
const express = require('express');
const jwt = require('jsonwebtoken');
const app = express();
const secret = 'your_private_secret';

// Middleware for authenticating JWT
app.use((req, res, next) => {
    const authHeader = req.headers['authorization'];
    const token = authHeader && authHeader.split(' ')[1];

    if (!token) {
        return res.status(401).send('Access denied. No token provided.');
    }

    try {
        const decoded = jwt.verify(token, secret);
        req.user = decoded;
        next();
    } catch (error) {
        res.status(400).send('Invalid token.');
    }
});
```

Conclusion

Implementing JWT and OAuth 2.0 scopes in API security strategies not only ensures robust authentication but also provides precise control over user access levels. These methods protect APIs by securing transactions and defining clear access boundaries, thereby maintaining high security and operational integrity in digital interactions.

Chapter Four

Efficient Data Management

Data Caching Techniques: Different caching strategies to enhance performance

In contemporary software development, effectively utilizing data caching strategies is fundamental to enhancing application performance. This involves temporarily storing critical data in readily accessible storage systems, thereby reducing reliance on slower backend processes. This article explores various caching strategies that are designed to optimize data retrieval times and lighten the load on primary resources, thereby improving overall system responsiveness.

The Role of Data Caching

Data caching is aimed at facilitating faster data access by preserving copies of frequently accessed data in high-speed storage areas. This is particularly useful for data that is costly to generate or retrieve, thereby enhancing efficiency and responsiveness, especially in environments experiencing heavy user demand.

Diverse Caching Strategies

Selecting the right caching strategy is crucial for maximizing application performance. Here are several effective strategies employed in various operational scenarios:

1. In-memory Caching

This strategy involves storing data within the server's RAM, making it extremely quick to retrieve. It is ideal for handling small to medium-sized data sets that require rapid access.

In-memory Caching Systems Include:

- **Redis**: This open-source data structure store is capable of serving as a database, cache, and message broker.

- **Memcached**: A distributed memory object caching system that is used to speed up dynamic web applications by reducing database load.

2. Database Caching

Caching at the database level involves storing the results of database queries so that identical future queries fetch data faster by avoiding repeated query execution.

Practical Use Case:

- Storing the results of frequently executed queries to avoid repeated database hits.

3. Distributed Caching

Suitable for applications spread across multiple servers, distributed caching synchronizes cached data across various nodes to manage larger data volumes and maintain data consistency.

Tools for Distributed Caching:

- **Apache Ignite**: A distributed database and caching platform that focuses on allowing memory-centric storage and processing.

- **Hazelcast**: An in-memory computing platform that provides distributed caching capabilities.

4. CDN Caching

Utilizing CDNs involves caching static resources like images and scripts on servers distributed across various geographical locations to reduce latency and enhance content delivery speed.

Example of CDN Usage:

- Deploying static assets across a CDN to ensure faster loading times for users worldwide.

5. Application-Level Caching

This form of caching saves data generated during application processes, useful for data like user session information or personalized HTML content.

Example Implementation in Python using Flask:

```python
from flask import Flask, jsonify
from flask_caching import Cache

app = Flask(__name__)
cache = Cache(app, config={'CACHE_TYPE': 'simple'})
```

```
@app.route('/heavy')
@cache.cached(timeout=120)  # Cache this view for 120 seconds
def heavy_computation():
    result = intensive_compute_function()
    return jsonify(result)


def intensive_compute_function():
    # Complex computation logic
    return {"data": "Result of heavy computation"}
```

Best Practices for Caching

- **Expiration Policies**: Clearly define when cached data should be refreshed or discarded to avoid serving stale data.

- **Performance Monitoring**: Regularly assess the cache's effectiveness and adjust settings based on performance metrics like hit rates.

- **Data Security**: Ensure that any sensitive data stored in caches is securely encrypted, especially in distributed caching scenarios.

Conclusion

Implementing strategic data caching is critical for improving application performance and user experience by ensuring quick data access and reducing the demand on core resources. By adopting suitable caching strategies, developers can significantly enhance both the speed and efficiency of their applications. Each caching technique offers unique advantages and should be chosen based on the specific requirements and context of the application's operational environment.

Database Scalability: Optimizing database interactions for large-scale applications

Database scalability is essential in maintaining the efficiency and reliability of applications as they grow to accommodate more data, transactions, and concurrent users. Effective optimization of database interactions is critical for sustaining performance under scaling conditions. This article explores a variety of strategies to enhance database scalability, focusing on practical implementations and solutions.

Core Concepts of Database Scalability

Database scalability can be achieved through **vertical scaling** and **horizontal scaling**.

- **Vertical Scaling** involves augmenting the existing hardware of a server, such as adding more RAM, CPU power, or storage. This method is straightforward but often limited by physical constraints and cost.

- **Horizontal Scaling**, or scaling out, entails adding more servers to distribute the database workload across multiple machines. This approach is more complex but essential for achieving high scalability and availability.

Effective Database Scalability Strategies

1. Database Sharding

Sharding involves distributing data across multiple database servers, each holding a segment of the total data. This method reduces the burden on any single server and enhances performance by allowing parallel data processing.

Practical Example: Data can be sharded based on a key attribute like user ID, ensuring that all related data is stored on the same shard, minimizing complex cross-shard operations.

2. Read Replicas

Read replicas enhance read scalability by replicating the primary database to secondary databases that handle read queries. This configuration reduces the load on the primary database, which continues to handle all write operations.

Cloud Implementation Note: Services such as AWS RDS and Google Cloud SQL facilitate easy management of read replicas, including automatic failover protocols.

3. Partitioning

Partitioning splits a database into discrete parts that can be managed independently, potentially across different nodes. This can be done horizontally (splitting rows) or vertically (splitting columns).

Example: Partitioning user data by month to improve the efficiency of queries that access a specific month's data.

4. Caching

Caching temporarily stores copies of frequently accessed data in faster storage systems. This reduces repeated database queries, saving time and resources.

Example Code with Redis:

```python
import redis
from your_database import get_data

cache = redis.Redis(host='localhost', port=6379, db=0)

def get_user_info(user_id):
    # Attempt to get data from cache
    data = cache.get(user_id)
    if data:
        return data  # Return cached data if available

    # Data not in cache, pull from database and cache it
    data = get_data('SELECT * FROM users WHERE id = ?', [user_id])
    cache.setex(user_id, 3600, data)  # Cache for 1 hour
    return data
```

5. Efficient Indexing

Creating indexes on frequently accessed data fields can drastically improve query performance. Indexes facilitate quick data retrieval, significantly reducing search time.

Indexing Strategy: Evaluate query patterns to determine which fields are most often accessed and index those fields to maximize query efficiency.

6. Asynchronous Processing

Offloading certain operations to be processed asynchronously can improve application responsiveness. This is suitable for operations where immediate consistency is not crucial.

Implementation Example: Using message queues like RabbitMQ to handle tasks such as sending notifications or processing background jobs can reduce direct load on the database.

Conclusion

Enhancing database scalability through strategic implementation of sharding, read replicas, partitioning, caching, indexing, and asynchronous processing is vital for supporting the growth of large-scale applications. These techniques not only help manage increased data and user demands but also ensure that databases continue to perform optimally as they scale. By effectively employing these strategies, organizations can ensure robust performance and high availability of their database systems.

Chapter Five

Rate Limiting and Throttling

Implementing Rate Limiting: Techniques and tools for controlling traffic

In the digital realm, rate limiting is crucial for managing network traffic effectively and ensuring robust online service performance. It involves setting constraints on how many requests a user or service can make to an API or server within a defined period, thus preventing resource overuse and enhancing system security and stability. This exposition outlines various methods and tools for efficiently implementing rate limiting, including practical implementations.

Essentials of Rate Limiting

Rate limiting is utilized to shield services from potential abuse and to maintain equitable resource distribution among users. This mechanism is vital for preventing service disruptions caused by excessive traffic, whether from legitimate users or malicious attacks.

Strategic Approaches to Rate Limiting

Implementing rate limiting can be approached through multiple techniques, each suitable for specific service requirements:

1. Fixed Window Rate Limiting

This straightforward method involves defining a maximum number of allowed requests within a set time window (e.g., per minute, per hour). It is easy to implement but may lead to traffic spikes at the time window boundaries, potentially resulting in performance fluctuations.

2. Sliding Window Log Rate Limiting

A more granular approach, this method logs each request's timestamp, allowing the server to dynamically count requests in a sliding time window. This technique helps smooth traffic intake but requires more resources to manage the logs.

3. Token Bucket Algorithm

This algorithm permits short bursts of requests by allocating tokens that regenerate over time. Each request consumes a token, and as long as tokens are available, requests are processed. This is effective for managing overall throughput with flexibility for occasional spikes.

4. Leaky Bucket Algorithm

Designed to even out the request flow, the leaky bucket algorithm processes requests at a steady rate, filling up with incoming requests and emptying at a set rate. This prevents bursts of traffic from overwhelming the system.

Tools for Rate Limiting

Several tools and software solutions facilitate rate limiting, catering to different platforms and infrastructures:

Nginx

Nginx provides built-in support for rate limiting through the **limit_req** directive, making it a convenient option for environments already utilizing Nginx.

Sample Nginx Configuration:

```
http {
    limit_req_zone $binary_remote_addr zone=one:10m rate=10r/s;

    server {
        location /service/ {
            limit_req zone=one;
        }
    }
}
```

This setup restricts requests to 10 per second, suitable for services needing steady traffic control.

Cloudflare

For environments integrated with Cloudflare, setting up rate limiting is streamlined through its user-friendly dashboard, offering robust traffic management capabilities.

Node.js with Express-rate-limit

In Node.js applications, especially those using Express, the **express-rate-limit** middleware provides an easy way to implement rate limiting.

Node.js Example:

```javascript
const rateLimit = require('express-rate-limit');

const apiLimiter = rateLimit({
  windowMs: 15 * 60 * 1000, // 15 minutes
  max: 100 // limit each IP to 100 requests per windowMs
});

// Apply the rate limiting middleware to API calls
app.use('/api/', apiLimiter);
```

Rate Limiting Best Practices

- **Transparent Policies**: It's critical to clearly communicate the rate limiting policies to users to manage expectations and minimize user dissatisfaction.

- **Dynamic Limits**: Adapt rate limiting thresholds based on real-time analytics to balance user needs with system capabilities.

- **Regular Monitoring**: Keep track of rate limiting performance and adjust parameters to fine-tune resource allocation and user experience.

Conclusion

Rate limiting is indispensable for safeguarding APIs and servers from overuse while ensuring reliable and continuous service availability. By selecting and integrating appropriate rate limiting strategies and tools, developers can protect their systems and optimize user interactions. Continuous evaluation and adjustment of rate limiting settings are recommended to respond to changing traffic patterns and system demands effectively.

Benefits of Throttling: How throttling can prevent system overloads and improve user experience

Throttling is an essential technique in traffic management and server load control within digital environments, particularly when it's crucial to allocate system resources wisely. By intentionally reducing the speed of processed operations, throttling helps avert system overloads, maintains equitable resource distribution, and ultimately enhances the user experience. This discussion examines the diverse advantages of throttling and demonstrates how it can be strategically applied to bolster system resilience and improve user satisfaction.

Throttling Explained

Throttling is a sophisticated form of rate limiting that manages the number of operations a system handles over a specified time. Unlike standard rate limiting, which blocks excess requests once a threshold is reached, throttling delays requests to balance the load on the system. This method ensures ongoing service availability and system responsiveness, even during high demand.

Advantages of Throttling

1. Prevention of System Overloads

Throttling's primary advantage is its ability to keep servers from becoming overloaded, which can slow down service or cause crashes. By controlling the volume of processed requests, throttling keeps system operations within their capacity limits, ensuring consistent stability and reliability.

2. Ensures Fair Usage

Throttling upholds fair usage policies by preventing any user or group from consuming a disproportionate amount of resources. In shared resource environments, throttling ensures that all users have equal access to services, thus increasing overall user satisfaction.

3. Enhances User Experience

Throttling minimizes potential spikes in response times during peak traffic periods, offering a more uniform and predictable user experience. This reliability can significantly improve users' perceptions of the service, as performance remains consistent.

4. Cost-Effective Resource Utilization

Through throttling, organizations can effectively manage operational costs by optimizing existing infrastructure usage. This approach allows for handling peak demands without immediately resorting to expensive resource upgrades, thus managing costs more efficiently.

5. Reduces DDoS Attack Risks

Throttling also helps mitigate the risk of Distributed Denial of Service (DDoS) attacks by limiting the number of requests handled. This reduces the attack's effectiveness and ensures the system remains available to legitimate users.

Practical Implementation of Throttling

Throttling can be implemented using various tools and middleware across different programming environments. Here is an example using the Express framework in Node.js to illustrate a simple throttling setup:

```javascript
const express = require('express');
const rateLimit = require('express-rate-limit');

// Configure rate limiting
const apiLimiter = rateLimit({
  windowMs: 15 * 60 * 1000, // 15 minutes
  max: 100, // limit each IP to 100 requests per window
  standardHeaders: true, // Return rate limit info in the `RateLimit-*` headers
  legacyHeaders: false, // Disable the `X-RateLimit-*` headers
  handler: function (req, res, /*next*/) {
    res.status(429).json({
      message: "Too many requests, please try again later."
    });
  }
});
```

```javascript
const app = express();

// Apply rate limiting to all requests
app.use(apiLimiter);

app.get('/', (req, res) => {
  res.send('Hello World!');
});

app.listen(3000, () => {
  console.log('Server is running on port 3000');
});
```

This setup creates a throttle mechanism where each IP is allowed up to 100 requests every 15 minutes. Exceeding this limit prompts a 429 status code, advising the user to try again later.

Conclusion

Implementing throttling is crucial for maintaining the operational integrity and performance of web services. By effectively managing how traffic is handled, throttling not only prevents service disruptions but also promotes a more equitable and satisfactory experience for all users. It is an indispensable strategy in modern web application management, crucial for sustainable resource management and efficient service delivery.

Chapter Six

API Gateway Optimization

Role of API Gateways: Centralizing common functionalities through gateways

API gateways are essential components in the architecture of modern applications, particularly those based on microservices. They serve as a central point that manages incoming API requests by providing a single entry point for various services. This approach simplifies interactions, enhances security, and improves performance by centralizing common functionalities. This article explores the crucial role of API gateways, detailing their functionalities, benefits, and practical implementation strategies.

Role and Functions of API Gateways

An API gateway consolidates several critical functions that enhance the management and delivery of services:

1. Routing Requests

The gateway directs incoming API calls to the correct microservice based on the route and characteristics of the request, facilitating efficient and accurate request handling.

2. Authentication and Security Measures

API gateways enhance security by implementing authentication and authorization checks before forwarding requests to backend services. This centralizes security management and offloads responsibility from individual services.

3. Rate Limiting

API gateways manage the flow of data by enforcing rate limiting and throttling policies. This prevents any single consumer from overloading the system, ensuring equitable resource usage and system stability.

4. Load Balancing

By distributing incoming requests evenly across multiple service instances, API gateways optimize resource utilization and prevent any single service from becoming a bottleneck, thereby enhancing reliability and response times.

5. Caching Responses

API gateways improve response times and reduce backend load by caching the outputs of service calls. This allows them to serve cached responses for common requests without repeatedly processing the same operations.

6. Transforming Requests and Responses

The gateway can modify requests and responses as they pass through, including converting between different data formats or protocols, which ensures compatibility between disparate client expectations and backend capabilities.

Advantages of Implementing API Gateways

- **Simplified Client Architecture**: Clients interact with a single consolidated endpoint rather than individual services, simplifying the network architecture and reducing client-side complexity.

- **Consistent Security Layer**: By centralizing security mechanisms, API gateways provide a consistent and robust security layer across all backend services.

- **Flexibility and Modularity**: API gateways allow backend services to evolve independently, as changes to services do not necessarily require changes to the client-side code.

- **Performance Enhancements**: Through functionalities like caching and load balancing, API gateways optimize the overall performance of API interactions, providing faster and more reliable responses to clients.

Implementing API Gateways

Choosing and configuring the right API gateway depends on the specific needs of the application. There are several open-source and commercial options available that provide extensive features:

Example of Setting Up Kong for Rate Limiting:

```
{
  "name": "rate-limiting",
  "config": {
    "minute": 30,
    "policy": "local"
  },
```

```
"service": {
  "id": "service_identifier_here"
  }
}
```

This snippet configures Kong to limit requests to 30 per minute for a specified service, illustrating how API gateways can manage traffic effectively.

Conclusion

API gateways are vital for managing the complexities of modern applications, especially those built with a microservices architecture. They consolidate essential functions such as routing, security, and performance enhancements into a single, manageable point. Effectively implemented, API gateways facilitate smoother operations, bolster security measures, and ensure efficient resource management, making them indispensable for scalable, robust applications. Through strategic configuration and deployment, organizations can leverage API gateways to significantly improve operational efficiency and user satisfaction.

Customizing API Gateways: How to tailor API gateways for performance enhancements

API gateways are central components in modern digital architectures, particularly when utilizing microservices. These gateways facilitate efficient data flow between clients and services while safeguarding communications. Tailoring API gateways to meet specific organizational needs and performance targets involves strategic enhancements that go beyond basic configurations. This discussion delves into how

API gateways can be customized to optimize performance, detailing specific enhancements and implementations.

Tailoring API Gateways for Enhanced Performance

Effectively customizing an API gateway requires an in-depth understanding of the organization's specific needs and the technical capabilities of the gateway. Such customization is pivotal for boosting performance, enhancing security, and ensuring efficient operations under various conditions. Here are key areas for customization:

1. Caching Strategies

Optimizing caching can significantly enhance performance by reducing backend load and speeding up response times. Customizing caching rules according to particular use cases and data volatility can lead to major performance improvements.

Example: Implementing differentiated caching policies within the gateway for static and dynamic content, adjusting the TTL (Time-To-Live) based on the nature of the content.

2. Adaptive Rate Limiting and Throttling

Customizing rate limits to accommodate different user levels ensures that backend systems are protected from overload while optimizing user access. Adjusting these parameters can enhance user experience and system responsiveness.

Example: Applying distinct rate limits for various user tiers by decoding user information from authentication tokens allows for greater flexibility and optimized access.

3. Advanced Load Balancing Techniques

Employing sophisticated load balancing algorithms can improve the efficiency of request distribution across servers, enhancing overall system responsiveness and reducing latency.

Example: Using a least connections strategy helps direct traffic to the server with the fewest active connections, optimizing resource use and potentially lowering response times.

4. Security Customizations

API gateways come equipped with fundamental security features, but expanding on these through custom security measures such as IDS (Intrusion Detection Systems) and tailored firewall rules can provide superior protection.

Example: Integrating custom security protocols to immediately block or flag suspected malicious activities based on observed patterns in API traffic.

5. Protocol Transformation

Transforming communication protocols within the gateway to align with client and server requirements can ensure seamless interactions and extend legacy system integrations.

Example: Converting SOAP to RESTful API calls within the gateway enables older systems to interface seamlessly with newer, REST-based services without modifying client-side code.

Practical Implementation Example

Using Nginx as an API gateway to set up customized caching demonstrates how specific configurations can be applied to enhance performance:

```
http {
    proxy_cache_path /data/nginx/cache levels=1:2 keys_zone=api_cache:10m
        max_size=10g
                    inactive=60m use_temp_path=off;

    server {
        location /api {
            proxy_pass http://backend;
            proxy_cache api_cache;
            proxy_cache_valid 200 302 30s;
            proxy_cache_valid 404 1m;
        }
    }
}
```

This configuration in Nginx sets up a caching strategy where API responses are cached differently based on their status codes, optimizing data retrieval based on response type and frequency.

Conclusion

Customizing API gateways is crucial for achieving optimal performance, reliability, and security in application delivery. By implementing strategic customizations such as effective caching, refined rate limiting, advanced load balancing, enhanced security measures, and protocol adaptations, organizations can ensure that their API gateways are not only functional but also finely tuned to their specific operational needs. These enhancements not only improve efficiency but also contribute to better user experiences and higher service availability, underpinning the critical role of API gateways in contemporary web application ecosystems.

Chapter Seven

Load Balancing Techniques

Types of Load Balancers: Overview of different load balancer types and their use cases

Load balancers are crucial in managing network traffic across servers to ensure no single server is overly burdened. They help maintain system stability and enhance application performance by effectively distributing incoming requests. This article examines various load balancer types, detailing their operational mechanisms and ideal use cases to provide insights into their strategic deployment in network architectures.

Introduction to Load Balancers

A load balancer serves as a pivotal component in network management, routing client requests across several servers. It optimizes the use of server resources, prevents overloads, and ensures that applications run efficiently without any server facing excessive demand.

Classification and Applications of Load Balancers

1. Round Robin Load Balancer

This type of load balancer allocates requests cyclically and equitably among the available servers. It cycles through servers, assigning requests in a straightforward sequential order.

Use Case: This approach is best suited for setups where servers have similar processing capabilities and where session persistence is not necessary.

2. Least Connections Load Balancer

This load balancer targets the server with the fewest active connections, adjusting traffic distribution based on real-time server load, which can vary significantly.

Use Case: It's particularly beneficial in environments where session lengths vary or where servers differ in performance.

3. IP Hash Load Balancer

This method utilizes a hash of the client's IP address to direct all of a client's requests to the same server, maintaining a consistent user session.

Use Case: Crucial for applications that require user session persistence across multiple interactions.

4. Weighted Load Balancing

In this approach, servers are assigned weights based on their capacity or performance metrics, with higher-capacity servers handling a larger share of requests.

Use Case: Ideal for networks where servers vary in their capabilities, ensuring that more powerful servers handle more traffic.

5. Dynamic Load Balancing

This sophisticated form of load balancing evaluates server performance and health in real time, dynamically adjusting the distribution of requests to manage server loads proactively.

Use Case: Essential for mission-critical applications that require high availability and minimal response times.

Implementing a Load Balancer with Nginx

Nginx can be configured as a simple yet effective round-robin load balancer, demonstrating how basic load balancing can be implemented:

```
http {
    upstream myapp1 {
        server srv1.example.com;
        server srv2.example.com;
        server srv3.example.com;
    }

    server {
        listen 80;

        location / {
            proxy_pass http://myapp1;
        }
    }
}
```

This configuration ensures that traffic is evenly distributed among three servers, enhancing the network's ability to manage load without any server being overwhelmed.

Benefits of Using Load Balancers

- **Optimized Performance**: By distributing the load evenly, load balancers prevent server overload and ensure all requests are processed efficiently.

- **Seamless Scalability**: Load balancers facilitate the smooth scaling of services by managing additional servers without service interruptions.

- **Reliability and Redundancy**: Traffic can be rerouted from less capable servers to those with spare capacity, increasing the reliability of services.

Conclusion

Load balancers are indispensable for efficient network management, ensuring that traffic is evenly distributed, and servers operate within their optimal capacity. Understanding different types of load balancers helps in selecting the right one based on specific operational needs, enhancing system performance, and ensuring scalability and reliability. Whether implementing a simple round-robin or a complex dynamic load balancer, these systems play a critical role in maintaining robust, efficient, and scalable server environments.

Load Balancing Algorithms: How to choose and implement the right algorithm for your needs

Load balancing is crucial for distributing incoming web traffic evenly across a number of servers, ensuring no single server is overwhelmed, which enhances application performance and reliability. Properly choosing and implementing a suitable load balancing algorithm is key to managing network traffic effectively and optimizing server performance. This article discusses various load balancing algorithms, highlighting their functions and helping you determine the best choice for your specific needs.

Introduction to Load Balancing Algorithms

Load balancing algorithms are essential for defining how traffic should be directed across servers to optimize resource use and prevent overloads. Each algorithm offers unique benefits and is suited to specific network conditions and server capacities.

1. Round Robin

This is one of the most straightforward load balancing techniques, where requests are distributed evenly across all servers in a cyclical manner. It is very effective in environments where servers have roughly equivalent capabilities and request processing times are similar.

Example Setup:

```
upstream backend {
    server server1.example.com;
    server server2.example.com;
    server server3.example.com;
}
```

2. Least Connections

This algorithm routes traffic to the server with the fewest active connections, accounting for real-time server load. It is especially suited to environments where request load is uneven or server response times vary.

Example Setup:

```
upstream backend {
    least_conn;
    server server1.example.com;
    server server2.example.com;
    server server3.example.com;
}
```

3. IP Hash

The IP Hash algorithm directs requests based on a hash of the client's IP address. This approach ensures that users are consistently served by the same server, which can be crucial for maintaining user session integrity.

4. Weighted Load Balancing

In environments where server capabilities vary, weighted load balancing can allocate requests according to server capacity. Servers with higher weights handle more requests, balancing the load according to available resources.

Example Setup:

```
upstream backend {
    server server1.example.com weight=3;
    server server2.example.com weight=2;
    server server3.example.com weight=1;
}
```

5. Dynamic Load Balancing

Utilizing real-time data on server health and load, dynamic load balancing algorithms can adapt traffic distribution dynamically. This responsiveness is ideal for critical applications that demand high availability and minimal downtime.

Factors to Consider When Choosing a Load Balancing Algorithm

Selecting the right load balancing algorithm requires considering various factors:

- **Consistency of Workload**: Whether the workload is uniform across requests or varies significantly.

- **Server Specifications**: The homogeneity or diversity in server performance and capacity within the environment.

- **Session Persistence Requirements**: The need for maintaining user sessions, which might favor algorithms like IP Hash.

- **Adaptability and Scalability**: The ability to scale the server environment dynamically without service interruptions.

Implementing a Load Balancer with Nginx

Setting up a load balancer involves configuring a network solution like Nginx to manage server traffic. Here's how you can implement a Least Connections strategy using Nginx:

1. **Install Nginx**: Ensure Nginx is installed on the gateway or the dedicated machine that will manage traffic.

2. **Configure Load Balancing**:

   o Modify the Nginx configuration file, typically located at **/etc/nginx/nginx.conf**.

   o Set up an upstream block with the **least_conn** directive to enable dynamic server selection based on connections.

   o Define a server block to manage how traffic is handled.

```
http {
    upstream backend {
        least_conn;
        server server1.example.com;
        server server2.example.com;
        server server3.example.com;
    }

    server {
        listen 80;

        location / {
            proxy_pass http://backend;
        }
    }
}
```

3. **Validate and Deploy**: Test the new settings to ensure they function correctly before going live.

Conclusion

Selecting and implementing the appropriate load balancing algorithm is essential for ensuring efficient traffic management and server reliability. By evaluating your specific requirements and server environment, you can choose an algorithm that optimizes performance and supports seamless scalability. Whether using a simple Round Robin or a complex dynamic method, effective load balancing is key to maintaining robust and responsive network operations.

Chapter Eight

Asynchronous APIs and Event-Driven Design

Benefits of Asynchronous Communication: How asynchrony can improve scalability

Asynchronous communication plays a critical role in modern software architectures, especially in systems utilizing microservices or distributed frameworks. This communication strategy, where interactions between sender and receiver do not require immediate response times, contrasts sharply with synchronous communication, which demands that the sender wait for the receiver's acknowledgment before proceeding. The asynchronous approach not only boosts scalability but also enhances the efficiency and responsiveness of applications. This article delves into the numerous benefits of asynchronous communication and its pivotal role in expanding system capabilities.

Understanding Asynchronous Communication

In asynchronous communication frameworks, interactions between different system components or processes do not require both parties to engage simultaneously. This method is particularly beneficial in computational tasks where waiting for responses can lead to inefficient resource utilization and unnecessary idle time.

Benefits of Asynchronous Communication in Scalability

1. Enhanced Resource Efficiency

Asynchronous mechanisms allow systems to maximize resource utilization by eliminating idle wait times. Processes can perform additional tasks while awaiting responses, leading to improved throughput and overall system efficiency.

2. Increased Responsiveness

Applications that implement asynchronous communication can manage more user requests simultaneously. This is achieved by handling lengthy processes in the background, thereby maintaining fluid user interactions and significantly boosting user experience.

3. Robust Fault Tolerance

Asynchronous communication enhances the fault tolerance of systems. The decoupled nature of this communication style means that a failure in one component does not halt the entire system. Components can queue tasks and later process them when the system stabilizes, thereby maintaining continuous operation.

4. Adaptability to Fluctuating Workloads

Asynchronous systems are adept at managing sudden or unpredictable changes in workload. They achieve this by queuing incoming requests and processing them as resources permit, which is crucial for maintaining service quality during peak traffic periods.

5. Simplified Integration of Services

In environments where multiple services communicate, asynchronous messaging simplifies connections by allowing services to operate independently without strict synchronization. This facilitates easier scaling and integration of services within the architecture.

Implementing Asynchronous Communication

Message queues or event-driven architectures are common methods for implementing asynchronous communication. RabbitMQ is a popular choice for setting up asynchronous message handling systems:

```python
import pika

# Initialize a connection
connection = pika.BlockingConnection(pika.ConnectionParameters('localhost'))
channel = connection.channel()

# Create a message queue
channel.queue_declare(queue='hello')

# Enqueue a message
channel.basic_publish(exchange='',
                      routing_key='hello',
                      body='Hello, World!')

print(" [x] Sent 'Hello, World!'")
connection.close()
```

In this implementation using RabbitMQ, a message is sent without requiring the sender to pause for a receiver's readiness, showcasing asynchronous communication.

Conclusion

Embracing asynchronous communication is fundamental for scaling applications effectively. It provides substantial benefits in terms of resource utilization, system responsiveness, and operational continuity. Asynchronous methods are particularly valuable in complex systems where high throughput and reliability are necessary. Implementing these methods through technologies such as message brokers and event-driven systems is crucial for developing scalable, efficient, and resilient software architectures. The strategic adoption of asynchronous communication ensures that modern applications can meet the demands of increased scale and complexity.

Implementing Webhooks and WebSockets: Real-world applications of asynchronous APIs

In contemporary web development, leveraging asynchronous APIs like Webhooks and WebSockets is essential for crafting dynamic and responsive web applications. These technologies enhance server-client interactions, facilitating operations without the need for continuous page refreshes or incessant server checks. This article examines the deployment of Webhooks and WebSockets, highlighting their real-world applications and implementation strategies.

Exploring Webhooks and WebSockets

Webhooks are automated messages sent from applications when specified events occur, functioning as HTTP callbacks that facilitate seamless interactions between different systems.

WebSockets establish a persistent, two-way interactive communication session between a user's browser and a server. This protocol is invaluable for applications that demand real-time responsiveness and user interaction without the traditional request-response model.

Practical Applications of Webhooks

The flexibility of Webhooks makes them highly effective for automating and synchronizing cross-application processes. Here are some practical uses:

1. Enhancing E-Commerce Systems

Webhooks can be configured to update inventory or trigger order fulfillment processes instantly after a sale is confirmed, streamlining operations in e-commerce platforms.

Implementation Example:

```python
# A simple Flask route to handle Webhook events
from flask import Flask, request, Response

app = Flask(__name__)

@app.route('/webhook', methods=['POST'])
def webhook_handler():
    data = request.json
    # Execute an action such as updating inventory
    print("Order processed:", data['order_id'])
    return Response(status=200)

if __name__ == '__main__':
    app.run(port=5000)
```

This Python Flask server example listens for webhook notifications to process actions like inventory updates upon receiving transaction confirmations.

255

2. Real-Time Notifications

Webhooks enable applications to send real-time alerts or updates directly to users or other systems, significantly enhancing user engagement and operational efficiency.

Practical Applications of WebSockets

WebSockets are pivotal for developing interactive applications that require a live connection between the client and server. Some key applications include:

1. Real-Time Data Dashboards

WebSockets excel in scenarios requiring live data updates, such as analytics dashboards or performance monitoring systems, by providing instantaneous data streaming.

Example Code:

```javascript
// Example of a WebSocket server setup in Node.js
const WebSocket = require('ws');
const server = new WebSocket.Server({ port: 8080 });

server.on('connection', function (socket) {
    console.log('A client connected');
    socket.send('Connected to server');

    socket.on('message', function (msg) {
        console.log('Received:', msg);
    });

    setInterval(() => {
        socket.send('Update: ' + new Date().toLocaleTimeString());
    }, 1000);
});
```

This JavaScript snippet sets up a WebSocket server that sends timely updates to clients, suitable for dashboards that monitor data in real-time.

2. Interactive Communication Applications

Whether for chat applications or collaborative tools, WebSockets provide the necessary infrastructure for real-time, bidirectional communication, facilitating a seamless interactive experience for users.

Conclusion

Webhooks and WebSockets significantly empower web developers to enhance application interactivity and operational efficiency. These asynchronous APIs are integral for building applications that require immediate data updates and interactions without latency. By implementing Webhooks and WebSockets, developers can create scalable, responsive, and highly engaging web applications that meet the demands of modern users. Understanding and utilizing these technologies are pivotal for any developer aiming to deliver cutting-edge web solutions.

Chapter Nine

API Caching Strategies

When and Where to Cache: Best practices for caching within the API lifecycle

Caching is an essential technique in the API lifecycle that boosts performance by temporarily storing critical data or results from complex computations in a readily accessible space. This strategy significantly enhances API responsiveness and lightens the load on backend systems. This article explores the best practices for effectively implementing caching at different stages of the API lifecycle, offering insights into when and where to apply these practices optimally.

Essentials of Caching

Caching involves temporarily storing frequently accessed data in a cache—a temporary storage area, to speed up data retrieval in future requests. Proper caching decreases the time taken to fetch data and reduces the strain on server resources, leading to more scalable API operations.

Key Practices for Caching in the API Lifecycle

1. Identify Suitable Data for Caching

It's crucial to select the right type of data for caching:

- **Static Data**: Data that changes infrequently but is requested often, such as user settings or geographic details, is ideal for caching.

- **Resource-Intensive Data**: Information that requires significant resources to generate, like results from complex queries or processed data, should be cached.

Data that changes very frequently may not be the best candidate for caching due to the overhead of keeping the cache updated.

2. Select the Appropriate Caching Level

Different levels of caching provide unique benefits:

- **Client-Side Caching**: Reduces network calls by storing data locally on the user's browser, often controlled through HTTP cache headers.

- **Server-Side Caching**: This can be implemented within the application or via a dedicated caching system such as Redis or Memcached, which serves data quickly to various application instances.

3. Set Effective Cache Expiry Policies

Proper cache management requires an efficient expiration strategy:

- **Time-Based Expiry**: Cache items are set to expire after a predetermined duration.

- **Event-Driven Expiry**: Cache items are invalidated in response to specific events, like data updates.

For instance, an API that delivers weather forecasts might refresh its cache every 30 minutes to ensure the data remains current.

4. Employ Conditional Requests

Using conditional requests with HTTP headers such as **If-None-Match** or **If-Modified-Since** helps manage server responses based on the client's cached data state.

```python
from flask import Flask, request, jsonify

app = Flask(__name__)

@app.route('/resource')
def get_resource():
    resource = retrieve_data()
    last_modified = resource['last_modified']
    if 'If-Modified-Since' in request.headers and request.headers['If-Modified
        -Since'] >= last_modified:
        return ('', 304)  # Not Modified
    else:
        response = jsonify(resource)
        response.headers['Last-Modified'] = last_modified
        return response
```

5. Regularly Review and Adapt Caching Techniques

It's vital to continuously monitor the effectiveness of your caching strategy. Analyzing metrics like cache hit rates can help adjust approaches to ensure maximum efficiency.

Conclusion

Implementing effective caching within the API lifecycle is vital for enhancing performance, reducing latency, and optimizing server load. By carefully determining which data to cache, choosing the right caching level, setting strategic expiration policies, and utilizing conditional requests, developers can significantly improve their API's scalability and efficiency. Monitoring and adjusting caching strategies based on ongoing performance feedback is crucial to maintaining a high-performing API. Done correctly, caching not only speeds up API response times but also improves the overall user experience, making it an indispensable aspect of modern API architecture.

Tools for API Caching: Review of software and hardware solutions

In API development, caching is a fundamental strategy to boost performance, lower response times, and reduce server demands. Effective caching enhances user interactions by ensuring quicker data access and more efficient processing. Developers have a variety of both software and hardware tools at their disposal for caching. This article reviews prominent caching solutions and discusses their practical applications.

Overview of Software and Hardware Caching Tools

1. Redis

Redis is an open-source, in-memory data structure store that functions as a database, cache, and message broker, supporting various data structures like strings, hashes, and lists. It is known for its quick data access speeds and versatility in handling real-time application data.

Key Features:

- **Data Persistence**: Offers configurable persistence capabilities to ensure data durability.

- **Atomic Capabilities**: Provides atomic operations on its data types, supporting complex data manipulations.

- **Messaging Support**: Includes capabilities for publish/subscribe messaging systems.

Sample Code for Implementation:

```python
import redis

# Connect to the Redis server
redis_connection = redis.Redis(host='localhost', port=6379, db=0)

# Setting a value in the cache
redis_connection.set('key', 'value')

# Retrieving a value from the cache
print(redis_connection.get('key'))
```

2. Memcached

Memcached is a distributed memory object caching system that speeds up web applications by caching data and objects in RAM to reduce the number of times an external data source must be read.

Key Features:

- **Simplicity**: Memcached is easy to use and implement, ideal for basic caching needs.

- **Scalability**: Designed for easy horizontal scaling by adding more servers.

- **Transient Storage**: It focuses on in-memory storage for quick data retrieval.

Sample Code for Implementation:

```
import memcache

# Connect to Memcached server
memcache_client = memcache.Client(['127.0.0.1:11211'], debug=0)

# Save data in the cache
memcache_client.set("key", "value", time=120)

# Retrieve data from the cache
print(memcache_client.get("key"))
```

Hardware Solutions for Caching

1. F5 BIG-IP Local Traffic Manager (LTM)

F5 BIG-IP LTM is a hardware-based solution that optimizes web application performance through load balancing, SSL offloading, and HTTP caching, tailored for enterprise environments that demand high availability and extensive traffic management.

Key Features:

- **SSL Offloading**: Reduces the burden on servers by handling encryption and decryption operations.

- **Advanced Traffic Management**: Utilizes a full proxy architecture for precise traffic control.

- **Programming Flexibility**: Offers iRules for customized traffic direction based on specific needs.

263

2. A10 Networks Thunder ADC

A10's Thunder ADC is an application delivery controller designed for high-performance data centers, providing server load balancing and advanced traffic management.

Key Features:

- **Efficient Traffic Handling**: Manages complex data center traffic flows to enhance application delivery.

- **SSL Visibility**: Decrypts encrypted traffic to allow for more informed caching decisions.

- **Custom Scripting**: Enables detailed traffic management adjustments through scripting tools.

Conclusion

Selecting the right caching tool for API services hinges on specific requirements such as performance needs, scalability, and security considerations. Software tools like Redis and Memcached provide quick and easy caching solutions suitable for a range of applications from small to large scale. Meanwhile, hardware tools like F5 BIG-IP LTM and A10 Networks Thunder ADC offer robust solutions for larger enterprises requiring detailed traffic management and enhanced security. By incorporating these tools into their API infrastructure, developers can greatly improve application performance and user experience.

Chapter Ten

Versioning for Continuous Improvement

Strategies for API Versioning: How to handle API changes without disrupting users

API versioning is a vital practice that allows for the evolution and enhancement of software applications without interrupting the service for existing users. As APIs evolve over time, incorporating new features and making necessary adjustments, it's crucial to manage these changes in a way that doesn't negatively impact the existing API consumers. Implementing a well-thought-out versioning strategy ensures that older versions remain supported while new versions can coexist alongside them. This article outlines effective strategies for API versioning, providing insights into best practices for seamless transitions between API versions.

Exploring API Versioning

API versioning involves systematically managing changes to an API so that multiple versions can be supported simultaneously. This approach allows developers to introduce enhancements and new features while giving users ample time to transition without disruption. The main goal is to minimize "breaking changes" that could potentially disrupt applications that depend on the API.

Strategies for Effective API Versioning

1. Semantic Versioning (SemVer)

Semantic versioning is a widely adopted versioning scheme that uses a three-part version number (MAJOR.MINOR.PATCH) to indicate the type of changes made:

- **MAJOR version** indicates incompatible API changes,

- **MINOR version** indicates the addition of functionality in a backward-compatible manner,

- **PATCH version** indicates backward-compatible bug fixes.

SemVer helps to clearly communicate the impact of new versions to developers, providing an immediate understanding of the potential necessity for changes in their own applications.

2. URI Versioning

Incorporating the version number directly into the API's URI is a straightforward approach that clearly delineates different API versions.

Example:

```
https://api.example.com/v1/resource
https://api.example.com/v2/resource
```

This method is simple to implement and understand, although it can lead to code duplication and maintenance challenges if not carefully managed.

3. Parameter Versioning

This versioning strategy involves sending the API version as a query parameter in the request, which simplifies the URI structure and eases API endpoint management.

Example:

```
https://api.example.com/resource?version=1
https://api.example.com/resource?version=2
```

Parameter versioning offers flexibility but may obscure the versioning system from immediate visibility, potentially complicating documentation and client implementations.

4. Header Versioning

Using custom headers for versioning keeps the URL clean and makes version management transparent within the URI.

Example:

```
GET /resource HTTP/1.1
Host: api.example.com
Accept-Version: v1
```

This technique maintains a consistent URL structure but requires modifications to the header data on the client side, adding a layer of complexity to requests.

5. Content Negotiation

Versioning can also be achieved through content negotiation, using the Accept header to specify the version.

Example:

```
GET /resource HTTP/1.1
Host: api.example.com
Accept: application/vnd.example.v1+json
```

Content negotiation is flexible and leverages existing HTTP mechanisms, though it demands precise server-side handling to ensure correct response formats.

Best Practices in API Versioning

- **Comprehensive Documentation**: Maintain detailed documentation for all versions of your API, documenting any changes clearly to assist developers in understanding and implementing the API.

- **Clear Deprecation Guidelines**: Establish and communicate a deprecation policy, providing users with adequate notice and guidance for transitioning to newer versions.

- **Implement Hypermedia Links**: Utilize hypermedia as the engine of application state (HATEOAS) in your responses to help guide users through available resources and version changes.

- **Thorough Testing**: Employ robust testing strategies to ensure that updates do not compromise existing functionalities, with a focus on regression and API version tests.

- **Limit Active Versions**: Manage the number of active API versions to prevent overload and simplify maintenance, ensuring each version has a clear lifecycle and deprecation path.

Conclusion

Strategically versioning your API is crucial for managing its lifecycle effectively, allowing for ongoing improvement while supporting existing users. Choosing the right versioning strategy, whether it's through URIs, parameters, headers, or content negotiation, depends on your specific requirements and the nature of your API. By applying these strategies thoughtfully and consistently, you can ensure a smooth evolution of your API services and maintain robust, user-friendly interfaces over time.

Deprecation Policies: Best practices for phasing out older API versions

Deprecation policies play a critical role in API lifecycle management by outlining how to effectively phase out older versions of APIs. This ensures that both developers and users are well-prepared for updates, facilitating a smooth transition to newer versions while minimizing disruptions. Establishing and executing well-defined deprecation strategies not only helps in maintaining an organized and current API offering but also supports continuous improvement and adoption of new features. This article discusses the best practices for developing and applying deprecation policies for APIs.

Fundamentals of Deprecation Policies

A deprecation policy is a formal strategy that communicates the discontinuation plans of an API or a particular version of an API. It includes important details such as the deprecation timeline, support options available during the transition, and instructions for migrating to the new version. This ensures that users are neither caught off guard by changes nor experience service disruptions as they switch to updated versions.

Effective Practices for Deprecation Policies

1. Transparent Communication

It's crucial to communicate deprecation plans clearly and proactively to ensure users can prepare adequately. Key elements to convey include:

- The rationale for deprecating the API,

- The specific timeline leading up to the removal,

- End-of-life (EOL) date,

- Support options during the transition period,

- Directions for adopting newer versions.

Example of a Deprecation Announcement:

```
{
    "message": "Please note that API v1.0 will be deprecated on January 1, 2025. We
        encourage you to transition to API v2.0 by this date. For migration support,
        please visit [link]."
}
```

2. Comprehensive Migration Guides

Provide users with thorough migration guides that detail the process for transitioning from an older API version to a newer one. Include any changes in functionality and sample code snippets to facilitate understanding and adaptation.

Example Code Transition:

```
# Transition from v1.0 to v2.0 example
# v1.0
response = api.client.item.fetch('123')
# v2.0
response = api.client.product.get('123')
```

3. Robust Support During Transition

Maintain robust support channels during the API deprecation period. Offer assistance through help desks, FAQ sections, webinars, and direct outreach to ensure users can navigate the changes without significant issues.

4. Implementing Deprecation Alerts

Utilize HTTP headers to automatically inform developers of deprecated APIs when they make calls to such endpoints.

Example of Using HTTP Headers:

```
Deprecation: date="20250101"
Sunset: date="20250501"
```

5. Phased Deprecation Approach

Roll out the deprecation in stages to minimize impact. Start with notifications and documentation updates, followed by reminders, and introduce functionality reductions if necessary as the sunset date approaches.

6. Tracking API Usage

Monitor how much the deprecated API versions are still in use to gauge the urgency of communication and support needed.

Usage analytics can help tailor outreach efforts to ensure all users are aware and prepared for the upcoming changes.

7. Consider Legal and Compliance Issues

Align the deprecation strategy with legal and regulatory standards, particularly for APIs handling sensitive data. Ensuring compliance and data security is critical throughout the deprecation process.

Conclusion

Creating a strategic deprecation policy for APIs is essential for managing the evolution of technology within any platform. By communicating clearly, providing detailed migration instructions, supporting users through the transition, and monitoring the process, organizations can ensure a seamless update experience. This not only keeps the API portfolio fresh and aligned with technological advancements but also maintains user trust and satisfaction. Effective deprecation strategies are key to adaptive, forward-looking API management.

Chapter Eleven

Advanced Testing for Robust APIs

Stress and Load Testing: Techniques to test APIs under high load

Stress and load testing are essential practices for assessing how well APIs can handle expected and extreme user traffic. These tests are crucial for determining if APIs are robust enough to sustain performance under normal operations and peak loads without failure. Applying thorough testing techniques ensures that potential performance bottlenecks are identified, resource utilization is optimized, and end-users experience reliable service. This article provides insights into effective strategies for conducting stress and load testing on APIs.

Fundamentals of Stress and Load Testing

Load Testing is performed to understand how an API behaves under typical user traffic, replicating normal operational conditions to validate if the API can maintain its performance stability over time.

Stress Testing is more aggressive, aiming to push the system beyond its normal capacity to determine its absolute limits. It helps identify how the system reacts under extreme load and the point at which it fails.

Effective Techniques for API Stress and Load Testing

1. Establish Clear Testing Goals

It's important to clearly define the goals of your testing efforts. Whether it's to determine how many simultaneous users the API can handle, or to find out how it performs under stressful conditions, having clear goals helps tailor the testing process to yield meaningful insights.

2. Select Suitable Testing Tools

Several robust tools are available for facilitating stress and load testing, including:

- **JMeter**: An open-source tool ideal for performance testing.

- **LoadRunner**: Known for its detailed analysis capabilities.

- **Artillery**: Great for creating complex test scenarios.

Example with JMeter:

```xml
<!-- JMeter Test Plan for simulating user load -->
<jmeterTestPlan>
  <hashTree>
    <ThreadGroup guiclass="ThreadGroupGui" testclass="ThreadGroup" testname
      ="Simulated Users" enabled="true">
      <stringProp name="ThreadGroup.num_threads">100</stringProp>
      <stringProp name="ThreadGroup.ramp_time">10</stringProp>
    </ThreadGroup>
    <hashTree>
      <HTTPSamplerProxy guiclass="HttpTestSampleGui" testclass="HTTPSamplerProxy"
        testname="API Request" enabled="true">
        <stringProp name="HTTPSampler.path">/api/target</stringProp>
      </HTTPSamplerProxy>
    </hashTree>
  </hashTree>
</jmeterTestPlan>
```

3. Mimic Real-User Interactions

Develop tests that closely simulate the various types of requests users will make to the API to ensure the tests are realistic and cover all potential user interactions.

4. Monitor Key Performance Indicators

During testing, it's crucial to track performance metrics such as:

- Response times,

- Error rates,

- Throughput,

- Server resource usage.

These metrics will help pinpoint when and why performance issues occur.

5. Implement Incremental Testing

Begin with a small number of users and gradually increase the load. This method helps determine the specific load level at which the API begins to falter.

6. Optimize Based on Findings

Post-testing, analyze the outcomes to identify any performance issues or failures. Use this data to make informed decisions on how to enhance the API, whether by code optimization, scaling resources, or improving error handling.

7. Conduct Repeated Tests

Perform the tests repeatedly to ensure the API's performance remains consistent across different conditions and over time. Regular testing confirms the API's reliability and stability.

Conclusion

Stress and load testing are crucial for ensuring that APIs are capable of handling both normal and peak traffic conditions effectively. These testing practices not only verify the API's operational capabilities but also ensure it can deliver a reliable, efficient service without disruptions. By meticulously planning and executing these tests, developers can enhance the robustness and dependability of their APIs, leading to improved service quality and user satisfaction.

Security Testing: Ensuring your API is secure from attacks

Security testing is crucial for ensuring that APIs are protected against potential cyber threats, a fundamental component of API management that uncovers vulnerabilities and strengthens security mechanisms. In today's landscape of frequent data breaches and security incidents, robust API security is essential. This type of testing simulates various attack scenarios to help fortify APIs against unauthorized access and safeguard sensitive information. This article discusses effective methods and strategies for conducting comprehensive security testing on APIs.

Introduction to API Security Testing

API security testing aims to identify vulnerabilities within an API's protective measures and assess its ability to maintain data integrity and availability under malicious conditions. This process is vital for preventing unauthorized data access and ensuring that APIs adhere to their intended functional behaviors under all circumstances.

Crucial Strategies for API Security Testing

1. Establish Security Benchmarks

Begin with a clear understanding of your API's security needs, including data sensitivity and compliance requirements. This foundation will guide the specific tests that need to be conducted.

2. Perform Vulnerability Assessments

Critical to security testing are vulnerability assessments, which include:

- **Static Analysis**: Examining the codebase for security vulnerabilities without executing the code.

- **Dynamic Analysis**: Testing the API while it is running to identify runtime vulnerabilities.

Tools such as OWASP ZAP and Burp Suite are often used for these analyses.

Example of employing OWASP ZAP:

```
# Using OWASP ZAP for a quick security scan
zap-cli quick-scan --self-contained --start-options '-config api.disablekey=true'
   --api-key='none' http://example-api.com
```

3. Execute Penetration Testing

Penetration testing mimics real-world attacks to see how well the API can defend itself against unauthorized access and manipulation. Pen testing can be categorized as:

- **White Box Testing**: Testing with an internal understanding of the API.

- **Black Box Testing**: Testing without any prior knowledge of the API's internal workings, similar to an external hacker.

4. Assess Authentication and Authorization Mechanisms

It's critical to verify that the API correctly handles user identity verification and resource access permissions:

- **Authentication Testing** ensures that the API properly verifies user identities.

- **Authorization Testing** checks that users can access only the resources they are permitted to access.

5. Evaluate Input Validation and Sanitization

To protect against SQL injections, XSS, and other injection attacks, it's essential that all data inputs and outputs are thoroughly validated and sanitized:

- **Input Validation Testing** ensures robust processing of incoming data.

- **Output Sanitization Testing** makes sure that outputs do not expose sensitive data or create opportunities for data leakage.

6. Test Rate Limiting and Throttling Mechanisms

These tests are vital for preventing denial-of-service (DoS) attacks, ensuring that the API can handle unexpected volumes of requests by implementing controls such as:

- **Rate Limit Tests** to gauge how the API copes with a high number of legitimate requests.

- **Throttling Tests** to check how the API performs under resource strain.

7. Continuous Security Updates and Patch Testing

Maintain the security of your API by regularly updating security measures and testing the effectiveness of new security patches.

Best Practices in API Security Testing

- **Update Testing Procedures Regularly**: As security threats evolve, so should your testing techniques.

- **Automate Security Tests**: Embed security testing within the CI/CD pipeline to ensure continuous security oversight.

- **Educate Development Teams**: Regular training sessions on the latest security threats and mitigation techniques can help developers create more secure code.

- **Keep Comprehensive Logs**: Detailed logging of security tests can aid in diagnosing issues and understanding attack patterns after a security incident.

Conclusion

Conducting thorough security testing is indispensable for maintaining robust API security. Through systematic evaluation using various testing strategies, you can identify vulnerabilities and strengthen your API against potential threats. Regular and meticulous security testing not only protects data but also enhances user trust in the reliability and security of your API.

Chapter Twelve

Deployment Strategies for High Availability

Automated Deployments: Tools and practices for CI/CD

Automated deployments are pivotal in contemporary software development, streamlining the process of delivering consistent and reliable software updates. By integrating automated deployment practices, organizations can minimize errors, reduce the time to market, and enhance the overall reliability of their software releases. Continuous Integration (CI) and Continuous Deployment (CD) are key methodologies that facilitate these efficiencies. This article examines a variety of tools and practices that are fundamental to successful CI/CD implementations.

Overview of CI/CD

Continuous Integration (CI) is a development practice where developers frequently merge code changes into a central repository, followed by automated builds and tests. The main advantage of CI is that it allows you to detect issues early in the development cycle.

Continuous Deployment (CD) builds on CI by automatically deploying the code to a production or testing environment after the build phase. This ensures that the software can be deployed at any moment, enhancing the feedback loop with end-users and stakeholders.

Core Tools for CI/CD

Several tools have been designed to support the CI/CD pipeline by automating the software delivery process. These tools automate various steps such as code commits, testing, and deployments. Here are some essential tools widely adopted in the industry:

1. Jenkins

Jenkins is a powerful open-source automation server used to implement CI/CD workflows. It supports various plugins which extend its capabilities to meet diverse project requirements.

Example Jenkins Pipeline Script:

```
pipeline {
    agent any
    stages {
        stage('Build') {
            steps {
                echo 'Building project...'
                // Insert build commands here
            }
        }
        stage('Test') {
            steps {
                echo 'Executing tests...'
                // Insert test commands here
            }
        }
        stage('Deploy') {
            steps {
                echo 'Deploying application...'
                // Insert deployment commands here
            }
        }
    }
}
```

2. GitLab CI/CD

GitLab provides a comprehensive suite for software development through its single application, which includes built-in CI/CD capabilities. It allows for seamless integration with the GitLab version control system to automate the phases of build, test, and deploy within the GitLab platform.

Example .gitlab-ci.yml:

```yaml
stages:
  - build
  - test
  - deploy

build_job:
  stage: build
  script:
    - echo "Building application..."
    - build_script

test_job:
  stage: test
  script:
    - echo "Running tests..."
    - test_script

deploy_job:
  stage: deploy
  script:
    - echo "Deploying application..."
    - deploy_script
```

3. CircleCI

CircleCI is renowned for its quick setup and integration with GitHub and Bitbucket, providing robust CI/CD services that work across multiple environments.

4. Travis CI

Travis CI is favored in projects hosted on GitHub, offering automated testing and deployment services. It's known for its easy configuration and integration with GitHub repositories.

Best Practices for Effective CI/CD

1. Automate Extensively

Automate all stages from code integration to deployment to ensure consistency and reduce manual errors.

2. Use Version Control

Implement version control solutions to manage code changes effectively, using platforms like Git to facilitate collaboration and tracking.

3. Optimize Build Times

Strive to keep the build and test phases as efficient as possible to maintain a swift development pace.

4. Implement Infrastructure as Code

Manage your CI/CD configurations using code to maintain consistency and accountability through version control systems.

5. Monitor Systematically

Continuously monitor the CI/CD pipeline to ensure operations are smooth and to quickly identify any disruptions in the deployment phases.

6. Prioritize Security

Incorporate security practices throughout the CI/CD pipeline to safeguard against vulnerabilities from the outset.

Conclusion

CI/CD is an essential component of modern software development strategies, facilitating rapid and reliable software delivery. Utilizing tools such as Jenkins, GitLab CI/CD, CircleCI, and Travis CI enables teams to automate their development workflows, significantly boosting productivity and efficiency. By adhering to best practices such as comprehensive automation, efficient build processes, and robust security integration, organizations can enhance their deployment capabilities and achieve continuous improvement in their software development processes.

High Availability Architectures: Ensuring your API is always accessible

High availability architectures are crucial for maintaining uninterrupted access to APIs, ensuring they remain functional and responsive regardless of system failures or heavy traffic loads. This approach is vital for businesses dependent on continuous API availability, helping to reduce downtime and guarantee consistent user interactions. This article delves into the essential elements and methodologies necessary to construct robust high availability architectures for APIs.

Fundamentals of High Availability

High availability refers to the design of systems that are operational nearly all the time, minimizing both planned and unplanned downtime. For APIs, achieving high availability means ensuring the API is reliably responsive to requests, operating within expected time frames under various conditions, including high demand or component failures.

Crucial Elements of High Availability Architectures

1. Redundancy

At the heart of high availability is redundancy, the practice of duplicating key components of a system to increase reliability. For APIs, this involves several layers:

- **Server Redundancy**: Utilizing multiple servers across diverse geographic locations to ensure continuous availability even if one server fails.

- **Database Redundancy**: Employing primary and secondary databases so that the secondary can take over operations without interruption if the primary database fails.

2. Load Balancing

Load balancing effectively distributes incoming API requests across multiple servers to optimize resource use, enhance throughput, and reduce response times. This can be managed via hardware or software solutions.

Example configuration using Nginx for load balancing:

```
http {
    upstream myapi {
        server server1.example.com;
        server server2.example.com;
    }

    server {
        listen 80;

        location / {
            proxy_pass http://myapi;
        }
    }
}
```

This setup in Nginx helps distribute user requests evenly across two servers, enhancing the API's availability.

3. Failover Mechanisms

Failover processes ensure that if the primary system fails, a backup system immediately takes over with minimal service interruption. Techniques include:

- **Automatic Failover**: Systems switch to a standby operational mode automatically if the primary setup fails.

- **Failover Clusters**: These are configurations where multiple servers work together, ready to continue operations if one server fails.

4. Continuous Monitoring

Ongoing monitoring is essential for detecting and resolving potential issues before they affect availability. Modern tools can track server health, traffic flows, and other vital metrics in real time.

- **Tools like Prometheus and Grafana** offer extensive capabilities for monitoring and visualizing API health metrics.

5. Component Decoupling

Creating a modular system where components operate independently reduces the risk of a single component failure taking down the entire API. Microservices architectures are ideal for this, as each service functions independently but communicates through defined APIs.

High Availability Best Practices

- **Geographical Distribution**: Spread out your infrastructure to avoid regionalized risks, such as power failures or natural disasters.

- **Automated Backups**: Regular, automated backups help safeguard data and ensure that it can be quickly restored.

- **Scalable Design**: Build systems that can scale out (add more resources) to meet growing demand smoothly.

- **Regular Testing**: Continuously test your high availability strategies, including failover protocols and disaster recovery plans, to ensure they work effectively when needed.

Conclusion

Developing a high availability architecture for APIs involves strategic layering of redundancy, load balancing, failover strategies, and proactive monitoring. By implementing these components, organizations can assure that their APIs deliver consistent performance and reliability, enhancing user satisfaction and safeguarding the business against the impacts of downtime. This comprehensive approach not only supports a superior user experience but also fortifies the organization's operational resilience.

Chapter Thirteen

Monitoring and Analytics

Monitoring Tools and Techniques: How to keep track of API performance and health

Effective monitoring of API performance and health is crucial for ensuring that these essential components of modern digital infrastructures operate reliably and efficiently. Proper monitoring strategies can help detect and resolve issues swiftly, maintaining service continuity and enhancing user experiences. This article explores various tools and approaches for proficiently tracking API performance and health.

The Role of API Monitoring

Effective API monitoring allows IT teams to swiftly identify performance bottlenecks, errors, and inefficiencies, crucial for maintaining high performance and minimal downtime. It involves tracking specific metrics that provide insights into how well APIs are performing and interacting within digital services.

Essential Metrics for Monitoring APIs

A comprehensive API monitoring strategy includes observing several key metrics that reflect the API's operational state:

- **Response Time**: Tracks the time it takes for an API to fulfill a request, where longer times may suggest performance issues.

- **Error Rates**: Monitors the rate of requests that result in errors, indicating potential reliability or functional problems.

- **Throughput**: Measures the volume of requests an API processes over a given time, essential for evaluating its capacity and scalability.

- **Availability**: Assesses whether the API is up and running and accessible by users, crucial for overall service reliability.

Top Tools for API Monitoring

Several sophisticated tools exist for monitoring APIs, each offering unique functionalities ranging from real-time data analytics to comprehensive alerting capabilities. Some of the leading tools include:

1. Prometheus

Prometheus is an open-source monitoring solution known for its robust data collection and querying capabilities, ideal for tracking time-series data related to API performance.

Prometheus Query Example for API Response Times:

```
histogram_quantile(0.95, sum(rate(api_response_time_seconds_bucket[5m])) by (le))
```

This query assesses the 95th percentile of API response times over five minutes, offering insight into performance under various loads.

2. Grafana

Grafana provides powerful visualization tools for monitoring data, enhancing the ability to understand and react to API performance metrics.

Setting Up a Grafana Dashboard: A Grafana dashboard can be set up to display Prometheus data, providing a graphical representation of key metrics like response times and error rates.

3. New Relic

New Relic offers a robust suite of monitoring tools that deliver deep insights into API and application performance, enabling detailed performance tracking and issue resolution.

4. Datadog

Datadog is a comprehensive monitoring service that integrates with various systems to offer real-time insights into API performance across multiple platforms.

Strategies for Effective API Monitoring

Adopting the right strategies for API monitoring can significantly enhance its effectiveness:

- **Real-Time Monitoring**: Implement tools that provide instantaneous feedback on API performance to identify and address issues promptly.

- **Threshold-Based Alerts**: Establish alerts for when performance metrics exceed predetermined thresholds to facilitate quick responses.

- **Comprehensive Log Management**: Incorporate advanced log management solutions to collect, analyze, and archive API logs, vital for troubleshooting and historical analysis.

- **Routine Synthetic Testing**: Conduct regular tests that simulate typical user behaviors to ensure all API components function together seamlessly.

Conclusion

Maintaining rigorous monitoring of API performance and health is essential for the reliability and efficiency of digital services. By leveraging advanced monitoring tools like Prometheus, Grafana, New Relic, and Datadog, and implementing strategic monitoring practices, organizations can ensure their APIs remain performant and reliable. This proactive approach not only improves user satisfaction but also bolsters the organization's ability to adapt to new challenges in the digital environment.

Analyzing Usage Patterns: Gaining insights from traffic patterns and user behaviors

Analyzing usage patterns is essential for organizations relying on digital platforms to deeply understand user interactions. By examining how users engage with services, companies can enhance service delivery, tailor user experiences, and make informed strategic decisions. This process involves gathering and analyzing data on user activities and behaviors within an application or website.

Significance of Usage Pattern Analysis

Analyzing user behaviors and traffic patterns allows organizations to pinpoint successful features and identify areas needing improvement. Benefits include:

- Enhancing product design based on user preferences and behaviors.

- Increasing user engagement through personalized experiences.

- Allocating resources more effectively by understanding peak usage times.

- Identifying and resolving performance issues that impact user satisfaction.

Collecting Data for Usage Analysis

The foundational step in usage pattern analysis is the systematic collection of data. This includes tracking various metrics that offer insights into how users navigate and interact with a platform. Key metrics include:

- **Page Views and User Sessions**: Metrics that track user visits and navigation paths within the site.

- **User Interactions**: Observations of user actions such as clicks, form submissions, and interaction times.

- **Traffic Sources**: Analysis of where traffic originates, whether through search engines, direct entries, or referral links.

- **Device Usage**: Information on the devices and browsers used by visitors to optimize platform compatibility and performance.

For instance, integrating Google Analytics involves embedding a simple tracking code within your website, which gathers vast amounts of user interaction data:

```
// Google Analytics script
window.dataLayer = window.dataLayer || [];
function gtag(){dataLayer.push(arguments);}
gtag('js', new Date());

// Setup Google Analytics with your specific tracking ID
gtag('config', 'YOUR_TRACKING_ID');
```

Tools and Techniques for Analyzing Usage Data

After collecting data, several analytical tools and methods can be used to interpret and visualize usage patterns:

1. Google Analytics

A robust tool that offers detailed insights into traffic patterns, user demographics, and interaction rates, helping refine user acquisition and retention strategies.

2. Heatmaps

Tools such as Hotjar or Crazy Egg that provide heatmap visualizations of where users click, how they scroll, and how much time they spend on specific parts of a page.

3. Advanced Behavioral Analytics

Platforms like Mixpanel or Amplitude offer in-depth analysis of user actions and track detailed pathways throughout an application, identifying common behaviors and user flows.

296

4. Segmentation Analysis

Breaking down user data into specific segments based on demographics, behaviors, or device types, allowing for more tailored and effective user experiences.

Implementing Insights from Usage Data

Insights derived from usage data analysis can lead to practical applications across various business areas:

- **Interface Optimization**: Adjusting design and navigation based on user feedback to improve functionality and user engagement.

- **Personalization Strategies**: Developing personalized experiences or content recommendations based on user activity patterns.

- **Resource Management**: Optimizing server capacity and backend resources in line with observed user demand patterns.

- **Feature Prioritization**: Focusing on enhancing popular features or reevaluating underperforming areas based on user engagement statistics.

Example: Using Predictive Analytics

Leveraging predictive analytics can provide forward-looking insights, allowing businesses to anticipate user actions and strategize accordingly. Using machine learning models, such as those built with Python's scikit-learn, organizations can predict user behaviors like churn or engagement levels:

```
from sklearn.model_selection import train_test_split
from sklearn.ensemble import RandomForestClassifier
import pandas as pd

# Loading user data
data = pd.read_csv('user_data.csv')
features = data[['session_duration', 'pages_visited', 'interactions_per_visit']]
labels = data['user_retention']

# Splitting the dataset for training and testing
X_train, X_test, y_train, y_test = train_test_split(features, labels, test_size=0
    .25, random_state=42)

# Training a Random Forest model
model = RandomForestClassifier()
model.fit(X_train, y_train)

# Predicting user retention
predictions = model.predict(X_test)
```

Conclusion

Understanding and analyzing usage patterns is a critical practice for enhancing digital service platforms. Through detailed data collection, sophisticated analytics, and strategic application of insights, organizations can significantly improve user experiences, optimize operational performance, and drive effective business decisions. This ongoing process is fundamental to adapting to evolving user needs and maintaining competitive advantage in the digital marketplace.

Chapter Fourteen

Case Studies of Scalable API

Implementations

Successful Implementations: Dissecting what worked for popular APIs

Successful API implementations serve as models for effective digital interaction, often setting standards in the tech industry. By examining the attributes that have led to the success of well-known APIs, developers can glean insights that inform the design and operation of their own APIs. This analysis explores the defining characteristics of successful API deployments, citing specific examples from industry leaders.

Defining Traits of Successful API Implementations

There are several key traits commonly observed in successful APIs that contribute to their effectiveness and widespread use:

1. **Ease of Use and Simplicity**: The best APIs are those that are straightforward to implement and use, with clear, concise documentation and simple endpoints.

2. **Consistent Reliability and High Performance**: Successful APIs deliver high performance and are reliable under a range of operational scenarios, maintaining low latency and supporting high transaction volumes.

3. **Scalable Architecture**: Leading APIs are designed to accommodate growth in user numbers and data volume effortlessly.

4. **Comprehensive Security Measures**: Effective security protocols are crucial, incorporating strong authentication, authorization, and data encryption to safeguard sensitive information.

5. **Effective Versioning Control**: Proper versioning allows APIs to evolve and improve without disrupting the existing user experience.

6. **Active Developer Community and Support**: A supportive and engaged community around an API can enhance its adoption and long-term viability.

Examples of Popular APIs

Google Maps API

Google Maps API is an exemplar of widespread API adoption due to its robust functionality and ease of integration in various applications globally.

Key Attributes:

- **Detailed Documentation**: Google offers exhaustive guides, examples, and tips for best practices.

- **Scalability**: It supports more than a billion users, demonstrating its capability to handle extensive scaling.

- **Rich Functionality**: With features like geolocation, directions, and street views, it enables developers to create comprehensive location-based services.

Sample Code:

```
function initMap() {
  const location = { lat: -34.397, lng: 150.644 };
  const map = new google.maps.Map(document.getElementById("map"), {
    zoom: 8,
    center: location,
  });
  const marker = new google.maps.Marker({
    position: location,
    map: map,
  });
}
```

This snippet illustrates initializing a map with a marker, showcasing the API's straightforward implementation.

Stripe API

Stripe's API is celebrated for its developer-oriented design, extensive documentation, and superior support.

Key Attributes:

- **Simplicity in Integration**: Stripe's API is designed to be intuitively understandable, making it easy for developers to integrate payment processing solutions swiftly.

- **Advanced Security**: Employs tokenization for handling sensitive payment information.

- **Developer Resources**: Provides a wealth of resources including libraries and SDKs across various programming languages, appealing to a broad developer audience.

Sample Code:

```python
import stripe
stripe.api_key = 'your_api_key_here'

charge = stripe.Charge.create(
    amount=2000,
    currency='usd',
    source='tok_visa',
    description='Payment for example@example.com'
)
```

This example demonstrates how to execute a payment charge, highlighting the API's functional ease.

Insights from Successful APIs

Studying APIs like Google Maps and Stripe reveals several actionable insights:

- **Focus on User Needs**: Design APIs with the end-user in mind, ensuring interfaces are intuitive and documentation is clear.

- **Ensure Robust Support and Documentation**: Comprehensive documentation and active support channels are critical in reducing barriers to adoption.

- **Prioritize Core Functionalities**: Successful APIs focus on delivering their primary services efficiently and reliably.

- **Security is Crucial**: In an era of heightened cyber threats, prioritizing security in API design is essential.

Conclusion

The characteristics shared by successful APIs include simplicity, reliability, scalability, security, effective versioning, and strong community support. These elements are critical for creating APIs that not only meet user needs but also foster broad adoption and satisfaction. Learning from established APIs provides valuable blueprints for developers aiming to build functional, secure, and widely used APIs.

Lessons from Scalability Failures: Common scalability pitfalls and how they were addressed

Scalability is a fundamental aspect of software development, particularly crucial for applications expected to handle increased user or data growth. Neglecting scalability during the initial stages of development or failing to adapt to new demands can lead to significant challenges. Analyzing these issues provides essential lessons on integrating scalability into systems effectively. Here, we dissect common scalability failures and discuss how they have been successfully remedied, providing insights to aid in future projects.

Common Scalability Pitfalls

1. **Database Performance Issues**: As user base and data access increase, databases often become a major bottleneck, exhibiting slow query times and transaction delays which degrade user experience.

2. **Inadequate Load Balancing**: Without proper load balancing, some servers may be overloaded while others are underutilized, leading to uneven resource distribution.

3. **Suboptimal Caching Strategies**: Effective caching reduces direct database queries, enhancing responsiveness. Poor caching can result in frequent, unnecessary database loads, which impede performance as demand escalates.

4. **Monolithic Design**: Monolithic architectures can complicate scaling efforts because scaling often requires duplicating the entire application, not just specific functionalities.

5. **Physical Resource Constraints**: The physical limitations of servers, including processing power and bandwidth, can restrict scalability. Transitioning to virtual or cloud-based infrastructures often addresses these limitations.

Solutions to Scalability Challenges

Enhancing Database Capability

To mitigate database bottlenecks, many organizations employ database sharding or migrate to more scalable database systems. Sharding divides a database into several pieces that can be distributed across multiple servers.

Example: A global messaging app may shard its database by continent to balance the load effectively across its server network.

Effective Load Distribution

Implementing robust load balancing mechanisms ensures that traffic is evenly distributed across available servers. This can be managed through software solutions like Nginx or hardware-based load balancers.

Example Nginx Configuration for Load Balancing:

```
http {
    upstream app_servers {
        server server1.example.com;
        server server2.example.com;
        server server3.example.com;
    }

    server {
        listen 80;

        location / {
            proxy_pass http://app_servers;
        }
    }
}
```

This setup helps distribute user requests across three servers, maintaining equilibrium in server load.

Improving Caching Mechanisms

Refining caching processes involves strategically storing data to reduce repetitive database queries. Technologies like Redis and Memcached are instrumental for their in-memory caching capabilities, which provide quick data access.

Example: During peak traffic, an online store might cache heavily requested product information to speed up response times.

Transitioning to Microservices

Shifting from a monolithic architecture to microservices allows individual components of an application to scale independently, which can lead to more efficient utilization of resources and easier scalability.

Example: An e-commerce platform could separate its billing, inventory, and customer service features into distinct microservices, each scaling according to its specific demands.

Utilizing Cloud Technologies

Cloud platforms provide scalable solutions that adapt to changing load demands without the need for physical infrastructure upgrades. Services like AWS Auto Scaling automatically adjust computing resources based on actual usage, ensuring efficient handling of load spikes.

Example: A media streaming service might use cloud-based auto-scaling to manage the influx of users during new content releases, ensuring consistent streaming quality.

Lessons from Scalability Corrections

1. **Anticipate Scalability Needs**: Design systems with scalability in mind from the outset to avoid complex modifications later.

2. **Continuously Monitor and Adapt**: Regular monitoring and timely adjustments can preempt scalability issues from escalating into more severe problems.

3. **Adopt Cloud Services**: Cloud computing offers flexible and economical solutions to scalability challenges, accommodating large-scale operations without substantial upfront investments.

4. **Cultivate Scalability Awareness**: Encourage a culture where scalability considerations are integral to the design and development phases, fostering long-term stability and growth.

Understanding and addressing scalability failures through strategic improvements and technological adaptations provides a blueprint for developing robust, scalable systems capable of supporting business growth and technological evolution.

Conclusion

Summary of Key Concepts: Reiterating the most important points from the book

This summary revisits the pivotal concepts explored throughout the book, serving as a concise guide and refresher to reinforce the fundamental principles discussed. It offers a synthesized view of the key lessons, aimed at facilitating practical application and deeper understanding for ongoing and future projects.

1. Core Principles of API Design

The book begins by establishing a strong foundation in the principles of API design. It stresses the importance of creating APIs that are functional, intuitive, secure, and capable of scaling effectively. Detailed discussion on RESTful principles highlights the significance of statelessness, clear resource identification, proper use of HTTP methods, and leveraging standard HTTP status codes for efficient error handling.

Example Code Snippet: Using HTTP Methods Correctly

```javascript
// Example of implementing RESTful endpoints with Express.js
const express = require('express');
const app = express();
const port = 3000;

// Handling GET requests to retrieve data
app.get('/api/items', (req, res) => {
  res.send('Received GET request');
});

// Handling POST requests to create data
app.post('/api/items', (req, res) => {
  res.status(201).send('Item created');
});

app.listen(port, () => {
  console.log(`Server running on port ${port}`);
});
```

2. API Security Essentials

Security is paramount in API design. The section on security outlines key authentication methods like OAuth and JWTs (JSON Web Tokens), and advocates for strong security measures including HTTPS, input validation, and periodic security audits to protect against vulnerabilities.

Important Reminder: Employ HTTPS to secure data transmissions and prevent data from being intercepted by unauthorized parties.

3. Strategies for API Versioning

Versioning is crucial for API longevity and user satisfaction. Various approaches such as URI versioning, parameter versioning, and header versioning are examined, with guidance on when each is most applicable. The importance of maintaining clear versioning policies to ensure smooth transitions for API users is emphasized.

Advice: Document changes meticulously and aim for backward compatibility to enhance user experience.

4. Optimizing Scalability and Performance

This segment addresses the challenges of scaling APIs and provides strategies for enhancing performance, such as implementing caching, employing load balancing, and adopting a microservices architecture. It includes advice on using monitoring tools to identify and resolve performance issues promptly.

Practical Tip: Implement Redis to cache data frequently accessed to decrease database load and speed up response times.

5. Fostering a Developer Community

The success of an API can be significantly influenced by its adoption and reception within the developer community. This chapter covers the importance of excellent documentation, active community engagement, and potentially open-sourcing the API to encourage a collaborative and vibrant developer ecosystem.

Key Insight: Regular interaction with the developer community can lead to a more robust and widely accepted API.

6. Emerging Trends and Future Directions

The concluding discussions speculate on future developments in API technology, including the integration of AI and machine learning and adapting to regulatory changes like GDPR. It advises on staying abreast of technological advances and regulatory shifts to keep APIs relevant and compliant.

Forward-Looking Thought: Keep informed of new technologies and regulatory standards to ensure your APIs remain at the forefront of innovation and compliance.

Conclusion

This summary encapsulates essential themes from the book, providing readers with a compact reference of core API design and management principles. It encourages ongoing review and application of these concepts to keep up with best practices and prepare for emerging challenges and opportunities in software development. The insights provided aim to assist developers in crafting APIs that are not only technically sound but also aligned with industry standards and future-ready.

Next Steps for Advancing API Mastery: Guidance on progressing towards even more complex API challenges

In today's rapidly evolving business and technological landscapes, continuous growth and adaptability are crucial for maintaining competitiveness and achieving sustainable success. With swift changes in market conditions, technologies, and consumer preferences, both individuals and organizations must adopt an approach of ongoing learning and flexibility. This approach not only secures a competitive advantage but also promotes a resilient professional trajectory or business model. Encouraging such growth and adaptability involves recognizing their importance, implementing effective strategies, and creating an environment that values and promotes constant evolution.

Importance of Continuous Growth and Adaptation

Continuous growth involves the relentless enhancement of skills, knowledge, and capabilities to stay relevant and effective in one's field. Adaptability refers to the capacity to quickly adjust to new challenges, information, or objectives. Together, these capabilities are crucial for managing the complexities and uncertainties of the modern professional environment.

For instance, in the tech sector, frequent updates in programming languages, evolving development methodologies, and changing tech standards are commonplace. Professionals committed to regular learning can adeptly manage these changes, ensuring their skills and methods remain pertinent and effective.

Strategies to Foster Continuous Growth and Adaptation

1. Establishing a Lifelong Learning Culture

It is essential to cultivate a culture that emphasizes lifelong learning. This involves setting personal learning goals and embedding educational activities into daily routines.

Example: A systems analyst might set an objective to master a new database technology each year, scheduling specific times each week for this purpose.

```python
# Example to schedule weekly time for learning new technologies such as Kubernetes
import calendar
import datetime

# Plan weekly dedicated learning sessions: every Tuesday afternoon
def schedule_learning_sessions(year):
    days = []
    for month in range(1, 13):
        month_calendar = calendar.monthcalendar(year, month)
        # Choose each Tuesday of the month for learning
        for week in month_calendar:
            if week[calendar.TUESDAY] != 0:
                days.append(datetime.date(year, month, week[calendar.TUESDAY]))
    return days

learning_days = schedule_learning_sessions(2024)
print("Scheduled Learning Days for 2024:", learning_days)
```

2. Encouraging Innovation and Embracing Risk

An environment where employees are encouraged to innovate and take calculated risks can significantly encourage growth. This might involve leading new projects, experimenting with new tools, or developing new operational processes. Recognizing successful innovations and reviewing the outcomes of less successful efforts constructively are both key.

3. Provision of Learning Resources

Ensuring that employees have access to educational resources such as courses, seminars, and workshops significantly aids in continual growth. Many organizations offer tuition assistance, subscriptions to learning platforms, or conduct in-house training sessions to support employee development.

4. Implementing Regular Feedback and Reflective Practices

Continuous feedback is vital for growth. This includes structured performance reviews and real-time feedback mechanisms, as well as fostering a practice of self-reflection on both successes and lessons from less successful endeavors.

5. Utilizing Technological Tools for Adaptability

Adopting advanced technological tools can greatly aid in adaptability. Tools like data analytics platforms, AI decision-making aids, or automated testing frameworks can help professionals quickly adapt to new information or changes in their operational environment.

Example: Using a simple machine learning model to predict outcomes based on historical data can help in making proactive adjustments.

```python
from sklearn.linear_model import LinearRegression
from sklearn.model_selection import train_test_split
from sklearn.metrics import mean_squared_error
import numpy as np

# Example data: Features of projects and their success outcomes
X = np.array([[150, 7, 6500], [190, 9, 8500], [130, 5, 4500]])
y = np.array([9, 10, 7])

# Train a regression model to forecast project success
X_train, X_test, y_train, y_test = train_test_split(X, y, test_size=0.25, random_state=2)
model = LinearRegression()
model.fit(X_train, y_train)
predictions = model.predict(X_test)
error = mean_squared_error(y_test, predictions)

print("Forecasted levels of project success:", predictions)
print("Prediction error:", error)
```

Conclusion

Encouraging continual growth and adaptation involves building an environment that prioritizes learning, innovation, and flexibility. By advocating for a culture of lifelong learning, supporting innovative risk-taking, providing necessary resources, ensuring regular feedback, and using advanced technology, individuals and organizations can effectively navigate and thrive amid ongoing changes. These strategies ensure professionals not only keep pace with developments but also actively contribute to the advancements in their fields.

Resources for Further Learning: Directing readers to additional materials and communities

In the rapidly evolving world of technology, continuous learning is pivotal for staying current with the latest trends and techniques in API development. This chapter guides readers to an array of resources that can facilitate further learning and engagement with vibrant communities. These resources include books, online courses, professional forums, and interactive platforms that cater to varying levels of expertise, from novices to seasoned developers.

Books

Books are an invaluable resource for deepening one's knowledge in a structured, comprehensive manner. Here are some essential readings that cover both foundational concepts and advanced topics in API design and development:

- **"Designing Data-Intensive Applications" by Martin Kleppmann** – This book is crucial for understanding the intricacies of building scalable, reliable systems.

- **"APIs: A Strategy Guide" by Daniel Jacobson, Greg Brail, and Dan Woods** – Offers strategic insights into creating APIs that can successfully serve your business goals.

- **"RESTful Web APIs" by Leonard Richardson, Mike Amundsen, and Sam Ruby** – Provides a deep dive into RESTful API design, offering practical advice and examples.

Online Courses

Online learning platforms offer a flexible way to learn at one's own pace, with courses ranging from beginner to advanced levels. Here are several reputable platforms offering courses relevant to API development:

- **Coursera**: Features courses like "API Design and Fundamentals of Google Cloud's Apigee API Platform" that teach API design principles and practical implementations.

- **Udemy**: Offers a variety of courses tailored to specific aspects of API development, including "REST API Design, Development & Management".

- **Pluralsight**: Known for its technology-focused courses, it provides in-depth learning paths for API development in various programming languages.

Video Tutorials and Webinars

For visual and auditory learners, video tutorials and webinars provide a dynamic way to learn. They offer the advantage of demonstrating concepts through live coding sessions or discussions. Channels and platforms to consider include:

- **YouTube**: Channels like Academind and Traversy Media regularly post tutorials and comprehensive guides on API development.

- **API Evangelist**: Hosts webinars featuring industry experts discussing strategies and best practices in API design.

Professional Forums and Community Groups

Engaging with community forums and groups can enhance learning through discussions, Q&A sessions, and networking with peers and experts. Some of the most active communities include:

- **Stack Overflow**: A vital resource for developers seeking advice or solutions to specific programming challenges.

- **GitHub**: Provides a platform to explore open-source projects and collaborate with other developers.

- **Reddit**: Subreddits like r/webdev and r/api offer platforms for discussions and sharing experiences with a community of developers.

Interactive Platforms

Interactive learning platforms allow developers to practice coding in real-time, offering immediate feedback and challenges that improve coding skills. Notable platforms include:

- **Postman**: While primarily a tool for API testing, Postman also offers learning collections that guide users through API development processes.

- **Codecademy**: Provides hands-on coding exercises specifically tailored to web development and APIs.

Conferences and Workshops

Attending industry conferences and workshops is another excellent way to stay informed about the latest trends and network with professionals. These events often feature workshops that provide hands-on experience with new tools and technologies. Notable conferences include:

- **API World**: The world's largest API conference, featuring technical talks, workshops, and sessions on building and deploying APIs.

- **APIdays**: A series of conferences held in various cities around the world, focusing on APIs and the impact they have on business and IT infrastructure.

Continuous Learning through Documentation

Lastly, never underestimate the power of reading and interacting with official documentation and API specs from reliable sources like developer portals from major tech companies (Google, Microsoft, Amazon Web Services). These are often the most up-to-date resources available for specific technologies.

Example Interaction with Official Documentation:

Navigating AWS documentation to implement an S3 bucket might involve:

```python
import boto3

# Initialize a session using your AWS SDK
session = boto3.Session(
    aws_access_key_id='YOUR_KEY',
    aws_secret_access_key='YOUR_SECRET',
    region_name='YOUR_REGION'
)

# Create an S3 service client
s3 = session.resource('s3')

# Create a new bucket
s3.create_bucket(Bucket='my-new-bucket')
```

Conclusion

The path to mastering API development is continuous and ever-evolving. The resources provided here serve as a foundation for further exploration and growth. By actively engaging with these materials and communities, developers can build a robust knowledge base that supports innovative and effective API solutions.

Introduction

Purpose of the Book: Explaining the advanced focus on architectural patterns and detailed system design

"API Design: A Pro-Level Guide to Architectural Patterns and System Design" targets seasoned software developers, architects, and systems designers who are poised to refine their proficiency in advanced API design. This book aims to expand on foundational API concepts by delving into complex architectural patterns and systems, focusing on designs that address intricate and evolving business challenges efficiently.

Purpose of the Book

The book's primary goal is to provide an advanced exploration of sophisticated architectural patterns and system design principles critical to developing state-of-the-art APIs. It is tailored to professionals who wish to transcend basic API design to embrace and implement highly scalable, flexible, and maintainable API architectures.

1. **Exploring Complex Architectural Patterns**: This book offers an in-depth look at advanced design patterns such as Microservices, Domain-Driven Design (DDD), Command Query Responsibility Segregation (CQRS), and Event Sourcing. These patterns are explored in detail to illustrate their application in

320

creating scalable and adaptable APIs that can efficiently handle changing business needs.

Example: In a chapter on CQRS, we might include a code example demonstrating the separation of read and write operations, which is crucial for enhancing performance:

```java
// Command Model - Handling the write operations
public class ProductCommandModel {
    public void handleAddProductCommand(AddProductCommand command) {
        // Logic to add product
    }
}
```

```java
// Query Model - Handling the read operations
public class ProductQueryModel {
    public ProductDTO getProductDetails(int productId) {
        // Logic to retrieve product details
    }
}
```

2. **Principles for Scalability and High Availability**: The book stresses the importance of designing APIs that are not only scalable but also highly available. It covers scaling techniques such as horizontal scaling, load balancing, and advanced caching strategies to prepare systems for increased loads while maintaining high performance.

3. **Advanced Security Practices**: Security is a paramount concern. The book thoroughly addresses implementing robust security measures including OAuth 2.0, JWT, and other security patterns to safeguard APIs against vulnerabilities.

4. **Optimization of System Performance**: It also provides insights into optimizing performance through effective data handling, caching, and asynchronous processing, with practical applications to demonstrate how these can significantly enhance performance.

5. **Real-World Case Studies**: Incorporating case studies from tech giants, the book shows how complex API designs are applied in large-scale environments, providing readers with a practical perspective on implementing advanced design principles.

6. **Preparing for Future API Trends**: The book concludes with a forward-looking perspective, discussing emerging technologies and trends such as GraphQL, serverless architectures, and AI in API development, preparing readers to adapt to future changes in the field.

Conclusion

"API Design: A Pro-Level Guide to Architectural Patterns and System Design" is crafted as an authoritative resource for professionals aiming to master advanced API design techniques. The book is designed not just to inform but also to inspire innovation by applying these sophisticated techniques in anticipation of future technological advancements. With detailed explorations, practical examples, and engaging case studies, this book equips readers to elevate their API design skills to new heights, ensuring they are well-prepared to meet and lead the next wave of API technology developments.

Expected Background: Recap of the knowledge and skills readers should have acquired from the previous books

As we embark on "API Design: A Pro-Level Guide to Architectural Patterns and System Design," it is crucial to outline the prerequisite knowledge and skills that readers should possess from the earlier books in the series. This ensures that the advanced topics covered in this volume are fully accessible and can be practically applied.

Recap of Foundational Knowledge

Readers of this series have been equipped with the essential principles of API design from the first book, "API Design: A Beginner's Guide to Understanding, Building, and Using APIs." Key learnings include:

1. **Basic API Design Principles**: Familiarity with RESTful design, including concepts of statelessness, client-server architecture, and cacheability. Proficiency in using HTTP methods (GET, POST, PUT, DELETE) correctly, and effectively employing HTTP status codes to relay various API responses and errors.

Example: Creating a RESTful API endpoint using Express.js:

```
const express = require('express');
const app = express();
app.get('/api/items', (req, res) => {
    res.send({ message: 'Items retrieved successfully'});
});
app.listen(3000, () => console.log('Server operational on port 3000'));
```

2. **Data Serialization Formats**: Understanding the use of JSON and XML for data serialization, recognizing their advantages and limitations, and selecting the appropriate format for specific scenarios.

3. **Basic Security Practices**: Knowledge of securing APIs using methods like basic authentication or API keys and the importance of HTTPS in safeguarding data transmission.

Intermediate Skills Developed

The second book, "API Design: A Middle-Level Guide to Customizing APIs for Scalability and Efficiency," introduced more sophisticated concepts geared towards optimizing and scaling APIs. Key competencies developed include:

1. **Intermediate Architectural Concepts**: Insights into session management, stateful versus stateless design, and introductory strategies for load balancing and horizontal scaling.

2. **Performance Optimization**: Understanding efficient caching, rate limiting to mitigate abuse, and basic asynchronous operations in APIs.

Example: Implementing rate limiting in Express.js:

```
const rateLimit = require('express-rate-limit');
const limiter = rateLimit({
    windowMs: 15 * 60 * 1000, // 15 minutes
    max: 100 // limit each IP to 100 requests per windowMs
});
app.use(limiter);
```

3. **Scalability Practices**: Grasping the deployment of microservices to deconstruct a monolithic API into independently scalable units.

4. **Advanced Security Enhancements**: An introduction to OAuth, understanding CORS, and implementing secure headers and tokens.

Expected Proficiency for Advanced API Design

In this third installment, readers are anticipated to have a robust understanding of both basic and intermediate concepts previously discussed. This volume seeks to expand on those by addressing complex design issues and sophisticated architectural patterns essential for crafting highly scalable, efficient, and secure APIs in expansive production environments.

We will explore:

- Detailed microservices architectures and their management.

- Complex security frameworks involving OAuth 2.0, OpenID Connect, and advanced encryption methods.

- High-level design strategies incorporating domain-driven design (DDD), command query responsibility segregation (CQRS), and event sourcing to manage intricate business operations efficiently.

Example: A snippet illustrating CQRS:

```java
// Command part
public class ProductCommand {
    void createProduct(ProductData data) {
        // Logic to create a product
    }
}

// Query part
public class ProductQuery {
    ProductData getProductById(String productId) {
        // Logic to retrieve product details
    }
}
```

Conclusion

"API Design: A Pro-Level Guide to Architectural Patterns and System Design" presupposes a solid grasp of foundational and intermediate API design principles. It is crafted to elevate these concepts further, empowering seasoned developers to solve complex problems with sophisticated solutions. This book is both a continuation and an expansion of the series, perfectly positioned to help experienced developers innovate and lead in API architecture.

Overview of Content: Brief introduction to what each chapter covers and the progression of topics

"API Design: A Pro-Level Guide to Architectural Patterns and System Design" meticulously guides seasoned developers through a series of complex and advanced topics related to API architecture. This book is structured to deepen your knowledge of sophisticated system design strategies, enhance scalability and efficiency, and refine your approach to securing APIs. Below is an overview of the content across various chapters, providing a roadmap for the progressive discussion of topics designed to elevate your expertise in API design.

Chapter 1: Advancing API Design Principles

The first chapter reintroduces essential API design concepts, preparing readers for the intricate discussions that will follow. It serves as a foundational bridge, ensuring a seamless transition into more advanced topics.

Chapter 2: Advanced Architectural Patterns

This chapter delves into complex architectures like Microservices, Serverless, and Service-Oriented Architecture (SOA). It discusses the advantages and challenges of each, providing context for their application in various scenarios.

Example:

```python
# Example of a basic microservice using Flask
from flask import Flask
app = Flask(__name__)

@app.route("/microservice")
def service():
    return "This is a basic example of a microservice."

if __name__ == "__main__":
    app.run(port=5000)
```

Chapter 3: Domain-Driven Design (DDD)

Exploring Domain-Driven Design, this chapter emphasizes aligning API architecture with business objectives, enhancing the relevance and effectiveness of your API designs.

Chapter 4: Command Query Responsibility Segregation (CQRS)

Here, CQRS is introduced as a strategy to enhance scalability and maintainability by separating read and write operations within an API. Practical examples illustrate how to apply CQRS principles effectively.

Example:

```java
// CQRS Command Model Example
public class UserCommandService {
    public void addUser(String userId, String userDetails) {
        // Logic to add a user
    }
}

// CQRS Query Model Example
public class UserQueryService {
    public String getUser(String userId) {
        // Logic to retrieve a user
        return "User details";
    }
}
```

Chapter 5: Event Sourcing

The discussion on Event Sourcing shows how APIs can be designed to record and replay events to reconstruct system states, enhancing data integrity and auditability.

Chapter 6: APIs with GraphQL

This chapter introduces GraphQL as a more flexible and efficient alternative to REST for managing data requests and explains how to set up a GraphQL server.

Chapter 7: Advanced API Security

Focusing on security, this chapter covers OAuth, OpenID Connect, and additional security frameworks essential for protecting API endpoints and sensitive data.

Chapter 8: Enhancing Scalability and Performance

Strategies for effectively scaling APIs to accommodate high traffic and data volumes are explored, including horizontal scaling, rate limiting, and the use of caching and load balancers.

Example:

```
# Nginx configuration for load balancing
upstream api_servers {
    server api1.example.com;
    server api2.example.com;
}
server {
    location / {
        proxy_pass http://api_servers;
    }
}
```

Chapter 9: Case Studies from Industry Leaders

Analyzing case studies from tech giants, this chapter provides insights into how successful companies implement complex

API designs to solve scalability, performance, and security challenges.

Chapter 10: The Future of API Design

The final chapter looks at emerging trends and technologies that are shaping the future of API development, including potential impacts from AI and machine learning innovations.

Conclusion

By detailing each chapter's focus, this overview sets the stage for a comprehensive learning experience. The book is designed to not only impart knowledge but also to equip you with practical skills and insights necessary to tackle advanced API design challenges. Upon completion, readers should be adept at implementing state-of-the-art API strategies, prepared to handle both present and future demands in the technology landscape.

Chapter One

Advanced Architectural Patterns

Overview of Modern Architectural Patterns: Microservices, serverless, event sourcing, and beyond

In today's dynamic software development landscape, embracing modern architectural patterns is essential for building efficient, scalable, and adaptable applications. Microservices, serverless computing, and event sourcing stand out as transformative strategies that align with current demands for flexibility, robustness, and quick deployment in complex distributed environments. This overview delves into these contemporary architectural paradigms, highlighting their characteristics, advantages, and ideal use cases.

Microservices Architecture

Microservices structure applications as a collection of small, autonomous services, each performing a specific function and communicating typically through HTTP APIs. This approach promotes modularity, making applications easier to understand, develop, test, and maintain.

Advantages:

- **Scalability**: Individual components can be scaled independently, allowing for more efficient resource use.

- **Development Agility**: Small, dedicated teams can manage services independently, accelerating development cycles.

- **System Resilience**: Failures in one service do not necessarily compromise the entire system, enhancing reliability.

Example Implementation in Node.js:

```
const express = require('express');
const app = express();
const PORT = process.env.PORT || 3000;
```

```
app.get('/api/product', (req, res) => {
    res.status(200).send('Product service is operational');
});

app.listen(PORT, () => console.log( Service running on port ${PORT} ));
```

This snippet represents a standalone microservice that could interact as part of a larger ecosystem, handling specific functionalities.

Serverless Architecture

Serverless computing abstracts server management from developers, focusing instead on code execution in response to events. This model is particularly effective for applications with fluctuating workloads.

Advantages:

- **Cost Efficiency**: Costs are tied directly to execution with no charges for idle capacity.

- **Auto-scaling**: Resources automatically adjust to the workload without manual intervention.

- **Enhanced Productivity**: Developers can concentrate on business logic and code, not on server configuration or maintenance.

Example Use Case: An AWS Lambda function can automatically process images uploaded to an Amazon S3 bucket, demonstrating how serverless functions trigger in response to specific events.

Event Sourcing

Event sourcing records every change to the application's state as a series of events. This method not only preserves the current state but also the complete history of state changes, facilitating precise audits and historical analysis.

Advantages:

- **Complete Audit Trails**: Every transaction or event is recorded, enabling detailed historical analysis.

- **Data Model Flexibility**: Data can be retroactively reprocessed or queried in different ways as new business requirements arise.

- **Error Recovery**: By replaying events up to the point of failure, systems can recover more gracefully.

Example Scenario: A banking application using event sourcing might log every deposit and withdrawal, allowing the system to reconstruct account states at any given time from the event log.

Exploring Advanced Architectural Concepts

Beyond the core patterns of microservices, serverless, and event sourcing, advanced concepts like **Domain-Driven Design (DDD)** and **CQRS (Command Query Responsibility Segregation)** push the envelope further. DDD focuses on aligning software designs closely with business needs, while CQRS separates the handling of command inputs from query outputs to optimize performance and scalability.

Modern architectural patterns provide the frameworks necessary for developers and organizations to construct applications that are not just performant but also strategically aligned with business objectives and capable of adapting to technological advancements. As software architecture continues to evolve, understanding and implementing these patterns will be crucial for developing sophisticated, scalable, and maintainable software solutions.

Choosing the Right Architecture: Factors affecting the decision on architectural patterns

Selecting the appropriate architecture for a software system is a pivotal decision that influences both the development process and the ultimate success of a project. System architects and developers must weigh various factors to decide on the most suitable architectural pattern for a project's specific requirements. Modern systems demand a nuanced approach where scalability, performance, maintainability, and alignment with business objectives are critically analyzed. This discussion highlights the key factors that guide the decision on architectural patterns, offering insights to facilitate informed choices that sync with project demands and strategic goals.

Business Requirements

The primary step in choosing the right architecture is to thoroughly understand the business requirements. The architecture should efficiently support the business's operational demands, strategic directions, and growth projections, avoiding unnecessary complexity or costs.

- **Scalability**: Projects expecting fluctuating or growing user bases and data loads require architectures that scale effortlessly. Microservices are particularly beneficial here due to their capacity for independent service scaling.

- **Performance Requirements**: For applications that need high-performance levels, such as real-time data processing or high-frequency trading platforms, architectures like event-driven or CQRS can offer efficient and rapid data handling capabilities.

Technical Constraints

The choice of architecture is often influenced by existing infrastructure, the technological proficiency of the development team, and preferred technologies, which can limit architectural options.

- **Legacy System Integration**: The necessity to integrate with existing legacy systems can determine the architectural choice. Microservices, for example, can facilitate such integration with their distinct, service-focused APIs.

- **Development Team Expertise**: The development team's familiarity with specific architectures or technologies can impact the selection process. New architectures might involve a learning curve that could extend development timelines and introduce risks.

Cost Considerations

Evaluating the cost implications, both immediate and long-term, is crucial when selecting an architecture. Different architectures can vary significantly in both initial deployment and ongoing operational costs.

- **Infrastructure Costs**: Serverless architectures, which only charge for the actual compute time used, can be cost-effective for applications with variable demand.

- **Development and Maintenance Costs**: Although architectures like microservices might incur higher initial setup costs due to their complexity, they could potentially reduce long-term maintenance costs due to their modular nature.

Flexibility and Maintainability

An ideal architecture should accommodate future changes and technology advancements with minimal reconfiguration.

- **Adaptability**: Flexible architectures that allow easy modifications and updates are preferred, especially in fast-evolving market sectors.

- **Decomposability**: Systems designed with loosely coupled components, such as in a microservices setup, tend to be easier to maintain and update than those with a monolithic structure.

Security Considerations

Security is a decisive factor, particularly for applications managing sensitive information or under regulatory scrutiny.

- **Data Security**: Architectures must support stringent data security measures, like end-to-end encryption and secure data exchanges typically facilitated through API gateways in microservices setups.

- **Compliance**: Certain architectures may better support compliance with regulatory standards such as GDPR or HIPAA, which can mandate specific security controls and data handling procedures.

Example Scenario: Opting for Microservices

Consider a company developing a scalable e-commerce platform needing robust integration capabilities with external systems like payment processors and inventory management tools.

Requirements:

- Ability to scale dynamically during high-traffic events.

- Flexibility to integrate seamlessly with various external services.

- Frequent, non-disruptive updates.

Decision:

- Microservices architecture is chosen for its ability to scale services on a per-demand basis, support agile deployment methodologies, and offer robust integration capabilities through defined APIs.

Conclusion

The decision to adopt a particular architectural pattern is multi-dimensional, affecting technical performance and the strategic viability of a project. By thoroughly assessing business needs, technical limitations, cost factors, flexibility, maintainability, and security needs, organizations can select an architecture that not only fits their current project criteria but also supports future growth and adjustments. Strategic architectural planning is essential to ensure effective and efficient project outcomes over its lifecycle.

Chapter Two

Domain-Driven Design (DDD) in APIs

Principles of DDD: Key concepts and strategies

Domain-Driven Design (DDD) is a sophisticated framework that guides the design and development of software to closely align with an organization's core business operations. Originally conceptualized by Eric Evans in "Domain-Driven Design: Tackling Complexity in the Heart of Software," DDD promotes a collaborative approach between software developers and domain experts to ensure the software reflects the intricate realities of the business environment. The goal of DDD is to simplify the development of complex systems by crafting a model that evolves with the business's core concepts.

Core Principles of DDD

Ubiquitous Language: This principle emphasizes the use of a common vocabulary shared between developers and domain experts throughout the project. This language should pervade all aspects of the project, from verbal discussions to written code and documentation, ensuring consistency and clarity across all forms of communication.

Example: In a library management system, terms such as "Book," "Patron," "Loan," and "Reservation" would be uniformly used across all communications and code.

```
public class Book {
    private String title;
    private String author;
    private String ISBN;
    // Methods for book management
}

public class Patron {
    private String patronId;
    private String name;
    // Methods for patron management
}
```

Strategic Design: This involves mapping out the large-scale structure of the system, defining boundaries, and detailing the relationships between different domains. It includes delineating bounded contexts, creating context maps, and organizing the overarching architecture.

- **Bounded Contexts**: These are crucial for managing complexity by defining clear delineations where specific models apply. Each bounded context handles a distinct segment of the domain, promoting modularity and decoupling systems.

Example: An e-commerce platform may include separate bounded contexts for handling Orders, Inventory, and Customer Profiles.

```
// Context for User Management
public class User {
    private String userId;
    private String email;
    // Methods for user interactions
}

// Context for Order Management
public class Order {
    private String orderId;
    private Date orderDate;
    // Methods for order processing
}
```

Tactical Design: Whereas strategic design addresses the macro-level structure, tactical design focuses on the modeling of entities within these contexts, specifying their behavior and lifecycle. Key elements include entities, value objects, aggregates, repositories, and domain events.

- **Entities** are defined by their continuous identity over time.

- **Value Objects** are immutable and described only by their properties.

- **Aggregates** act as a cluster of related objects that are treated as a unit.

- **Repositories** facilitate the storage and retrieval of aggregates.

- **Domain Events** capture significant occurrences within the domain.

Example:

```java
public class Order {
    private String orderId;
    private List<Item> items;
    private Date orderDate;

    public void addItem(Item item) {
        items.add(item);
    }
}

public class Item {
    private String productId;
    private int quantity;

    // Items are treated as part of the Order aggregate, without needing their own identity
}
```

Context Mapping

Understanding the interactions and boundaries between bounded contexts is essential for the integration of different parts of the system, helping to clarify how disparate models interact and connect.

Example: Mapping how the User Profile context communicates with the Order Processing context, detailing the flow of information and specifying the integration mechanisms used, such as REST APIs or event-driven messaging.

Implementing DDD

Adopting DDD is not merely a technical challenge but a shift in organizational culture, necessitating ongoing collaboration between domain experts and software teams. It involves regular iterative cycles to refine the domain model, ensuring it remains reflective of the business as it grows and evolves.

Example: Conducting frequent interactive workshops like Event Storming can help continuously refine the ubiquitous language and enhance the domain model by involving both domain experts and developers.

Conclusion

Domain-Driven Design offers a robust methodology for developing complex software systems that are deeply integrated with business strategies. By focusing on foundational concepts such as ubiquitous language, bounded contexts, and a strategic approach to design, DDD equips organizations to manage the complexities of their domains effectively, leading to software that is both functionally rich and highly adaptable to business needs.

Integrating DDD with Microservices: Practical implementations and case studies

Integrating Domain-Driven Design (DDD) with a microservices architecture is a strategic methodology that can profoundly benefit the development and management of complex software systems. This approach combines DDD's comprehensive domain modeling with the agility and scalability of microservices, presenting a structured yet flexible framework for building enterprise-level applications. This detailed discussion provides insights into practical implementations and explores real-world case studies to illustrate the effective synergy between DDD and microservices.

The Convergence of DDD and Microservices

DDD centers on crafting software models that reflect complex real-world scenarios, facilitating effective communication between domain experts and software developers. Microservices break down a system into small, autonomous services that manage specific functions and communicate through defined APIs. When DDD principles guide the creation of microservices, each service aligns with a distinct bounded context from the domain model, enhancing both clarity and functionality.

Benefits of This Integration:

- **Enhanced Modularity**: Services are designed around distinct domain models, minimizing dependencies and facilitating easier updates.

343

- **Scalability**: Services can scale independently according to the demands of their specific domain contexts, improving resource allocation.

- **Dedicated Expertise**: Teams can specialize in particular domains, optimizing development efficiency and deepening domain expertise.

Implementing the Strategy

The implementation of DDD in a microservices framework starts by identifying and defining bounded contexts. Each bounded context is a separate segment of the domain with its own model and language, which translates into individual microservices in the architecture.

Example: Consider a logistics system where different aspects such as shipment tracking, warehouse management, and customer relations are distinct bounded contexts.

```java
// Shipment Tracking Microservice
public class ShipmentService {
    public void trackShipment(String trackingNumber) {
        // Logic to track shipment
    }
    // Other domain-specific methods
}

// Warehouse Management Microservice
public class WarehouseService {
    public void updateInventory(String productCode, int quantity) {
        // Logic to update the warehouse inventory
    }
    // Other domain-specific methods
}
```

This code illustrates how each microservice handles domain-specific operations, maintaining clear boundaries and responsibilities.

Real-World Case Studies

Case Study 1: Banking Application A financial institution adopted DDD within their microservices setup to manage distinct banking functions such as account management, loan processing, and customer feedback. Each microservice was crafted around a bounded context, which simplified updates, scaling, and maintenance, leading to a more robust banking platform.

Case Study 2: E-commerce Platform An e-commerce giant redesigned their system with DDD-driven microservices, categorizing the system into product management, order fulfillment, and customer engagement. This modularity allowed them to manage heavy user traffic efficiently during peak sales periods and improved their ability to introduce new features rapidly.

Best Practices for Integration

- **Establish Clear Bounded Contexts**: Ensure that each microservice is strictly aligned with a bounded context to prevent service overlap and bloated implementations.

- **Consistent Ubiquitous Language**: Maintain a ubiquitous language within each bounded context to ensure consistency and clarity across the development team and domain experts.

345

- **Adopt Suitable Integration Techniques**: Employ effective integration techniques such as event-driven communication or API gateways to ensure microservices interact seamlessly while maintaining loose coupling.

Conclusion

The fusion of DDD with microservices provides a powerful approach to managing and developing complex software systems. This methodology not only ensures scalability and flexibility but also aligns software development closely with strategic business objectives. As demonstrated through practical examples and case studies, careful planning and execution of this integration yield a robust, capable system that supports both current functionalities and future growth.

Chapter Three

System Modularity and Decomposition

Breaking Down Complex Systems: Techniques for modularity

In today's software development landscape, managing complexity effectively is paramount. Achieving modularity, the practice of breaking down complex systems into smaller, manageable parts, is critical for ensuring systems are scalable, flexible, and maintainable. This discourse delves into several established techniques for fostering modularity in complex systems, including the adoption of microservices, component-based architecture, and domain-driven design.

Microservices Architecture

Microservices architecture structures applications as a collection of small, autonomous services. Each service operates independently, focusing on a single business function and communicates using lightweight mechanisms, typically through HTTP APIs. This architectural style is particularly suited for systems requiring high scalability and resilience.

Advantages:

- **Scalability**: Microservices allow parts of the application to scale independently, making it easier to manage resource allocation and system performance.

- **Flexibility**: This architecture supports the use of diverse technologies across different services, facilitating technological adaptability and updates.

- **Resilience**: Isolation of services means the failure of one does not affect the entire system, enhancing reliability.

Example:

```python
from flask import Flask, jsonify
app = Flask(__name__)

@app.route('/api/orders')
def get_orders():
    # Placeholder for fetching orders
    return jsonify({"orders": []})
```

This Python Flask application demonstrates a microservice responsible for handling orders, showcasing how such a service might function within a broader system.

Component-Based Architecture

Component-based architecture builds systems by integrating independent, well-defined components. Each component encloses a segment of functionality and exposes interfaces that other components can interact with. This setup promotes reusability and replaceability, reducing overall system complexity.

Advantages:

- **Reusability**: Components can be reused in various parts of an application or across different projects, reducing duplication and development efforts.

348

- **Maintainability**: Since components are isolated, updates or fixes can be done with minimal impact on other parts of the system.

- **Simplicity**: Decomposing functionality into separate components simplifies development and enhances system comprehension.

Example:

```
public interface AccountService {
    Account getAccount(String accountId);
}

public class AccountServiceImpl implements AccountService {
    public Account getAccount(String accountId) {
        // Implementation to retrieve an account
    }
}
```

Here, **AccountService** represents a component in a system designed to manage financial accounts, illustrating how components are defined and utilized.

Domain-Driven Design (DDD)

Domain-driven design (DDD) offers a methodology centered around aligning software design with business domain complexities. It emphasizes creating a model that reflects the domain intricacies, ensuring the software is directly tied to business requirements.

Advantages:

- **Integrated Design**: Fosters a unified understanding of the domain across all team members, leading to better-aligned software solutions.

349

- **Complexity Management**: Helps tackle intricate business logic and rules through a well-structured domain model.

- **Adaptability**: As business needs change, the domain model can evolve, facilitating easier updates and expansions.

Example:

```
public class Inventory {
    public void UpdateStock(Item item, int quantity) {
        // Code to update the inventory with the new quantity
    }
}
```

In this example, the **Inventory** class acts as part of a domain model managing inventory-related functionalities, encapsulating related actions.

Conclusion

Embracing modularity is essential for effectively managing the complexities of modern software systems. By implementing strategies such as microservices, component-based architectures, and domain-driven design, development teams can create more manageable, robust, and adaptable software. These approaches not only streamline development processes but also prepare systems to better adapt to ongoing technological advancements, ensuring long-term sustainability and effectiveness.

Benefits of a Modular Architecture: Maintenance, scalability, and flexibility

In the field of software development, adopting a modular architecture is becoming increasingly common, driven by its significant advantages in maintenance, scalability, and flexibility. This approach involves segmenting a software system into discrete modules that operate independently but are integrated to function cohesively. This segmentation simplifies management, facilitates updates, and enhances the system's adaptability, making it crucial for modern projects that demand high agility and robust functionality.

Advantages of Modular Architecture

1. Streamlined Maintenance

One of the standout benefits of modular architecture is the streamlined approach to maintenance it enables. By isolating specific functionalities into separate modules, developers can address updates or bugs in one module without impacting the integrity of others. This localization minimizes downtime and reduces the likelihood of bugs spreading across the system, thus boosting the system's stability and reliability.

Example: In a modular web application, distinct components like user authentication, payment processing, and order management might be handled by separate modules. An upgrade required on the payment module can be executed independently of the others, which lessens disruptions and mitigates risk.

```
// Modular example for payment processing in a Node.js application
const express = require('express');
const paymentRouter = express.Router();

paymentRouter.post('/process-payment', (req, res) => {
    // Code to handle payment processing
    res.send('Payment has been processed.');
});

module.exports = paymentRouter;
```

This snippet demonstrates how a payment processing module in an Express.js application can be individually maintained and updated, illustrating the modular approach.

2. Enhanced Scalability

Modular architecture facilitates scalability by enabling specific modules to be scaled according to their unique demands without affecting the entire system. This selective scaling is particularly advantageous in cloud environments where resources are allocated dynamically.

Example: In microservices architecture, which is inherently modular, different services such as user interaction and backend processing can scale independently based on usage patterns and load demands.

```
// Microservice example for handling user interactions
@Service
public class UserInteractionService {
    public ResponseEntity<String> handleInteraction(UserInteraction interaction) {
        // Code to process user interaction
        return ResponseEntity.ok("Interaction handled successfully.");
    }
}
```

Here, the **UserInteractionService** can be independently scaled to manage peak loads, showcasing how modularity supports effective resource management.

3. Greater Flexibility

Adopting a modular architecture provides flexibility in terms of technology stack and design choices within individual modules. Each module can use the technology that best fits its functional needs, allowing for easier updates and faster adoption of new technologies.

Example: A complex application may use different database technologies—SQL for transactional operations and NoSQL for handling large volumes of unstructured data, each within its respective module.

```python
# NoSQL database module example for handling large datasets
from pymongo import MongoClient

class BigDataHandler:
    def __init__(self):
        self.client = MongoClient('mongodb://localhost:27017/')
        self.db = self.client.big_data

    def storeData(self, data):
        self.db.data_collection.insert_one(data)
```

This Python class demonstrates a module designed for handling big data with MongoDB, illustrating the flexibility to implement specific technologies tailored to module needs.

Conclusion

The modular architecture approach provides substantial benefits, making it a preferred strategy in software development. By enabling independent development, testing, and scaling of different system components, modularity not only simplifies system management but also aligns software development more closely with dynamic business needs and technological advancements. This approach ensures that systems are both powerful in capability and adaptable to the fast-paced evolution of technology landscapes.

Chapter Four

Optimizing Data Architecture for APIs

Data Modeling Techniques: Advanced concepts in data organization for APIs

In the domain of API development, advanced data modeling techniques are indispensable for structuring and managing data efficiently. These techniques ensure that APIs are robust, scalable, and performant, catering optimally to specific data handling requirements. This exposition details several crucial advanced data modeling concepts that are essential for API developers, encompassing normalization, denormalization, data partitioning, and the adoption of NoSQL data models.

Normalization

Normalization is a methodical approach to reduce redundancy and enhance data integrity in databases by segregating data into various tables and establishing relationships through foreign keys. This approach is crucial for maintaining data accuracy and minimizing redundant storage, thereby streamlining database maintenance.

Example:

```sql
CREATE TABLE Users (
    UserID int NOT NULL,
    UserName varchar(255) NOT NULL,
    UserEmail varchar(255),
    PRIMARY KEY (UserID)
);

CREATE TABLE Orders (
    OrderID int NOT NULL,
    OrderDate date NOT NULL,
    UserID int,
    PRIMARY KEY (OrderID),
    FOREIGN KEY (UserID) REFERENCES Users(UserID)
);
```

In this SQL setup, the **Users** and **Orders** tables are normalized to avoid data duplication, where **Orders** references **Users**, ensuring that user information is stored once and efficiently referenced.

Denormalization

Denormalization involves integrating redundant data into a database system to enhance read performance, which is especially useful in read-heavy application scenarios. While it increases data duplication, it simplifies query operations by reducing the need for joins and potentially enhances performance.

Example:

```
CREATE TABLE Orders (
    OrderID int NOT NULL,
    OrderDate date NOT NULL,
    UserID int,
    UserName varchar(255),
    UserEmail varchar(255),
    PRIMARY KEY (OrderID)
);
```

This denormalized table structure includes user information directly within the **Orders** table, enabling quicker data retrieval at the cost of increased storage and potential upkeep due to redundant data.

Data Partitioning

Data partitioning splits a database into smaller segments, improving manageability and access speed. Horizontal partitioning divides data into rows across several databases or tables, whereas vertical partitioning separates data by columns.

Example:

```python
# Example of implementing horizontal partitioning in an API
def get_user_orders(user_id):
    partition_key = user_id % 4  # Assuming 4 partitions
    query = f"SELECT * FROM Orders_Partition_{partition_key} WHERE UserID = {user_id}"
    results = execute_query(query)
    return results
```

This Python example illustrates horizontal partitioning, where user orders are distributed across different tables, enhancing query performance by isolating data into manageable chunks.

NoSQL Data Models

NoSQL databases offer versatile data models suitable for handling structured, semi-structured, and unstructured data. These databases excel in scenarios requiring rapid access to vast amounts of data, where relational databases may falter.

Example:

```json
{
    "UserID": "1",
    "UserName": "JohnDoe",
    "Orders": [
        {"OrderID": "501", "OrderDate": "2021-09-15"},
        {"OrderID": "502", "OrderDate": "2021-09-16"}
    ]
}
```

This JSON document demonstrates how a document-based NoSQL database model can efficiently store and retrieve user and order data in a single document, eliminating the need for complex relational joins.

Conclusion

Advanced data modeling techniques like normalization, denormalization, data partitioning, and the utilization of NoSQL databases are critical for constructing efficient and scalable APIs. Selecting appropriate data modeling strategies based on the specific needs of the API and the characteristics of the data ensures enhanced API performance, scalability, and manageability. These methods provide developers with refined control over data structure and management, equipping APIs to efficiently handle diverse and dynamic data requirements.

Implementing Data Layers: Best practices in building scalable data back-ends

Developing a scalable data layer is fundamental for ensuring that back-end systems are robust and capable of handling increased loads efficiently. A strategically designed data layer facilitates optimal data storage and retrieval processes, which are essential for supporting system scalability. This article outlines the best practices for constructing scalable data back-ends, focusing on layer abstraction, appropriate database selection, data partitioning, and caching strategies.

Layer Abstraction

Abstraction within data layers means separating the data access mechanics from the business logic. This isolation allows for modifications in the database without affecting other parts of the application. This is often implemented through data access objects (DAOs) or repositories that centralize data interaction logic.

Example:

```java
public interface OrderRepository {
    Order findOrderById(String orderId);
    void save(Order order);
}

public class OrderRepositoryImpl implements OrderRepository {
    private DataSource dataSource;

    public OrderRepositoryImpl(DataSource dataSource) {
        this.dataSource = dataSource;
    }

    @Override
    public Order findOrderById(String orderId) {
        // Implementation to retrieve an order from the database
    }
```

```
@Override
public void save(Order order) {
    // Implementation to save an order to the database
}
}
```

This Java example shows how an **OrderRepository** abstracts the data access for orders, ensuring that the application's business logic remains decoupled from data management details.

Database Selection

Choosing the right database technology is crucial for building a scalable data layer. The choice should consider the application's specific needs, such as transaction complexity, data model, and the expected read/write loads. Relational databases like MySQL are suited for transaction-heavy applications, whereas NoSQL databases like MongoDB cater to applications with high write loads or those requiring flexible schema.

Example:

```python
# Utilizing MongoDB for flexible data storage
from pymongo import MongoClient

class CustomerRepository:
    def __init__(self):
        self.client = MongoClient('mongodb://localhost:27017/')
        self.db = self.client['customer_db']

    def find_by_id(self, customerId):
        return self.db.customers.find_one({"_id": customerId})

    def save(self, customer):
        self.db.customers.insert_one(customer)
```

This Python code utilizes MongoDB, demonstrating its use in handling dynamic, semi-structured data within a customer management system, taking advantage of its schema-less design.

Data Partitioning

Data partitioning involves dividing a database into distinct segments, which can be managed more efficiently. Horizontal partitioning (or sharding) distributes data across multiple databases based on a specific key, whereas vertical partitioning splits the data by its features, typically improving access speeds for particular queries.

Example:

```sql
-- SQL example demonstrating horizontal partitioning
CREATE TABLE customer_data_part1 (
    customer_id INT PRIMARY KEY,
    customer_name VARCHAR(255),
    CHECK (customer_id < 10000)
);
CREATE TABLE customer_data_part2 (
    customer_id INT PRIMARY KEY,
    customer_name VARCHAR(255),
    CHECK (customer_id >= 10000)
);
```

This SQL configuration shows horizontal partitioning where customer data is segmented into different tables based on customer ID, facilitating efficient data management and retrieval.

Caching

Caching is a strategy employed to reduce database load and enhance response times by storing copies of frequently accessed data in a rapidly accessible location. This can be implemented at various levels, from application-level caching using tools like Redis to database caching or even client-side caching for web applications.

Example:

```java
// Implementing caching using Redis in Java
import redis.clients.jedis.Jedis;

public class CacheManager {
    private Jedis jedis = new Jedis("localhost");

    public String getCachedOrder(String orderId) {
        return jedis.get("order:" + orderId);
    }

    public void cacheOrder(String orderId, String orderData) {
        jedis.set("order:" + orderId, orderData, "NX", "EX", 3600); // Cache with
            1-hour expiry
    }
}
```

In this example, Redis is used to cache order data, reducing the frequency and need for database queries by keeping temporary, quickly retrievable copies of data in memory.

Conclusion

Establishing a scalable data back-end is essential for modern applications, requiring a well-thought-out approach to data layer architecture, database technology selection, data partitioning, and caching. By adhering to these best practices, developers can ensure their back-end systems are not only efficient but also scalable and prepared to handle increased operational demands effectively. These strategies are foundational to developing advanced data management systems that support complex and growing applications.

Chapter Five

Advanced Security Practices

Enhanced Security Protocols: Deep dive into OAuth, OpenID Connect, and other security frameworks

In the current digital landscape, employing sophisticated security protocols such as OAuth, OpenID Connect, and other security frameworks is critical for protecting web applications and APIs. These protocols are designed to secure access and ensure user authentication across various digital platforms efficiently. This article examines these protocols, detailing their functionality, use cases, and guidelines for integrating them effectively to bolster security.

OAuth 2.0

OAuth 2.0 is a prominent authorization framework that enables third-party applications to obtain limited access to a user's data without exposing their credentials. It's particularly useful in applications that require secure interactions between different services.

Core Concepts:

- **Resource Owner**: The user who owns the data.

- **Client**: The application seeking access to the user's data.

- **Resource Server**: The server that stores the user's data.

- **Authorization Server**: The server that authenticates the resource owner and issues access tokens to the client.

Process Overview:

1. The client requests authorization from the user.

2. Once authorized, the client receives an authorization code.

3. The client exchanges this code for an access token at the authorization server.

4. The access token enables the client to request data from the resource server.

```python
import requests

def acquire_access_token(client_id, secret, code, redirect_uri):
    url = 'https://auth-server.com/token'
    payload = {
        'grant_type': 'authorization_code',
        'client_id': client_id,
        'client_secret': secret,
        'code': code,
        'redirect_uri': redirect_uri
    }
    token_response = requests.post(url, data=payload)
    return token_response.json().get('access_token')
```

This Python example showcases obtaining an access token by exchanging an authorization code, a critical operation in OAuth 2.0.

OpenID Connect

OpenID Connect extends OAuth 2.0 by introducing an authentication layer, allowing clients to verify the identity of users and access their profile information. It is widely used for single sign-on (SSO) functionalities across various services.

Essential Elements:

- **ID Token**: A token that contains the user's identity details.

- **UserInfo Endpoint**: A resource that returns claims about the user.

Implementation Flow:

1. The user authenticates with the OpenID provider.

2. The provider sends back an ID token and an access token.

3. The client uses the ID token to authenticate the user and establish a session.

```python
import jwt

def verify_user_identity(id_token, secret):
    return jwt.decode(id_token, secret, algorithms=['HS256'])
```

This function demonstrates how to verify a user's identity by decoding an ID token, critical for ensuring user authenticity in applications.

Other Security Protocols

Protocols like SAML and Kerberos are also vital in enhancing digital security, particularly within larger organizations.

SAML: Supports secure data exchange for authentication and authorization, often used for enabling SSO.

Kerberos: Utilizes strong cryptography to safely authenticate service requests between trusted hosts on unsecured networks.

Implementation Best Practices

- **Secure Token Handling**: Protect tokens to prevent unauthorized use and potential data breaches.

- **Routine Updates**: Keep all software components updated to safeguard against vulnerabilities.

- **Scoped Permissions**: Implement restrictive scopes and claims to limit access, reducing the impact of potential token compromises.

Conclusion

Utilizing advanced security protocols such as OAuth, OpenID Connect, SAML, and Kerberos is indispensable for securing digital interactions and protecting sensitive user information. By comprehending and deploying these protocols effectively, organizations can enhance their defense mechanisms against cyber threats. As digital security threats continue to evolve, the adoption of robust security measures and continuous improvement of security practices are essential for maintaining the integrity and trustworthiness of digital platforms.

Securing Service-to-Service Communications: Ensuring data integrity and confidentiality across services

In today's networked environments, safeguarding service-to-service communications is paramount to maintaining data integrity and confidentiality. Effective security protocols prevent unauthorized data access and ensure that information remains secure as it is transmitted across services. This discussion highlights key strategies and technologies essential for securing communications between services, focusing on mutual authentication, Transport Layer Security (TLS), message-level encryption, and the strategic implementation of API gateways.

Mutual Authentication

Mutual authentication is critical for ensuring that both parties in a communication verify each other's identities before any data is exchanged. This approach is vital to prevent identity spoofing and ensure that interactions are conducted only between verified parties.

TLS Mutual Authentication: Mutual TLS (mTLS) secures communications by requiring both the client and the server to present and validate digital certificates before establishing a trusted connection. This method is particularly effective over public or potentially insecure networks.

Example Configuration:

```java
import javax.net.ssl.SSLContext;
import javax.net.ssl.KeyManagerFactory;
import javax.net.ssl.TrustManagerFactory;
import java.security.KeyStore;
import java.io.FileInputStream;
import java.security.SecureRandom;
```

```java
public SSLContext initializeSSLContext(String keyStorePath, String
    keyStorePassword, String trustStorePath, String trustStorePassword) throws
    Exception {
    KeyStore keyStore = KeyStore.getInstance("JKS");
    keyStore.load(new FileInputStream(keyStorePath), keyStorePassword.toCharArray
        ());

    KeyStore trustStore = KeyStore.getInstance("JKS");
    trustStore.load(new FileInputStream(trustStorePath), trustStorePassword
        .toCharArray());

    KeyManagerFactory keyManagerFactory = KeyManagerFactory.getInstance
        (KeyManagerFactory.getDefaultAlgorithm());
    keyManagerFactory.init(keyStore, keyStorePassword.toCharArray());
```

```java
    TrustManagerFactory trustManagerFactory = TrustManagerFactory.getInstance
        (TrustManagerFactory.getDefaultAlgorithm());
    trustManagerFactory.init(trustStore);

    SSLContext sslContext = SSLContext.getInstance("TLS");
    sslContext.init(keyManagerFactory.getKeyManagers(), trustManagerFactory
        .getTrustManagers(), new SecureRandom());
    return sslContext;
}
```

This Java example sets up an SSLContext for mutual TLS, using certificates from key stores to ensure secure mutual authentication.

Transport Layer Security (TLS)

TLS plays a critical role in securing data transmissions, encrypting data to ensure privacy and protect it from tampering and eavesdropping.

TLS Implementation Tips:

- Utilize only strong, secure cipher suites.

- Enable perfect forward secrecy to safeguard encrypted data, even if encryption keys are later compromised.

- Regularly update your TLS protocols to combat emerging security vulnerabilities.

Message-Level Encryption

To further enhance security, encrypting messages themselves ensures that data remains protected, even after reaching its destination. This is especially relevant when data must be stored securely or processed further.

Example with JSON Web Encryption (JWE):

```
import org.jose4j.jwe.JsonWebEncryption;
import org.jose4j.keys.AesKey;
import java.security.Key;
```

```
public String encryptData(String plaintext, Key key) throws Exception {
    JsonWebEncryption jwe = new JsonWebEncryption();
    jwe.setPayload(plaintext);
    jwe.setAlgorithmHeaderValue("A256KW");
    jwe.setEncryptionMethodHeaderParameter("A256GCM");
    jwe.setKey(key);
    return jwe.getCompactSerialization();
}

public String decryptData(String ciphertext, Key key) throws Exception {
    JsonWebEncryption jwe = new JsonWebEncryption();
    jwe.setKey(key);
    jwe.setCompactSerialization(ciphertext);
    return jwe.getPayload();
}
```

This implementation demonstrates how to encrypt and decrypt messages using JSON Web Encryption, providing robust security for the contents of the messages.

API Gateways

API gateways are essential in managing and securing service-to-service communications. They enforce security policies, manage traffic flow, and monitor interactions, ensuring that communications are both secure and efficient.

Security Features of API Gateways:

- Authenticate and authorize service requests.

- Enforce rate limits and monitor service usage to prevent abuse.

- Detailed logging of all transactions for auditing and compliance.

Conclusion

Securing service-to-service communications in distributed environments involves employing a comprehensive set of security measures including mutual authentication, the strategic use of TLS, message-level encryption, and API gateways. These practices ensure that sensitive data is protected from unauthorized access and cyber threats, supporting secure and reliable interactions between services. Adopting these strategies is fundamental for organizations looking to maintain data security and operational integrity in modern digital landscapes.

Chapter Six

Fault Tolerance and Resilience

Building Resilient Systems: Patterns like Circuit Breaker, Bulkhead, and Retry

In modern software development, ensuring systems are robust and can gracefully handle and recover from failures is paramount. This resilience is critical for maintaining system availability and reliability in the face of unexpected disruptions. Design patterns such as Circuit Breaker, Bulkhead, and Retry are essential in crafting such resilient systems. These patterns provide mechanisms for systems to cope with failures, enhancing their stability and ensuring they continue to deliver optimal user experiences even under adverse conditions.

Circuit Breaker Pattern

The Circuit Breaker pattern prevents a system from carrying out an operation that's likely to fail, similar to how an electrical circuit breaker prevents overloads by stopping the flow of electricity. It helps to manage failures that might not be quickly resolved, avoiding resource wastage.

Operation Modes:

1. **Closed**: Normal operations continue, but failures are counted.

2. **Open**: Operations are halted for a designated timeout period, after which the circuit tries to reset.

3. **Half-Open**: Limited operations are allowed to test if the underlying issue has been resolved. Success resets the circuit; failure reopens it.

Example Usage:

```python
from circuitbreaker import circuit

@circuit(failure_threshold=5, recovery_timeout=20)
def unstable_operation():
    # Potentially failing operation
    pass
```

```python
try:
    unstable_operation()
except Exception as e:
    print(f"Operation blocked: {str(e)}")
```

In this Python example, the **unstable_operation** function is wrapped with a circuit breaker that triggers if five consecutive failures occur, blocking further attempts for 20 seconds.

Bulkhead Pattern

Inspired by the watertight compartments of ships, the Bulkhead pattern limits failures to specific areas of an application, preventing a failure in one area from cascading to others. This isolation improves fault tolerance within the system.

373

Implementations:

- **Separate Pools**: Assigning distinct pools of resources (threads, connections) to different areas of the application.

- **Service Isolation**: Isolating services so that the failure of one does not affect the others.

Example Configuration:

```java
ExecutorService serviceOne = Executors.newFixedThreadPool(10);
ExecutorService serviceTwo = Executors.newFixedThreadPool(10);

public void processServiceOne(Runnable task) {
    serviceOne.execute(task);
}

public void processServiceTwo(Runnable task) {
    serviceTwo.execute(task);
}
```

This Java snippet illustrates how different services can operate independently using separate thread pools, minimizing the risk of a slowdown in one service impacting another.

Retry Pattern

The Retry pattern is used when dealing with potentially transient failures, such as temporary network glitches. It involves attempting a failed operation multiple times before finally declaring it a failure, potentially overcoming temporary issues through repeated attempts.

Retry Logic:

- **Immediate Retry**: Re-attempt the failed operation immediately.

- **Exponential Backoff**: Introduce delays between retries that increase exponentially to reduce the load and likelihood of repeated failures.

Example Implementation:

```python
import time
import random

def attempt_operation(max_attempts, backoff):
    for i in range(max_attempts):
        try:
            # Flaky operation simulation
            print("Trying operation")
            if random.choice([True, False]):
                raise Exception("Operation failure")
            return "Operation successful"
        except Exception as e:
            print(f"Retry {i+1}: {str(e)}")
            time.sleep(backoff**i)  # exponential backoff
    return "Final failure after retries"

result = attempt_operation(3, 2)
print(result)
```

In this Python code, an operation is attempted up to three times with an exponential backoff starting at two seconds, accommodating for the possibility of resolving transient issues with time.

Conclusion

Incorporating resilience design patterns like Circuit Breaker, Bulkhead, and Retry into the architecture of systems significantly enhances their robustness. These patterns equip systems to effectively manage and mitigate failures, maintaining high availability and a seamless user experience despite potential disruptions. By implementing these strategies, developers can create software that not only survives but thrives under operational stress.

Disaster Recovery Planning: Ensuring continuous operation and data integrity

Disaster recovery planning is critical for businesses aiming to ensure uninterrupted operations and protect data integrity during unexpected disruptions. Effective disaster recovery strategies enable organizations to recover swiftly from scenarios like natural disasters, technological malfunctions, or operational mistakes, which might otherwise severely impact business continuity.

Fundamentals of Disaster Recovery

Disaster recovery involves structured protocols and strategies that equip organizations to restore essential functions promptly after disruptions. The chief objectives are minimizing operational downtime and reducing data loss to keep business processes running smoothly during crises.

Key Elements of Disaster Recovery Planning

1. **Risk Assessment and Business Impact Analysis (BIA):**

   o **Risk Assessment**: Identifies potential threats to IT systems and evaluates vulnerabilities that could impact operations.

   o **Business Impact Analysis**: Assesses the potential consequences of disruptions, identifies key systems and processes, and prioritizes their recovery based on the business's operational needs.

2. **Recovery Point Objective (RPO) and Recovery Time Objective (RTO):**

   o **RPO:** Indicates the maximum tolerable age of data that the business can recover from backups without substantial losses.

   o **RTO:** Defines the maximum allowable downtime after a disaster that the business processes can tolerate before the situation becomes critical.

3. **Data Backup Strategies:**

   o **Data Replication:** Maintains real-time duplication of data to a secondary location to ensure its availability.

   o **Backup Frequency:** Determines how often backups occur—daily, weekly, or continuously, based on the data's importance and the RPO.

4. **Disaster Recovery Sites:**

   o **Hot Site:** An operational facility equipped and ready to take over business operations instantly.

   o **Cold Site:** A location equipped with the necessary infrastructure but requires configuration and provisioning post-disaster.

- **Warm Site**: Offers a middle ground with some pre-installed systems and services, ready for quick activation.

5. **Disaster Recovery Plan Testing**:

   - Implements regular testing of the disaster recovery plan to ensure its effectiveness and the team's readiness to execute it.

6. **Plan Maintenance**:

   - Continually updates the disaster recovery plan to align with evolving business processes and technological developments, ensuring its ongoing relevance and effectiveness.

Example: Cloud-Based Disaster Recovery Implementation

Cloud-based platforms like AWS or Azure offer scalable, flexible, and cost-effective disaster recovery solutions. These platforms typically include capabilities for automated data replication and rapid failover to minimize downtime.

```
# AWS CLI commands for disaster recovery operations
# Creating a snapshot for disaster recovery backup
aws ec2 create-snapshot --volume-id vol-1234567890abcdef0 --description "Disaster
    Recovery Snapshot"

# Retrieving details of a specific snapshot
aws ec2 describe-snapshots --snapshot-ids snap-123456abcd

# Generating an AMI from a snapshot for quick recovery
aws ec2 register-image --name "Disaster-Recovery-AMI" --block-device-mappings
    DeviceName=/dev/sda1,Ebs={SnapshotId=snap-123456abcd}
```

This example showcases the use of AWS CLI for effective snapshot management, critical for rapid restoration of services to a specified recovery point.

Conclusion

Disaster recovery planning is essential for businesses to maintain continuous operation and safeguard data integrity amid potential disruptions. By implementing comprehensive risk assessments, effective backup strategies, and maintaining updated disaster recovery plans, organizations enhance their resilience and preparedness. Employing modern cloud technology further supports these efforts, ensuring businesses are equipped to handle and swiftly recover from disruptions, thereby ensuring long-term stability and reliability.

Chapter Seven

Scalable API Gateway Architectures

High-Performance Gateways: Design and customization for scale

High-performance gateways are crucial for managing the large-scale data flow between clients and backend services, ensuring that enterprises can efficiently handle increased traffic and complex data transactions. The design and customization of these gateways must be strategically approached to satisfy current operational demands and anticipate future growth and technological advancements. This article explores the essential design principles, architectural considerations, and customization techniques necessary for developing high-performance gateways that can support expansive applications effectively.

Fundamentals of High-Performance Gateways

A high-performance gateway serves as a critical node, managing and directing data traffic to ensure secure and efficient network operations. These gateways are engineered to manage numerous simultaneous connections, support high data throughput, and maintain low-latency communications. Essential features often include load balancing, security measures like authentication and rate limiting, and comprehensive API management.

Core Design Principles

1. **Scalability**: Gateways must be designed to scale horizontally by adding more instances as needed, which is more effective than merely increasing the capacity of existing hardware (vertical scaling).

2. **High Availability**: Essential to gateway design is the implementation of redundant instances and automatic failover solutions to guarantee continuous operation during component failures.

3. **Security**: As primary traffic controllers, gateways must incorporate advanced security protocols, including SSL/TLS termination and comprehensive threat management, to safeguard data integrity.

4. **Performance Optimization**: Optimizing gateway performance might involve response caching, reducing data transformation, and employing efficient logging methods to enhance operational efficiency.

5. **Customizability**: Tailoring gateways to meet specific operational demands is vital, allowing for unique routing configurations, specialized authentication approaches, and other custom integrations.

Architectural Considerations

High-performance gateways generally combine several architectural elements:

- **Reverse Proxy**: Functions as an intermediary for requests from clients seeking resources from backend servers.

381

- **Load Balancer**: Distributes incoming network traffic across multiple backend servers to ensure even load distribution and increased redundancy.

- **API Manager**: Manages the APIs' entire lifecycle, from deployment and security to traffic management and analysis.

Customization Techniques

Customizing a high-performance gateway involves adjusting it to specific requirements and performance conditions. This could include:

- **Traffic Management**: Implementing algorithms that dynamically adjust routing and load balancing based on real-time server performance and network conditions.

- **Security Policies**: Developing specific security measures tailored to the application's needs, which might involve setting up custom authentication methods or integrating existing corporate security frameworks.

- **Caching Policies**: Determining optimal caching strategies to reduce backend load and improve response speed for frequently requested data.

Performance Tuning Example

Here is a practical example of setting up NGINX for load balancing, a common function for high-performance gateways:

```
http {
    upstream backend {
        server backend1.example.com weight=5;
        server backend2.example.com weight=5;
        server backend3.example.com weight=10;
    }

    server {
        listen 80;

        location / {
            proxy_pass http://backend;
            proxy_set_header Host $host;
            proxy_set_header X-Real-IP $remote_addr;
            proxy_set_header X-Forwarded-For $proxy_add_x_forwarded_for;
            proxy_set_header X-Forwarded-Proto $scheme;
        }
    }
}
```

This NGINX configuration demonstrates a basic load balancing setup where traffic is distributed among three servers with specified weights, indicating their handling capacity.

Conclusion

Creating and customizing high-performance gateways necessitates a profound comprehension of network architecture, performance enhancement strategies, and security protocols. By focusing on scalability, reliability, and customization, developers can construct gateways that robustly support the demands of large-scale, high-traffic applications. Employing standard solutions like NGINX or tailored systems, the appropriate gateway design can significantly improve the efficiency and resilience of enterprise applications.

Managing API Traffic: Techniques for routing, load balancing, and managing peak loads

Effectively managing API traffic is crucial for ensuring system resilience, enhancing user experiences, and maintaining operational efficacy as organizations experience growth and increased digital interactions. Employing advanced methods for routing, load balancing, and handling peak traffic loads is essential. This article explores various approaches for efficiently managing API traffic, focusing on effective routing, load balancing, and managing high traffic situations.

Techniques for Routing

Optimal routing of API traffic ensures that incoming requests are directed efficiently to the appropriate backend services, thus reducing latency and enhancing system responsiveness.

1. Path-Based Routing: This method directs traffic based on URL paths, facilitating the routing of requests to different services based on distinct URL segments.

Example using NGINX for Path-Based Routing:

```
server {
    location /service1/ {
        proxy_pass http://backend-service1;
    }
    location /service2/ {
        proxy_pass http://backend-service2;
    }
}
```

This configuration in NGINX helps route traffic to various backend services according to the specific path in the URL.

2. Host-Based Routing: This strategy uses the hostname from the HTTP headers to route requests, allowing a single IP to serve multiple domains.

Example using NGINX for Host-Based Routing:

```
server {
    server_name service1.example.com;
    location / {
        proxy_pass http://backend-service1;
    }
}
server {
    server_name service2.example.com;
    location / {
        proxy_pass http://backend-service2;
    }
}
```

In this NGINX setup, requests are routed to different services based on the domain name accessed by the user.

Load Balancing Strategies

Load balancing is fundamental for evenly distributing incoming API requests across multiple servers, thus avoiding overloads and ensuring smooth performance.

1. Round Robin Load Balancing: This basic method evenly distributes incoming requests across all available servers.

2. Weighted Load Balancing: This approach assigns different weights to servers based on their processing capabilities, and distributes requests accordingly.

3. Dynamic Load Balancing: This dynamic method adjusts traffic distribution based on real-time analysis of server loads.

Example with HAProxy for Dynamic Load Balancing:

```
frontend api_frontend
    bind *:80
    default_backend api_backend

backend api_backend
    balance roundrobin
    server server1 192.168.0.1:80 weight 3
    server server2 192.168.0.2:80 weight 7
```

This HAProxy configuration demonstrates dynamic load balancing where traffic is distributed to servers based on assigned weights, allowing for more efficient resource use.

Managing High Traffic Loads

Addressing peak traffic effectively involves strategies to ensure APIs can handle spikes in traffic without performance degradation.

1. Rate Limiting: This method limits the number of requests a user can make within a specific period, smoothing out sudden spikes in demand.

2. Caching: By storing frequently accessed data temporarily, caching reduces backend load and speeds up response times.

3. Autoscaling: Autoscaling adjusts the number of active servers automatically based on the current traffic load, which is especially useful in cloud environments.

Example of Implementing Caching with Redis:

```python
import redis

cache = redis.Redis(host='localhost', port=6379, db=0)

def get_data(key):
    data = cache.get(key)
    if data is not None:
        return data  # Returning cached data
    else:
        data = fetch_data_from_db(key)   # Fetching data from the database
        cache.setex(key, 3600, data)   # Caching data for one hour
        return data
```

This Python script illustrates using Redis for caching, significantly decreasing database load by serving cached responses for frequent requests.

Conclusion

Managing API traffic effectively with robust routing, load balancing, and peak load management techniques is key for sustaining the reliability and efficiency of digital services. These methods ensure APIs are equipped to handle increased traffic, maintain availability, and provide consistent user experiences even during peak times. Implementing these strategies allows businesses to enhance their API infrastructure, support scalable growth, and optimize overall system performance.

Chapter Eight

State Management in Distributed Systems

Handling State Across Services: Strategies for statefulness in stateless environments

In the realm of modern software architectures, particularly those that utilize microservices, the challenge of maintaining state across services in environments designed to be stateless is increasingly prevalent. Stateless architectures—where each request is treated independently without requiring knowledge of past interactions—offer benefits like scalability and simplicity. However, some applications necessitate the retention of state information across multiple transactions or sessions. This necessitates specific strategies for effectively managing statefulness without compromising the architectural benefits. This article explores various approaches for effectively handling state across services in stateless settings.

Statefulness in Stateless Systems

Stateless architectures, such as those typical in RESTful APIs, do not store user state between requests. Each client request must carry all necessary information for the server to process it. Conversely, stateful applications retain data from user sessions that can be used in subsequent interactions. The challenge in stateless environments is to manage necessary state information while retaining the benefits of the stateless model.

Strategies for State Management

1. **Client-Side State Management:**

   o **Cookies and Local Storage**: One straightforward approach is to store the state on the client side, using mechanisms like cookies or local storage, suitable for small data amounts and can help reduce server load.

Example:

```
// Storing state information in local storage
localStorage.setItem('userSession', JSON.stringify(sessionData));
```

2. **Server-Side State Management:**

   o **Session Management**: For state that needs to be accessed by various services, utilizing a centralized session store like Redis allows for efficient state querying by all services.

Example using Redis:

```
import redis
redis_client = redis.Redis(host='localhost', port=6379, db=0)
redis_client.set('session_key', 'session_value')  # Storing session data
print(redis_client.get('session_key'))  # Retrieving session data
```

3. **Database-Driven State Management:**

   o **Persistent Storage**: Employing a database to store state information offers a reliable solution

389

for applications requiring durable state management and supports complex queries and transactional integrity.

Example:

```
INSERT INTO user_sessions (session_id, data) VALUES ('abc123', 'data_value');
SELECT data FROM user_sessions WHERE session_id = 'abc123';
```

4. **Distributed Cache:**

   o **In-Memory Data Grids**: Technologies such as Hazelcast or Apache Ignite provide in-memory data grids that facilitate quick access to distributed data and are ideal for large-scale state management.

Example using Hazelcast:

```
HazelcastInstance hazelcastInstance = Hazelcast.newHazelcastInstance();
Map<Integer, String> myMap = hazelcastInstance.getMap("myMap");
myMap.put(1, "value");
```

5. **State Aggregation Layer:**

   o **API Gateway**: Utilizing an API Gateway to aggregate requests and manage state can simplify the complexity of state management, handling functions like authentication, caching, and session management.

Example in API Gateway configuration:

```yaml
apiVersion: networking.istio.io/v1alpha3
kind: Gateway
metadata:
  name: example-gateway
spec:
  selector:
    istio: ingressgateway
  servers:
  - port:
      number: 80
      name: http
      protocol: HTTP
    hosts:
    - "my.example.com"
```

Considerations for State Management

- **Consistency**: It's essential that the state management strategy ensures consistency across services, especially in distributed systems.

- **Performance**: Implementing state management should not adversely affect the application's performance. In-memory solutions are often favored in performance-critical situations.

- **Reliability**: Strategies should include mechanisms for failover and redundancy to preserve state during system failures.

Conclusion

Handling state in environments designed to be stateless involves balancing between maintaining essential state information and maximizing the benefits of statelessness. By integrating one or more of the strategies outlined, developers can create robust, scalable architectures capable of managing the complexities associated with stateful interactions within stateless environments. Whether through client-side mechanisms, distributed caching, or a specialized state management layer, it is feasible to manage state across services effectively, enhancing the functionality and scalability of applications.

Session Management: Best practices for distributed session handling

Session management is crucial in distributed systems, particularly where applications are broken down into microservices. Effective management of user sessions ensures seamless user experiences and bolsters application security and performance. This article outlines best practices for handling sessions across distributed environments, emphasizing methods that enhance robustness, scalability, and security.

Key Concepts in Distributed Session Management

In distributed architectures, where services might be spread across different locations, managing session information becomes complex. The aim is to ensure session data is readily available to all parts of the application that need it, regardless of the user's entry point or the services' locations.

Best Practices for Managing Sessions in Distributed Systems

1. **Centralized Session Store:** Utilizing a centralized store for session data, such as Redis or Memcached, ensures all services can access session information efficiently. These systems are optimized for quick data retrieval and high availability, critical for maintaining session integrity across services.

Example using Redis:

```python
import redis

# Establishing a Redis connection
session_store = redis.StrictRedis(host='localhost', port=6379, db=0)

# Writing session data
session_store.set('session_id', 'user_data')

# Reading session data
user_data = session_store.get('session_id')
print(user_data)
```

This configuration allows any service within the application to access session data quickly, ensuring a consistent user experience.

2. **Session Stickiness:** In scenarios with load balancers that distribute requests across several servers, session stickiness ensures that requests from a single session consistently go to the server where the session was initiated. This is often managed at the load balancer level.

Example for configuring session stickiness:

```
backend app_backend
    balance roundrobin
    cookie SERVERID insert indirect nocache
    server app1 192.168.0.1:80 cookie app1 check
    server app2 192.168.0.2:80 cookie app2 check
```

This setup uses cookies to direct session-specific requests to the same server, aiding in maintaining session continuity.

3. **Token-Based Authentication:** Using JSON Web Tokens (JWT) simplifies session handling across services. Upon login, the user is issued a JWT that encodes all necessary session information, which is then verified by each service with each request.

Example of JWT usage:

```python
import jwt
import datetime

# Token generation
encoded_jwt = jwt.encode({'user_id': 123, 'exp': datetime.datetime.utcnow() +
    datetime.timedelta(seconds=600)}, 'secret', algorithm='HS256')
print(encoded_jwt)

# Token validation
decoded_jwt = jwt.decode(encoded_jwt, 'secret', algorithms=['HS256'])
print(decoded_jwt)
```

4. **Secure Session Data:** Transmission of session data should always be secured using HTTPS to protect against eavesdropping and tampering. Additionally, sensitive information within session tokens should be encrypted, and storing minimal sensitive data is advisable.

5. **Session Expiration and Invalidity:** Sessions should be configured to expire automatically to prevent abuse of stale session data. Furthermore, sessions must be invalidated immediately upon user logout or when no longer needed.

6. **Monitor and Audit Session Activity:** Continuously monitoring and auditing session activities helps in identifying and addressing unauthorized accesses or anomalies, thereby strengthening security.

Conclusion

Managing sessions effectively in distributed systems is critical for ensuring seamless operation and robust security in applications, especially those using microservices architecture. By centralizing session data, employing session stickiness, using token-based authentication, securing session transmissions, managing session lifecycles properly, and monitoring session activities, developers can create more secure, scalable, and user-friendly applications. These best practices offer a structured approach to session management in distributed environments, enabling applications to operate smoothly and securely at scale.

Chapter Nine

API Composition and Aggregation

Techniques for API Aggregation: Handling multiple data sources and backend services

API aggregation is crucial in today's software architectures, especially for organizations that handle data across multiple sources and backend services. By integrating data from various APIs into a unified interface, API aggregation facilitates more efficient data retrieval and enhances user interactions. This method streamlines development, boosts performance, and improves user experiences by presenting a unified data view across different services. This article examines critical strategies for API aggregation, focusing on how to effectively manage multiple data sources and backend services.

Exploring API Aggregation

API aggregation involves merging responses from multiple discrete API calls into one comprehensive response. This is particularly useful in microservices architectures, where distinct services manage different segments of business logic. Aggregation minimizes the number of client-side requests, which reduces network latency and increases data retrieval efficiency.

Strategies for Effective API Aggregation

1. **API Gateway Usage:** An API Gateway serves as a reverse proxy, receiving API requests, aggregating

necessary data from multiple backend services, and delivering a consolidated response. This layer simplifies the client interface and hides the complexity of backend systems.

Example Configuration:

```json
{
  "endpoint": "/api/user/profile",
  "method": "GET",
  "description": "Aggregates data from multiple services into a single response"
}
```

In this setup, the API Gateway handles requests by pulling data from user and profile services, amalgamating the information into a single output.

2. **Service Orchestration:** Orchestrating service involves coordinating multiple backend services to respond to an API request, which may include an orchestration layer that makes subsequent calls to different services, gathers responses, and combines them into one final output.

Orchestration Example in Node.js:

```javascript
const express = require('express');
const axios = require('axios');
const app = express();

app.get('/aggregate-data', async (req, res) => {
    try {
        const [userData, accountData] = await Promise.all([
            axios.get('http://user-service/users/1'),
            axios.get('http://account-service/accounts/1')
        ]);
        res.json({
            user: userData.data,
            account: accountData.data
        });
    } catch (error) {
        res.status(500).send('Aggregation Error');
    }
});

app.listen(3000, () => console.log('API Server running on port 3000'));
```

3. **API Chaining:** When the response from one API call dictates the request for another, API chaining is employed. This method sequentially connects API calls where each link in the chain depends on the previous one's response.

Chaining Example:

```javascript
async function aggregateUserAccount(user_id) {
    const user = await getUser(user_id);
    const account = await getAccount(user.account_id);
    return { user, account };
}
```

4. **Data Transformation and Caching:** Transforming data at the aggregation layer into a format suitable for client interaction is crucial. Caching these aggregated

398

responses can also improve performance by reducing the load on backend systems.

Example of Caching in Python:

```python
from cachetools import cached, TTLCache

cache = TTLCache(maxsize=100, ttl=300)  # Cache configuration

@cached(cache)
def retrieveAggregatedData(user_id):
    user_data = getUserData(user_id)
    account_data = getAccountData(user_data['account_id'])
    return { 'user': user_data, 'account': account_data }
```

Considerations in API Aggregation

- **Performance**: Minimize latency introduced by multiple network requests through concurrent calls, effective caching, and optimizing response sizes.

- **Error Management**: Robust mechanisms are essential to manage failures and ensure dependency resilience across API calls.

- **Security Measures**: Safeguard against exposing sensitive data inadvertently through strict access controls and data handling policies.

Conclusion

API aggregation is an effective strategy for managing multiple data sources and backend services within a microservices framework. By implementing an API Gateway, orchestrating service calls, chaining APIs, and applying data transformation and caching, developers can achieve a highly efficient, scalable, and secure system. These practices ensure that client interactions are smoother, network traffic is reduced, and users receive a cohesive experience across various services.

Best Practices in API Composition: Ensuring performance and reliability

API composition is essential in modern software development, particularly within frameworks like microservices where it integrates various backend services into a single streamlined interface. This process is pivotal for simplifying interactions for clients by consolidating multiple service responses into one effective response. This article provides a guide on the best practices for API composition to enhance performance and ensure reliability.

Fundamentals of API Composition

API composition is about merging data and functionality from several smaller, discrete API endpoints to create higher-level services. This approach helps microservices architectures by making client-side programming simpler and improving the overall user experience by presenting all relevant data through a unified endpoint.

Strategies for Robust API Composition

1. **Reduce Excessive Interactions:** Design composite APIs to limit the need for numerous interactions between the client and server or across services. This approach decreases the overhead associated with multiple API calls and enhances data retrieval efficiency.

Example:

```javascript
// Composite API for a user dashboard
app.get('/complete-user-data', async (req, res) => {
    const user = await userService.retrieveUserDetails(req.userId);
    const orders = await orderService.getUserOrders(req.userId);
    const account = await accountService.getAccountInfo(req.userId);
    res.json({ user, orders, account });
});
```

This endpoint serves as a single point for fetching all user-related information, thereby reducing the client's workload.

2. **Implement Asynchronous Mechanisms:** Employ asynchronous communication such as event-driven responses to improve system responsiveness and allow services to perform tasks in parallel, thus enhancing throughput.

Node.js Event-Driven Example:

```javascript
const EventEmitter = require('events');
const myEmitter = new EventEmitter();

// Asynchronously fetch user data
myEmitter.on('requestData', async (userId) => {
    const data = await userService.getUserData(userId);
    console.log('Fetched Data:', data);
});

// Trigger data request
myEmitter.emit('requestData', 101);
```

3. **Use an API Gateway:** An API Gateway can be used to manage complex service interactions, aggregate results from multiple microservices, handle authentication, and manage rate limiting. This centralizes the orchestration and simplifies client-side logic.

401

API Gateway Setup Example:

```yaml
apiVersion: networking.istio.io/v1beta1
kind: Gateway
metadata:
  name: central-api-gateway
spec:
  selector:
    istio: ingressgateway
  servers:
  - port:
      number: 80
      protocol: HTTP
    hosts:
      - "api.mycompany.com"
```

4. **Employ Aggressive Caching:** To reduce repeated data fetch operations, implement caching strategies at either the gateway or service level. This not only decreases latency but also reduces the load on backend systems.

Caching with Redis Example:

```python
import redis
cache = redis.Redis()

def getCachedData(key):
    data = cache.get(key)
    if data:
        return json.loads(data)  # Return cached data
    # Otherwise, fetch new data, cache it, and return
    newData = fetchData(key)
    cache.setex(key, 3600, json.dumps(newData))
    return newData
```

5. **Monitor and Optimize Performance:** Regularly monitoring the performance of APIs is crucial. Use

monitoring tools to track and analyze performance metrics and logs, which can help identify and rectify bottlenecks.

6. **Design for Failure:** Integrate resilience patterns such as retries, circuit breakers, and fallback mechanisms to ensure the system remains robust and reliable even when individual components fail.

Circuit Breaker Implementation:

```python
from pybreaker import CircuitBreaker
circuit_breaker = CircuitBreaker(fail_max=3, reset_timeout=60)

@circuit_breaker
def secureFetchData(key):
    return fetchData(key)
```

Conclusion

By adhering to these best practices in API composition, developers can build efficient, reliable, and scalable API services within a microservices architecture. Reducing client-side requests, using asynchronous methods, managing service interactions through an API Gateway, implementing effective caching strategies, continuously monitoring performance, and building fault-tolerant systems are all vital for delivering high-performance APIs. These strategies form the backbone of successful API integration and management across distributed systems.

Chapter Ten

Real-time Data Handling

Implementing Real-time APIs: WebSockets, server-sent events

Real-time APIs are crucial for developing dynamic, responsive web applications that require immediate and continuous communication between the server and the client. Technologies like WebSockets and Server-Sent Events (SSE) are instrumental in facilitating this real-time interaction by enabling servers to instantaneously push updates to clients. This article explores the implementation of WebSockets and SSE for real-time APIs, detailing their advantages, appropriate use cases, and practical implementation guidelines.

Fundamentals of Real-time APIs

Real-time APIs establish a persistent connection between the client and server, which allows for the instant transmission of data upon updates. Unlike traditional request/response models that necessitate periodic polling for updates, real-time APIs maintain an open channel for constant data flow. These APIs are especially beneficial in environments where immediate data synchronization is necessary, such as in interactive games, live financial trading platforms, or social media platforms where user interactions occur in real time.

Utilizing WebSockets

WebSockets create a bi-directional communication line between the client and server, which stays active throughout the session, allowing messages to be passed in both directions simultaneously without reopening connections.

Characteristics:

- **Bi-directional Communication:** Both the client and server can send messages independently at any time.

- **Low Overhead:** Persistent connections reduce the overhead seen with traditional HTTP connections.

- **Continuous Connection:** The connection remains open, enabling ongoing communication without session interruptions.

WebSocket Implementation Example:

```javascript
// Node.js WebSocket server using the 'ws' library
const WebSocket = require('ws');
const server = new WebSocket.Server({ port: 8080 });

server.on('connection', socket => {
    socket.on('message', message => {
        console.log('Server received:', message);
    });

    socket.send('Welcome message from server');
});

// WebSocket client in JavaScript
const client = new WebSocket('ws://localhost:8080');

client.onmessage = event => {
    console.log('Server message:', event.data);
};

client.send('Client message to server');
```

This demonstrates a basic WebSocket server and client where two-way communication is established, allowing for messages to be sent in either direction.

Implementing Server-Sent Events (SSE)

Server-Sent Events facilitate a one-directional data stream from the server to the client, perfect for applications where only the server communicates updates directly to the client.

Advantages:

- **Unidirectional Flow:** Information flows only from server to client.

- **HTTP-Based:** Utilizes conventional HTTP protocols, which simplifies implementation on existing web infrastructures.

- **Reconnection Protocol:** Automatically attempts to reconnect if the connection is lost.

SSE Usage Example:

```javascript
// Setting up an SSE endpoint in Node.js using Express
const express = require('express');
const app = express();

app.get('/real-time', function(req, res) {
    res.setHeader('Content-Type', 'text/event-stream');
    res.setHeader('Cache-Control', 'no-cache');

    // Send real-time updates
    const interval = setInterval(() => {
        res.write(`data: ${new Date().toLocaleTimeString()}\n\n`);
    }, 1000);
```

```
    req.on('close', () => {
        clearInterval(interval);
        res.end();
    });
});

app.listen(3000, () => {
    console.log('SSE server operational on port 3000');
});
```

This server continuously sends updates to the client, demonstrating SSE's capability to stream data in real-time.

Conclusion

Choosing between WebSockets and Server-Sent Events depends on your specific application needs. WebSockets are best suited for interactive, two-way communication scenarios like live chats or gaming applications. Conversely, SSE is ideal for applications such as live news feeds or stock tickers, where the server needs to send frequent updates to the client. Integrating these technologies into web applications can significantly enhance user interaction and responsiveness, offering richer and more engaging user experiences.

Challenges and Solutions: Handling synchronization, latency, and throughput

Managing synchronization, latency, and throughput presents substantial challenges in distributed and networked environments, affecting the performance and reliability of applications that demand real-time capabilities or span extensive geographic regions. This article examines these pivotal challenges, proposes effective solutions, and provides practical code examples to aid implementation.

1. Synchronization Issues

In distributed systems, synchronization is critical to ensure consistent and orderly operations across various system nodes. However, achieving effective synchronization can be daunting due to network delays, clock discrepancies, and the unpredictable nature of distributed environments.

Solution: Clock Synchronization and Logical Ordering

Implementing protocols such as the Network Time Protocol (NTP) helps synchronize clocks to within milliseconds of Coordinated Universal Time (UTC). For event sequencing without precise clock synchronization, logical clocks like Lamport timestamps prove beneficial.

Lamport Timestamps Example:

```python
def send_event(ts):
    ts += 1  # Increment timestamp for the next event
    return ts

def receive_event(local_ts, incoming_ts):
    local_ts = max(local_ts, incoming_ts) + 1
    return local_ts
```

This Python snippet illustrates using Lamport timestamps to maintain consistent event ordering in a distributed system, allowing all nodes to agree on the event sequence.

2. Latency Challenges

Latency, or the delay in data transmission from source to destination, can significantly affect user experience, particularly in real-time applications.

Solution: Network Path Optimization and Content Delivery Networks

Minimizing transmission hops and using Content Delivery Networks (CDN) can effectively reduce latency. CDNs store data geographically closer to users, reducing the distance data travels.

CDN Configuration Example:

```
// Setting up a CDN to minimize latency
cdn.configure({
    origin: 'base-server.com',
    contentPath: '/multimedia/*',
    ttl: 3600, // Cache time-to-live
    locations: ['North America', 'Europe', 'Asia']
});
```

This JavaScript code sets up a CDN to cache multimedia content at edge locations close to users, enhancing access speed and reducing latency.

3. Throughput Constraints

Throughput—the rate at which data transfers successfully—may be restricted by network bandwidth, server capacity, or application design, particularly under high demand.

Solution: Load Balancing and Data Streamlining

Using load balancers to distribute incoming traffic across several servers can optimize throughput. Streamlining data processing and employing data compression also aid in maximizing throughput.

Load Balancing with Nginx Example:

```
http {
    upstream app_cluster {
        server instance1.example.com;
        server instance2.example.com;
        server instance3.example.com;
    }
```

```
    server {
        location / {
            proxy_pass http://app_cluster;
            proxy_next_upstream error timeout invalid_header http_500 http_502
                http_503 http_504;
        }
    }
}
```

This Nginx script demonstrates distributing traffic across multiple servers to manage loads efficiently and enhance throughput.

Conclusion

Addressing synchronization, latency, and throughput in distributed systems involves strategic planning, network management, and sophisticated software solutions. By synchronizing clocks, optimizing network routes, leveraging CDNs, and implementing load balancing, developers can resolve many of the prevalent challenges in distributed environments. These strategies ensure that applications are robust, responsive, and scalable, capable of handling the demands of complex distributed operations.

Chapter Eleven

Advanced Versioning Techniques

Strategic API Versioning: Managing multiple active versions

Strategic API versioning is essential in managing the lifecycle of APIs and ensuring that they continue to serve their purpose as technology and client needs evolve. Maintaining multiple active versions of an API allows providers to introduce new features, correct issues, and optimize functionality without disrupting existing users. This article explores effective practices for managing multiple active API versions, focusing on methods that enable seamless transitions and maintain system integrity.

Significance of API Versioning

API versioning is crucial for several reasons:

- **Backward Compatibility:** Ensures that older applications continue to function even as new versions are rolled out.

- **Client Transitioning:** Allows clients to migrate to newer versions at their own pace without being forced to adapt immediately.

- **Controlled Deprecation:** Facilitates the retirement of outdated features in a managed, predictable manner.

Effective API Versioning Strategies

1. Common Versioning Techniques

Different versioning techniques can be applied depending on the scenario, including URL versioning, header versioning, and query parameter versioning:

- **URL Versioning:** Places the version number directly in the API path (e.g., /api/v1/resource). This approach is straightforward but can lead to clutter as the number of versions grows.

- **Header Versioning:** Incorporates version information within HTTP headers, keeping URLs clean but potentially complicating client and server interactions.

- **Query String Versioning:** Uses query parameters to indicate version (e.g., /api/resource?version=1). This method is simple to implement but might conflict with caching mechanisms and is less transparent.

URL Versioning Example:

```javascript
const express = require('express');
const app = express();

app.get('/api/v1/books', (req, res) => {
    res.send('Fetching books list from version 1');
});

app.get('/api/v2/books', (req, res) => {
    res.send('Fetching books list from version 2 with new features');
});

app.listen(3000, () => console.log('API server operational with multiple versions'));
```

2. Managing Multiple Versions

When multiple versions are active, particular management practices are necessary:

- **Documentation:** Each version should be documented thoroughly to guide developers through the differences and use cases.

- **Endpoint Management:** Ensure that endpoints for each version are managed separately to prevent updates in one version from impacting another.

- **Deprecation Strategy:** Communicate the lifespan and deprecation plans for each version clearly to users to manage expectations and transition plans.

Deprecation Header Example:

```
HTTP/1.1 200 OK
Content-Type: application/json
Deprecation: version="1"; date="2023-01-01"
Sunset: Tue, 01 Jan 2024 00:00:00 GMT

{
    "message": "Version 1 will soon be deprecated. Please transition to version 2."
}
```

3. Facilitating Version Transitions

Smooth transitions between versions can be achieved through several approaches:

- **Parallel Versioning:** Keep old and new versions running concurrently to give clients time to adapt.

- **Version Negotiation:** Enable clients to select which version they interact with, either through specific endpoints or header settings.

- **Transformation Middleware:** Use server-side middleware to adapt responses to fit the expected formats of different API versions.

Middleware Example for Version Negotiation:

```
app.use((req, res, next) => {
    const version = req.headers['Accept-Version'];
    req.url = version === '2' ? `/v2${req.url}` : `/v1${req.url}`;
    next();
});
```

Conclusion

Effectively managing multiple active versions of an API involves careful planning and execution. Employing clear versioning techniques, maintaining detailed documentation for each version, and enabling smooth transitions between versions are all best practices that help ensure APIs remain functional and relevant over time. By implementing these strategies, organizations can provide flexibility to their clients and stability to their systems, ultimately supporting the ongoing evolution of technology and user needs.

Handling Breaking Changes: Minimizing disruption in client applications

Managing breaking changes effectively is crucial in API development to ensure stability and maintain user trust while evolving and enhancing API functionalities. Breaking changes,

415

which include modifications that could disrupt existing client applications—such as changes to endpoint URLs, alterations in response formats, or the removal of features—require careful handling to prevent client-side issues and dissatisfaction. This article outlines effective strategies for mitigating the impact of such changes on client applications.

Understanding the Impact of Breaking Changes

Breaking changes can manifest in various ways, each potentially affecting how client applications interact with the API:

- **Endpoint Adjustments:** Changes to endpoint paths, query parameters, or HTTP methods can lead to failures in existing integrations.

- **Data Format Alterations:** Modifying the structure of the JSON response, such as changing key names, data types, or converting data structures (e.g., arrays to objects), might result in errors in client applications that expect data in a specific format.

- **Behavior Modifications:** Updates that alter the logic of how the API functions can cause unexpected results for existing clients.

Strategies for Mitigating Breaking Changes

1. Implement Semantic Versioning

Semantic versioning is a systematic method to manage versions of an API and communicate changes to users. It is structured as MAJOR.MINOR.PATCH:

- **MAJOR:** Indicates breaking changes that may affect existing functionalities.

- **MINOR:** Introduces new, backward-compatible features.

- **PATCH:** Provides backward-compatible bug fixes.

This versioning strategy aids clients in understanding the implications of updates and deciding the appropriate timing for adopting changes.

Semantic Versioning Example:

```
Initial version: 1.0.0
After adding new features: 1.1.0
After making breaking changes: 2.0.0
```

2. Establish a Clear Deprecation Policy

A well-defined deprecation policy helps manage the transition to new API versions. Key components include:

- **Advance Notice:** Notify users well before making significant changes via documentation, direct communications, and API responses.

- **Transition Period:** Provide a timeline that allows clients ample time to adapt to new API versions.

- **Support for Legacy Versions:** Maintain older API versions for a set period, ensuring users have sufficient time to transition without disruption.

Deprecation Header Example:

```
HTTP/1.1 200 OK
Content-Type: application/json
Deprecation: version="1"; date="2023-01-01"
Sunset: Sat, 01 Jan 2024 00:00:00 GMT


{
    "notice": "Version 1 will be deprecated soon. Please migrate to version 2."
}
```

3. Enhance Documentation

Comprehensive documentation for each API version is crucial. It should clearly outline the changes, especially breaking ones, and provide migration guides and examples to facilitate a smooth transition.

Documentation Example:

```
API Version 2.0.0 - Release Notes
-------------------------------------
Changes:
- Endpoint `/getUsers` is now `/fetchUsers`.
- Property `totalUsers` in responses is renamed to `userCount`.

Additions:
- Introduced new endpoint `/findUsers` for advanced searches.

Corrections:
- Corrected errors in the `/fetchUsers` response format regarding user timestamps.
```

4. Employ Feature Flags

Feature flags allow new features or significant changes to be rolled out selectively and tested by subsets of users in production environments. This strategy can isolate new developments from the main operational API, enabling safer testing and phased rollouts.

418

Feature Flag Implementation Example:

```
app.get('/api/products', (req, res) => {
    if (featureFlags.newFeaturesEnabled(req.user)) {
        return handleNewProductRequest(req, res);
    }
    return handleOldProductRequest(req, res);
});
```

Conclusion

Effectively managing breaking changes in APIs is essential for ensuring a reliable service as it evolves. By employing strategies such as semantic versioning, a clear deprecation policy, comprehensive documentation, and feature flags, API providers can minimize disruptions and maintain a positive relationship with their users. These practices help ensure that transitions are seamless and that both new and existing functionalities are supported throughout the lifecycle of the API.

Chapter Twelve

Performance Optimization and Caching

Advanced Caching Strategies: Edge caching, cache invalidation patterns

In today's digital landscape, sophisticated caching strategies are essential for boosting performance and enhancing the scalability of web applications. Advanced techniques like edge caching and nuanced cache invalidation patterns are critical for optimizing data retrieval and minimizing the burden on servers. This article delves into these advanced caching methods, explaining their implementation and advantages.

Edge Caching Explained

Edge caching refers to the technique of storing content replicas at multiple network locations nearer to end-users—typically at the network's "edge." This strategy is central to Content Delivery Networks (CDNs) and aims to accelerate content delivery by minimizing the distance data travels to the user.

Advantages of Edge Caching:

- **Reduced Latency:** Storing content closer to users cuts down transmission time, thus enhancing response speeds.

- **Lowered Server Load:** With edge caching, many requests are resolved at the edge, significantly reducing the traffic to the origin server.

- **Enhanced User Experience:** Quicker loading times and reduced latency contribute to a more responsive and satisfying user experience.

Example of Edge Caching Configuration:

```
# Example NGINX setup for edge caching
location /content/ {
    proxy_cache edge_cache;
    proxy_pass http://my-origin-server.com;
    proxy_cache_valid 200 24h;  # Keep valid HTTP 200 responses for 24 hours
    proxy_cache_use_stale error timeout invalid_response http_500 http_502
        http_503 http_504;
}
```

This configuration snippet for NGINX demonstrates setting up edge caching for static content, which allows for direct content delivery to users while alleviating load on the primary server.

Cache Invalidation Strategies

Proper cache invalidation is a fundamental component of effective caching. It determines when a cached item is outdated and should be refreshed or removed. Properly managed cache invalidation ensures users access current information, maintaining system accuracy and user trust.

Key Cache Invalidation Patterns:

1. **Time-based Expiration:**

   o This basic invalidation strategy assigns an expiration time to cache entries. Once this time passes, the cache considers these entries stale or automatically deletes them.

- ○ **Example:** Setting a 24-hour Time to Live (TTL) for cached entries.

2. **Change-based Invalidation:**

   - ○ This approach invalidates cache entries following data modifications. It's more intricate but guarantees that cached data remains current.

   - ○ **Example:** Implementing a notification system that triggers cache invalidation when underlying data is modified.

3. **Tag-based Invalidation:**

   - ○ In tag-based invalidation, cache entries are tagged by category, and all entries under a tag are invalidated together. This method is useful for bulk invalidation actions.

   - ○ **Example:** Assigning tags based on user activity and invalidating all related tags when significant changes occur.

Implementation of Tag-based Invalidation:

```python
# Python caching example with tag-based invalidation
from cachetools import cached, TTLCache, hashkey

cache = TTLCache(maxsize=100, ttl=86400)  # Define cache with a one-day TTL
```

```
@cached(cache, key=lambda user, tag: hashkey(user, tag))
def fetch_user_info(user, tag):
    # Fetch user information logic
    return some_data

def clear_cache(user, tag):
    # Invalidate cache based on user and tag
    try:
        del cache[hashkey(user, tag)]
    except KeyError:
        pass
```

This Python script illustrates using a caching library to manage data by tags. It allows specific cache entries associated with a user tag to be invalidated, ensuring the cache does not serve stale data.

Conclusion

Implementing advanced caching strategies like edge caching and detailed cache invalidation schemes is essential for modern web applications aimed at delivering optimal performance. These techniques not only improve data access speeds and reduce server load but also enhance the reliability and user experience of the application. Effective cache management, especially regarding invalidation, ensures that users always receive the most current information, maintaining the integrity and efficiency of the application.

Performance Tuning: Profiling and optimizing API endpoints

Performance tuning for API endpoints is vital in ensuring that web services operate efficiently and are scalable. This critical task involves initial profiling to identify performance bottlenecks and subsequent optimization strategies to enhance efficiency. Profiling provides a detailed examination of how an API performs under different conditions, pinpointing areas that require improvement. This article discusses essential techniques for profiling and optimizing API endpoints, with practical examples to illustrate these methods.

The Role of Profiling

Profiling is the foundational step in performance tuning, focusing on collecting and analyzing runtime data to assess how resources are utilized. Metrics such as response times, CPU usage, memory usage, and database query times are crucial. The aim is to discover which parts of the API are slow or inefficient and determine the underlying reasons.

Tools for Profiling APIs:

- **Application Performance Management (APM) Tools:** Solutions like New Relic, Datadog, and AppDynamics offer comprehensive monitoring capabilities that track performance across the application stack.

- **Profiling Libraries:** For more granular insights, libraries such as cProfile for Python or Clinic.js for Node.js are useful in diagnosing code-level performance issues.

Example of Profiling with cProfile in Python:

```python
import cProfile
import re

def retrieve_data():
    # Simulates a database data retrieval function
    pass

def manipulate_data():
    # Simulates data manipulation
    pass

def api_call():
    retrieve_data()
    manipulate_data()

cProfile.run('api_call()')
```

This example employs Python's cProfile module to profile an api_call function, identifying time-consuming operations or resource-heavy sections.

Optimizing API Endpoints

After profiling, the next step is applying optimization strategies to address the identified bottlenecks. Whether it's refining database queries, implementing caching mechanisms, or rearchitecting certain components, each optimization targets specific performance issues.

1. Database Query Optimization

Improving database interactions is often necessary to boost API response times. Slow queries can drastically affect performance, making them prime candidates for optimization.

- **Techniques:** Strategies include adding indexes to frequently accessed columns, minimizing joins, and

425

analyzing query execution plans to pinpoint inefficiencies.

- **Tools:** Database management tools and APMs can provide insights into query performance and help fine-tune SQL commands.

Example of Enhancing SQL Query Efficiency:

```
-- Before Optimization
SELECT * FROM users JOIN orders ON users.id = orders.user_id WHERE users.age > 30;

-- After Optimization with indexing
CREATE INDEX idx_age ON users(age);
SELECT * FROM users USE INDEX (idx_age) JOIN orders ON users.id = orders.user_id
    WHERE users.age > 30;
```

This SQL example shows how adding an index on the age column can expedite query processing by reducing the search space.

2. Implementing Caching

Caching is a powerful strategy to decrease server load and improve response times by storing copies of frequently accessed data.

- **Approach:** Effective caching can be applied at various levels, including the application, database, or through dedicated caching systems like Redis.

- **Considerations:** It's crucial to manage cache life cycles and invalidation properly to avoid serving outdated data.

Example of Caching with Redis in Python:

```python
import redis

cache = redis.Redis(host='localhost', port=6379, db=0)
```

```python
def fetch_user(user_id):
    # Try to get data from cache first
    if (user := cache.get(user_id)):
        return user  # Return cached user data

    # If not in cache, retrieve from database
    user = simulate_database_fetch(user_id)
    cache.setex(user_id, 3600, user)  # Cache the data with a TTL of one hour
    return user
```

This script illustrates using Redis to cache user data, effectively reducing database query frequency for frequent requests.

Conclusion

Tuning the performance of API endpoints through careful profiling and targeted optimizations is crucial for maintaining efficient, scalable web services. By accurately identifying performance bottlenecks and applying appropriate optimizations such as query refinement and caching, developers can ensure their APIs handle increased load efficiently and continue to provide fast, reliable service. This proactive approach to API management significantly enhances user experience and maintains the robustness of the web infrastructure.

Chapter Thirteen

Advanced Deployment Patterns

Containerization and Orchestration: Using Docker, Kubernetes for API deployments

Containerization and orchestration represent cornerstone technologies in today's software development landscape, crucial for deploying and managing API services efficiently. These methodologies enable developers to encapsulate applications within containers and manage them across systems, ensuring high scalability and reliability. Docker and Kubernetes lead these fields, offering sophisticated tools that facilitate robust container management and orchestration. This discussion delves into leveraging Docker and Kubernetes for deploying APIs, focusing on their integration to enhance performance and manageability.

Containerization via Docker

Docker provides a platform for containerization, allowing developers to package applications along with their dependencies into containers. These containers are executable units that contain all necessary components to run the application, ensuring it operates uniformly across different computing environments.

Benefits of Docker:

- **Environmental Consistency:** Docker containers offer consistent environments throughout development, testing, and production phases, reducing discrepancies and bugs.

- **Resource Efficiency:** Containers utilize the host system's operating system and consume fewer resources than traditional virtual machines, leading to faster start-ups and more efficient operations.

Example of a Docker Configuration:

```
# Base image with Python runtime
FROM python:3.7-slim

# Set the working directory in the container
WORKDIR /app
```

```
# Copy the application files to the container
COPY . /app

# Install dependencies from requirements.txt
RUN pip install --no-cache-dir -r requirements.txt

# Expose port 80 for the application
EXPOSE 80

# Environment variable for the application
ENV NAME App

# Command to run the application
CMD ["python", "app.py"]
```

This Dockerfile demonstrates how to prepare a Docker container that can run a Python application, showcasing the simplicity of setting up and deploying applications with Docker.

Kubernetes for Advanced Orchestration

Kubernetes extends Docker's capabilities by providing an orchestration layer for managing containerized applications across a cluster of machines. It automates the deployment, scaling, and operations of containerized applications.

Advantages of Kubernetes:

- **Automated Scaling:** Kubernetes allows applications to respond to changes in demand automatically by adjusting the number of running container instances.

- **Efficient Load Balancing:** It automatically distributes application traffic across containers to ensure efficient load handling and maximum application uptime.

Kubernetes Configuration Example:

```yaml
apiVersion: apps/v1
kind: Deployment
metadata:
  name: api-deployment

spec:
  replicas: 3
  selector:
    matchLabels:
      component: api
  template:
    metadata:
      labels:
        component: api
    spec:
      containers:
        - name: api-container
          image: myapi:1.0
          ports:
            - containerPort: 80
```

This configuration snippet for Kubernetes outlines a deployment strategy for an API, specifying three replicas to maintain high availability and load distribution.

Combining Docker and Kubernetes for API Deployment

Integrating Docker with Kubernetes provides a streamlined approach to deploying and scaling web APIs. Docker packages the API and its environment into a container, which Kubernetes then deploys across a server cluster, managing the lifecycle and scalability.

Operational Workflow:

1. **Build the Container:** Develop a Docker container for the API using the provided Dockerfile.

2. **Upload to a Registry:** Push the Docker container to a registry like Docker Hub.

3. **Orchestrate Deployment:** Utilize Kubernetes to deploy the container from the registry, managing its distribution and scaling across available servers.

Conclusion

The integration of containerization with orchestration through Docker and Kubernetes offers a compelling framework for deploying and managing APIs effectively. Docker simplifies the creation and distribution of containerized applications, ensuring they run consistently across different environments. Kubernetes enhances this by automating complex operational tasks such as scaling, load balancing, and health monitoring. Together, they provide a robust infrastructure for deploying

APIs that are scalable, reliable, and easy to manage, aligning with agile development practices and modern IT requirements. This combined approach not only reduces infrastructure complexity but also empowers developers to focus more on development and less on deployment concerns.

Blue/Green and Canary Releases: Techniques for zero-downtime deployments

Blue/Green and Canary releases are advanced deployment strategies designed to ensure continuous application availability and minimize service interruptions during updates. These methods are critical for maintaining a seamless user experience and high service reliability, allowing organizations to deploy updates with minimal risk.

Blue/Green Deployment Strategy

The Blue/Green deployment method involves maintaining two identical production environments. One, the Blue environment, runs the current live version of the application, while the other, the Green environment, hosts the new version. This setup allows for quick traffic switching between the two environments, providing an effective safety net for rapid rollback if issues arise with the new release.

Advantages:

- **Rapid Rollback:** Traffic can be swiftly redirected back to the Blue environment if the Green deployment encounters problems, minimizing downtime.

- **Risk Mitigation:** The new version can undergo thorough live testing in the Green environment without affecting the current live version, ensuring stability before full deployment.

Practical Example: In environments like AWS, you might configure two identical groups of instances—one for each environment. After the Green environment has been validated, traffic can be redirected from Blue to Green by updating DNS settings or load balancer configurations.

```
# Example command for updating DNS settings in AWS
aws route53 change-resource-record-sets --hosted-zone-id YOUR_ZONE_ID --change
    -batch file://dns-update.json
```

This command updates the DNS records to point to the Green environment, effectively shifting traffic to the new version.

Canary Release Technique

Canary releases involve gradually rolling out the new version to a small percentage of users before a wider release. This method allows developers to monitor the new version's performance and gather user feedback under real conditions, thereby reducing the risk of widespread impact.

Advantages:

- **Controlled Exposure:** Initially, only a small group of users is exposed to the new version, increasing gradually based on confidence in the release.

- **Immediate User Feedback:** This method captures real user interactions and feedback, providing valuable

433

insights into the application's performance in a live setting.

Implementation Example: Using Kubernetes, you can manage a canary release by adjusting the number of pods serving the new version of your application. This gradual increase in pods allows you to control the percentage of traffic that experiences the new release.

```yaml
# Kubernetes setup for a canary deployment
apiVersion: apps/v1
kind: Deployment
metadata:
  name: myapp-canary
spec:
  replicas: 5
  selector:
    matchLabels:
      app: myapp
  template:
    metadata:
      labels:
        app: myapp
    spec:
      containers:
      - name: myapp
        image: myapp:new
```

```yaml
        ports:
        - containerPort: 80
---
apiVersion: v1
kind: Service
metadata:
  name: myapp-service
spec:
  ports:
    - protocol: TCP
      port: 80
      targetPort: 80
  selector:
    app: myapp
```

In this configuration, a fraction of the pods run the new version (myapp:new), gradually introducing the update to users, allowing performance monitoring and risk assessment before full deployment.

Integrating Both Methods for Enhanced Deployment

While both Blue/Green and Canary release strategies are effective on their own, integrating them can maximize deployment safety and efficiency. For example, a canary phase could be used to gauge the new version's stability before executing a full Blue/Green switch. This combination allows for detailed monitoring and testing, minimizing potential disruption from new software versions.

Conclusion

Blue/Green and Canary releases are essential for organizations striving for zero-downtime deployments and aiming to enhance deployment reliability. By enabling extensive testing in production-like conditions and allowing for incremental user exposure, these strategies significantly lower the risks associated with software updates. As deployment practices evolve alongside DevOps methodologies, these techniques become increasingly vital in delivering robust, user-centric software updates seamlessly and safely.

Chapter Fourteen

Monitoring, Logging, and Telemetry

Comprehensive Monitoring Strategies: Implementing effective system-wide monitoring

Developing and implementing a robust monitoring strategy is fundamental for ensuring the health and efficiency of IT infrastructures. Comprehensive monitoring provides crucial insights into system operations, helping to preemptively address issues, enhance system performance, maintain security, and adhere to compliance mandates. This discussion outlines the essential elements of an effective system-wide monitoring framework, incorporating various tools and techniques to secure extensive oversight across all components.

The Significance of Comprehensive Monitoring

Comprehensive monitoring is pivotal for:

- **Proactive Problem Management:** Identifying and resolving issues before they impact end-users.

- **Optimization of Performance:** Pinpointing system inefficiencies to boost overall performance.

- **Security Monitoring:** Detecting unusual activities that could signal security incidents.

- **Regulatory Compliance:** Ensuring systems adhere to relevant standards and facilitating necessary reporting protocols.

This strategy involves the aggregation and evaluation of data across all facets of IT infrastructure, encompassing applications, networks, servers, and security systems.

Core Aspects of a Comprehensive Monitoring Strategy

1. Real-Time Performance Monitoring

This involves the ongoing surveillance of vital system metrics to confirm operational norms are maintained. Metrics monitored include CPU usage, memory usage, disk activity, network bandwidth, and application response times.

Tools to Consider:

- **Nagios:** A robust tool for monitoring network services, server resources, and hosts.

- **Zabbix:** Capable of real-time monitoring of numerous metrics from diverse sources, including devices and applications.

Example of Real-Time Monitoring with Zabbix:

```
# Monitor CPU load
Host: Server1
Item: system.cpu.load[percpu,avg1]
Trigger: {Server1:system.cpu.load[percpu,avg1].last()} > 5
Action: Alert the system administrator
```

This example shows how Zabbix can monitor CPU load, issuing alerts when predefined thresholds are exceeded, allowing for swift administrative action.

2. Log Management and Analysis

Logs are invaluable for post-issue diagnostics and provide ongoing insights into the operational state of IT systems. Effective log management ensures that event logs are systematically collected, analyzed, and stored.

Relevant Tools:

- **ELK Stack (Elasticsearch, Logstash, Kibana):** Enables comprehensive log management from collection through to analysis and visualization.

- **Splunk:** Known for its robust data collection, indexing, and analytical visualizations pertaining to machine-generated data.

Log Analysis Using ELK Stack Example:

```
# Logstash configuration for system log processing
input {
  file {
    path => "/var/log/messages"
    type => "syslog"
  }
}
```

```
filter {
  grok {
    match => { "message" => "%{SYSLOGTIMESTAMP:timestamp} %{SYSLOGHOST:host}
        %{DATA:program}(?:\[%{POSINT:pid}\])?: %{GREEDYDATA:message}" }
  }
}
output {
  elasticsearch {
    hosts => ["localhost:9200"]
    index => "system-logs-%{+YYYY.MM.dd}"
  }
}
```

This configuration demonstrates how Logstash processes and forwards logs to Elasticsearch, where they are indexed daily for efficient analysis.

3. Network Traffic Analysis

Monitoring network traffic is essential for spotting potential security threats and identifying failures. Analysis of network packets helps administrators understand traffic flows and spot unusual patterns that could indicate issues.

Key Tools:

- **Wireshark:** This tool analyzes the contents of network frames in detail, which is crucial for troubleshooting complex issues.

- **SolarWinds Network Performance Monitor:** Offers extensive network performance monitoring capabilities, essential for maintaining robust network health.

4. Application Performance Management (APM)

APM is crucial for ensuring applications perform optimally and meet user expectations. These tools provide insights into application behavior, helping to trace issues down to the code level.

Recommended Tools:

- **Dynatrace:** Provides deep monitoring capabilities across the entire application stack.

- **AppDynamics:** Specializes in deep-dive diagnostics into application performance, enabling precise pinpointing of issues at the transaction level.

Conclusion

A well-structured monitoring strategy is vital for effective IT management, crucial for ensuring systems are reliable, performant, and secure. By integrating a comprehensive suite of monitoring tools that cover various IT infrastructure aspects—from logs and networks to applications and performance metrics—organizations can gain critical insights necessary for proactive management and continuous improvement of their IT environments. This holistic monitoring approach not only aids in swift issue resolution but also facilitates strategic planning and ongoing enhancements of IT operations.

Utilizing Logs and Metrics: Tools and practices for deep system insights

Harnessing logs and metrics is crucial for in-depth understanding and effective management of system performances and anomalies. These resources are vital for troubleshooting, optimizing performance, enhancing security, and ensuring compliance within IT operations. This article explores the various tools and methodologies necessary for effectively utilizing logs and metrics to derive extensive system insights, which aid in proactive management and strategic planning.

Significance of Logs and Metrics

Logs and metrics act as fundamental diagnostic tools, providing critical information that supports:

- **Issue Diagnostics:** Quick identification and rectification of problems.

- **Performance Tracking:** Ongoing observation of system performance, identifying trends and irregularities.

- **Security Monitoring:** Early detection of potential security threats.

- **Compliance Assurance:** Compliance with legal and regulatory standards through detailed auditing.

Properly managed logs and metrics enable comprehensive analysis of both historical and real-time data, facilitating predictive analytics and capacity planning.

Tools for Effective Management of Logs and Metrics

Selecting appropriate tools for managing logs and metrics depends on the specific needs such as the size of the infrastructure, the complexity of the systems, and the depth of insights required.

1. Log Management Tools

These tools are designed to aggregate, organize, and analyze log data from multiple sources, making it accessible and useful for deeper insights.

Key Log Management Tools:

- **ELK Stack (Elasticsearch, Logstash, Kibana):** This trio works together to enable effective searching, processing, and visualizing of log data. Elasticsearch indexes the data, Logstash processes it, and Kibana presents the data visually.

- **Splunk:** Offers advanced capabilities for collecting, indexing, and visualizing log data, helping uncover valuable insights from machine-generated data.

Configuration Example for ELK Stack:

```
# Configuration for Logstash to process and index system logs
input {
  file {
    path => "/var/log/*.log"
    start_position => "beginning"
  }
}
filter {
  grok {
    match => { "message" => "%{SYSLOGBASE}" }
  }
}
output {
  elasticsearch {
    hosts => ["http://localhost:9200"]
    index => "logs-%{+YYYY.MM.dd}"
  }
}
```

This setup enables Logstash to ingest and process system logs, sending them to Elasticsearch for indexing and further analysis.

2. Metrics Collection Tools

These tools focus on gathering and analyzing data points related to the performance of systems and applications.

Prominent Metrics Collection Tools:

- **Prometheus:** An open-source monitoring toolkit well-suited for recording real-time metrics in a time-series database.

- **Graphite:** Known for storing and rendering time-series data, Graphite facilitates real-time monitoring.

Sample Prometheus Configuration:

```
global:
  scrape_interval: 15s

scrape_configs:
  - job_name: 'example'
    static_configs:
      - targets: ['localhost:9090']
```

This Prometheus setup is configured to scrape metrics every 15 seconds, providing a consistent flow of performance data.

Best Practices for Logs and Metrics Utilization

1. Broad Scope Collection

It's critical to collect logs and metrics from all crucial system components to gain a comprehensive view of your IT infrastructure's health.

2. Real-Time Monitoring and Alerts

Setting up real-time monitoring with automated alerts is essential for swiftly identifying and addressing potential issues as they arise.

3. Advanced Data Analysis and Visualization

Leveraging advanced tools for data analysis and visualization can transform raw data into insightful, actionable information. Visual dashboards simplify the interpretation of complex datasets.

4. Secure Data Management

Ensure that logs and metrics are stored securely and access is strictly controlled to meet security and compliance requirements.

Conclusion

Effectively leveraging logs and metrics is vital for proactive IT infrastructure management. By employing advanced log and metrics management tools and adhering to best practices in data analysis, security, and real-time monitoring, organizations can significantly enhance their operational effectiveness and strategic decision-making. These efforts provide not only swift troubleshooting capabilities but also valuable insights for long-term system optimization and planning.

Chapter Fifteen

Case Studies and Lessons Learned

Analyzing Successful Implementations: What top companies are doing right

In the current competitive business landscape, the most successful companies stand out by meticulously enhancing their operational tactics and embracing progressive technologies. This discussion delves into the practices these leading firms employ effectively, providing a framework that can guide other organizations looking to emulate this success.

Prioritizing Customer-Centric Innovations

Top firms consistently put the customer at the forefront by developing solutions that significantly improve the user experience. This includes offering customized services, intuitive interfaces, and proactive support systems. Amazon, for example, has reshaped the retail space by focusing on customer satisfaction with features like rapid delivery, easy-to-navigate shopping interfaces, and personalized product suggestions.

Strategic Approach:

- **Data-Driven Customization:** Harnessing analytics to tailor products and interactions to individual customer preferences enhances engagement and builds loyalty.

446

```python
# Example Python script for customizing product recommendations using machine learning
import pandas as pd
from sklearn.cluster import KMeans

# Loading customer data
data = pd.read_csv('customer_purchases.csv')

# Clustering customers based on features to personalize recommendations
kmeans = KMeans(n_clusters=5)
data['cluster'] = kmeans.fit_predict(data[['age', 'total_spend']])

# Suggest products based on customer cluster
product_recommendations = data.groupby('cluster')['top_product'].agg(pd.Series.mode)
print(product_recommendations)
```

Embracing Digital Transformation

Successful organizations deeply embed digital transformation into their strategic initiatives. They leverage emerging technologies such as artificial intelligence, machine learning, and the Internet of Things (IoT) to enhance efficiency and reduce overhead costs. Nike, for instance, integrates AI to refine product designs and streamline supply chain operations, enhancing consumer engagement and operational efficiency.

Strategic Approach:

- **Integrating Automation and AI:** Employing automation and artificial intelligence not only streamlines processes but also improves decision-making and analytics.

447

```
# Python example for AI-driven decision-making in operations
import numpy as np
from sklearn.linear_model import LogisticRegression

# Example data points representing operational decisions
X = np.array([[1, 2], [2, 3], [3, 4], [4, 5]])
y = np.array([0, 1, 0, 1])

# Training a logistic regression model for predictive decision-making
model = LogisticRegression()
model.fit(X, y)

# Using the model to make decisions based on new data
decision_data = np.array([[2, 3], [3, 5]])
predictions = model.predict(decision_data)
print("Decisions based on new data:", predictions)
```

Implementing Agile Methodologies

Agility in project management and product development is a hallmark of leading companies. These firms use agile methodologies to swiftly adapt to changes and user feedback, supporting quick iterations and robust collaboration. Google's adoption of agile techniques facilitates its rapid innovation cycle, enabling timely updates to its products and services.

Strategic Approach:

- **Iterative Development with Continuous Feedback:** Adopting agile practices like Scrum or Kanban to foster rapid development cycles and continual integration of user feedback.

Ethical Operations and Sustainability

More than ever, successful companies recognize the importance of sustainability and ethical practices. Aligning with societal values not only enhances brand reputation but also meets the increasing consumer demand for responsible business practices. Patagonia's commitment to environmental sustainability and ethical operations deeply resonates with its customer base, strengthening brand loyalty.

Strategic Approach:

- **Sustainable Business Practices:** Integrating eco-friendly processes throughout the organization supports environmental sustainability and enhances corporate responsibility.

Conclusion

Exploring what successful companies do well uncovers several consistent strategies: focusing on customer-centric innovations, leveraging digital transformation, maintaining agility, and committing to ethical practices. By understanding and incorporating these approaches, other businesses can elevate their operational effectiveness and secure a competitive edge. This analysis serves as a roadmap for organizations aspiring to replicate the success of industry leaders, emphasizing the critical roles of adaptability, customer interaction, and ethical governance in achieving business excellence.

Learning from Complex Failures: Pitfalls and recovery strategies in high-profile API projects

In the sophisticated landscape of software development, particularly with high-profile API projects, learning from failures is as critical as celebrating successes. Such setbacks provide invaluable lessons that drive improvements and foster resilience in systems. This piece examines typical challenges encountered in API projects and discusses effective recovery strategies, serving as a blueprint for navigating and learning from these complex scenarios.

Typical Challenges in High-Profile API Projects

1. **Insufficient Initial Planning:** Many API projects falter due to a lack of rigorous upfront planning and poorly defined requirements. A well-defined scope and clear requirements are essential for the API to fulfill its intended functions effectively.

2. **Deficient API Design and Integration:** Ineffective API design can lead to significant issues such as poor modularity, overly complex interfaces, and integration difficulties with existing systems. These design flaws complicate maintenance and hinder scalability.

3. **Lapses in Testing and Quality Assurance:** Inadequate testing or incomplete coverage can leave critical bugs and security vulnerabilities undetected until after deployment, making them expensive and challenging to resolve.

4. **Security Shortcomings:** APIs are susceptible to security risks if they lack strong encryption, properly secured endpoints, and robust authentication and authorization controls, exposing sensitive data to potential breaches.

5. **Underestimated Scalability Needs:** Failing to anticipate the actual load and traffic can lead to scalability issues, negatively impacting performance and reliability when the API is most needed.

Strategies for Effective Recovery

1. **Detailed Post-Mortem Analysis:** Conducting a thorough examination after a failure is crucial. This involves dissecting what went wrong and why, to prevent future occurrences.

Framework for Post-Mortem Analysis:

```
## Post-Mortem for [API Project]
### Incident Details
 - **Description of the Incident**
 - **Timing and Duration**
 - **Stakeholders Involved**
 - **Impact on Operations**

### Analysis of Causes
 - **Technical Breakdowns**
 - **Process Inefficiencies**
 - **Contributions of Human Error**
```

```
### Extracted Lessons
 - **Insights Gained**
 - **Effective Recovery Measures**
 - **Identified Weaknesses**

### Corrective Measures
 - **Immediate Rectifications**
 - **Strategic Changes for Long-Term Improvements**
```

2. **Iterative Redesign and Testing:** Revising the API's architecture might be necessary to address fundamental design issues. This should involve best practices such as

451

creating clean, well-documented interfaces and building with scalability in mind.

Example of API Redesign for Improved Error Handling:

```javascript
// Refining an API endpoint to enhance error handling and user feedback
app.get('/api/items', async (req, res) => {
  try {
    const items = await fetchItems();
    res.json(items);
  } catch (error) {
    res.status(500).json({ error: 'Failed to retrieve items' });
  }
});
```

3. **Strengthening Security Measures:** Enhancing the security features of the API is imperative, including updating authentication methods, adding encryption, and tightening access controls.

Example of Implementing Enhanced Security:

```javascript
// Example of enhancing API security in a Node.js application
app.use((req, res, next) => {
  const token = req.headers['authorization'];
  if (token === 'expected_secure_token') {
    next();
  } else {
    res.status(403).json({ error: 'Unauthorized access' });
  }
});
```

4. **Optimizing for Performance:** Addressing performance shortfalls by optimizing existing code, better resource allocation, and implementing scalable architectures ensures the API can handle increased loads efficiently.

Example of Performance Optimization:

```python
# Using caching to reduce load times for frequently requested data
from flask import Flask
from flask_caching import Cache

app = Flask(__name__)
cache = Cache(app, config={'CACHE_TYPE': 'simple'})

@app.route('/api/popular')
@cache.cached(timeout=120)  # Cache the result for 120 seconds
def get_popular_items():
    return jsonify({"items": "List of popular items"})
```

Conclusion

Navigating the intricacies of high-profile API project failures involves identifying the root causes, applying lessons learned, and making strategic adjustments. By adopting a methodical approach to post-mortem analysis, redesigning APIs for resilience, bolstering security, and ensuring scalability, organizations can convert challenges into opportunities for growth and development. This continuous learning cycle is vital for mastering API project complexities and achieving sustained success.

Conclusion

Summarizing Advanced Concepts: Revisiting the key lessons and advanced strategies discussed

In the intricate domain of software development, mastering the advanced strategies of API design and management is crucial for technological and operational success. This review revisits essential teachings and methodologies that are central to sophisticated API management, aiming to consolidate these concepts into a comprehensive overview that highlights their significance and practical application.

Core Lessons in Advanced API Strategies

1. **Foundations of API Design:** Superior API design is critical and should adhere to well-established principles such as RESTful standards, which stress statelessness, separation of concerns between the client and server, and uniform interfaces. Proper API design ensures it is user-friendly, maintainable, and scalable.

Example: Crafting a RESTful API Endpoint

```python
from flask import Flask, jsonify, request

app = Flask(__name__)

@app.route('/api/users/<int:user_id>', methods=['GET'])
def get_user(user_id):
    user = fetch_user_by_id(user_id)  # Assume a function that retrieves user data
    if user:
        return jsonify(user), 200
    else:
        return jsonify({"error": "User not found"}), 404
```

2. **Robust API Security:** Security measures are paramount in API development. Techniques such as implementing OAuth for authentication, employing HTTPS for secure communications, and safeguarding against common threats are crucial for maintaining secure API endpoints.

Example: OAuth 2.0 Implementation for API Security

```python
from flask import Flask, request, jsonify
from flask_oauthlib.provider import OAuth2Provider

app = Flask(__name__)
oauth = OAuth2Provider(app)

@app.route('/api/data')
@oauth.require_oauth('data')
def data_api():
    return jsonify({'data': 'Secure data accessed'})
```

3. **Optimizing API Performance:** Performance optimization is key, particularly under high traffic conditions. Techniques like caching, asynchronous operations, and rate limiting are vital for improving throughput and minimizing latency.

Example: Caching in APIs

```python
from flask import Flask, jsonify
from flask_caching import Cache

app = Flask(__name__)
cache = Cache(app, config={'CACHE_TYPE': 'simple'})

@app.route('/api/resource')
@cache.cached(timeout=50)
def get_resource():
    result = intensive_computation()  # Assume an intensive computation function
    return jsonify(result)
```

4. **Scalability Practices:** Scalability is essential for APIs, especially those serving large-scale systems. Techniques like load balancing, database optimization, and microservices architecture facilitate scalable solutions that adapt to varying load conditions.

Example: SQL Indexing for Scalable Queries

```sql
CREATE INDEX idx_user_id ON users(user_id);
```

5. **Comprehensive Error Handling:** Effective error management enhances API reliability and user satisfaction. Implementing detailed error logging, standardized response formats, and proactive monitoring for irregularities are practices that contribute to robust error handling.

Example: Standardized API Error Handling

```python
@app.errorhandler(404)
def not_found_error(e):
    return jsonify(error=str(e)), 404
```

6. **Continuous Integration and Deployment:** Embracing CI/CD practices ensures APIs are continuously updated, tested, and deployed with minimal human intervention, maintaining high-quality standards and operational continuity.

Example: Configuring a CI/CD Pipeline

```
# Example GitLab CI/CD pipeline configuration
stages:
  - test
  - deploy

test_job:
  stage: test
  script: pytest

deploy_job:
  stage: deploy
  script: deploy_script.sh
  only:
    - master
```

Conclusion

Understanding and implementing advanced API strategies are indispensable for developers aiming to build robust, efficient, and secure APIs. This summary not only reaffirms the importance of these advanced concepts but also provides a framework for their practical application, ensuring that professionals in the field can build upon solid principles to manage and enhance their API solutions effectively. This structured recap serves as a guide for further exploration and proficiency in sophisticated API development and management.

Future Trends in API Design: Predictions and upcoming innovations

In today's fast-paced tech environment, APIs (Application Programming Interfaces) are crucial for enabling effective communication between diverse software platforms. Their design impacts everything from scalability to user interaction and integration capabilities. As technology progresses and user preferences evolve, a slew of emerging trends promises to revolutionize API design, pushing the boundaries of what these interfaces can achieve. This discussion highlights these trends, forecasting the innovations that are set to reshape API development and deployment.

1. The Rise of GraphQL

GraphQL's ability to allow developers to pull exactly what they need from a single request is making it a favored alternative to REST. Its adoption streamlines operations and cuts down on unnecessary data transfers, making it particularly advantageous for mobile apps and intricate systems.

Example: Crafting a GraphQL API

```javascript
const { graphql, buildSchema } = require('graphql');

// Constructing a GraphQL schema
const schema = buildSchema(`
  type Query {
    welcome: String
  }
`);

// Root resolver functions
const root = {
  welcome: () => 'Welcome to the API',
};

// Running a GraphQL query
graphql(schema, '{ welcome }', root).then((response) => {
  console.log(response);
});
```

2. Automated API Integration

The advancements in artificial intelligence and machine learning are paving the way for more automated API integrations. This trend is expected to reduce manual coding significantly, accelerate the integration process, and potentially lead to tools that can automatically generate API clients and documentation, thereby enhancing developer productivity.

3. AI-Enhanced API Security

Given the increasing sophistication of cyber threats, integrating AI and machine learning into API security frameworks is becoming a necessity. These technologies are adept at detecting unusual patterns that may indicate threats, allowing for immediate and automated security measures.

Example: Machine Learning for Detecting Anomalies in API Traffic

```python
from sklearn.ensemble import IsolationForest
import numpy as np

# Simulating API traffic data
data = np.array([[10], [12], [11], [21], [19], [17], [13], [23]])

# Isolation Forest model to detect anomalies
clf = IsolationForest(random_state=42)
clf.fit(data)

# Detecting a potential anomaly
is_anomaly = clf.predict([[100]])  # Anomalous traffic
print("Anomaly Detected" if is_anomaly[0] == -1 else "Normal")
```

4. Adoption of Event-Driven Architectures

As industries push towards real-time data processing and the Internet of Things (IoT), the adoption of event-driven architectures (EDAs) is increasing. APIs in these architectures react to specific events, facilitating immediate data handling and enabling swift decision-making processes.

5. Serverless Computing for API Deployment

Serverless computing is revolutionizing API deployment, allowing developers to focus on coding without server management. This model adapts seamlessly to varying loads, ensuring cost efficiency and eliminating the need for manual scaling.

6. Greater Regulation and Standardization

With increasing focus on data security and privacy, more stringent API standards and compliance regulations are expected to be implemented, particularly in sectors dealing with sensitive information. These standards aim to boost security, enhance reliability, and ensure transparency.

Conclusion

The future of API design is marked by smarter, more efficient, and more secure methodologies. Innovations like GraphQL, AI in security, serverless computing, and automated integrations are steering this transformation, promising to enhance the way businesses utilize and benefit from APIs. As these trends mature, they will undoubtedly set new benchmarks in API development, ensuring more robust and innovative digital ecosystems.

Continuing Professional Development: Resources and pathways for ongoing learning and expertise enhancement

In today's swiftly changing technology sector, continuous professional development (CPD) is critical for IT professionals aiming to stay relevant and excel in their careers. CPD involves actively maintaining and enhancing one's knowledge and skills through a variety of educational paths and experiences. This discussion outlines the key resources and methods available for ongoing learning and skill enhancement, providing insights into how professionals can continue to develop their expertise in the field of technology.

Overview of CPD

CPD is an ongoing process that encompasses a range of educational and practical experiences designed to foster career growth and skill proficiency. This development can be achieved through formal coursework, informal learning practices, or direct professional experiences, with the goal of not just maintaining but elevating a professional's capability to deliver high-quality services.

Formal Academic Courses and Certification Programs

Formal education and professional certifications are traditional and highly structured paths to CPD. Many universities and specialized institutions offer relevant courses and certification programs that validate expertise in specific technical areas or methodologies.

Example:

- **Certified Information Systems Security Professional (CISSP)**: This is a key certification for professionals in the cybersecurity arena, highlighting the critical nature of security within IT infrastructures.

Online Educational Platforms

The proliferation of online educational platforms has opened up new avenues for flexible, self-paced learning. Platforms such as Coursera, Udemy, and Pluralsight offer extensive courses on a wide range of topics, from introductory programming to complex data science and machine learning techniques.

Code Example:

```python
# Example Python script for a beginner's machine learning course
from sklearn import datasets
from sklearn.svm import SVC

# Load sample data
iris = datasets.load_iris()
X, y = iris.data, iris.target

# Fit a SVM model
model = SVC()
model.fit(X, y)

# Display predictions
print("Class Predictions:", model.predict(X))
```

Engaging in Workshops, Seminars, and Technical Conferences

Participation in workshops, seminars, and industry conferences is invaluable for CPD. These events not only offer exposure to the latest industry trends and technologies but also provide networking opportunities with other professionals and experts.

Example:

- **AWS re**

: This conference is a prime venue for IT professionals to learn about new AWS technologies and best practices in cloud architecture from the foremost experts.

Networking and Peer Learning

Engaging with peers through networking and professional groups offers practical insights and shared learning opportunities. This informal style of learning is driven by real-world applications and problem-solving.

Project-Based Learning and Practical Application

Hands-on experience through engaging in new projects or roles is critically important for deepening skills. Practical application of theoretical knowledge in real-world scenarios enhances understanding and expertise.

Example:

- **Contributing to Open Source Projects**: Active participation in projects on platforms like GitHub can significantly enhance coding skills and software development understanding.

```
# Command line example for engaging with an open source project
git clone https://github.com/someopensource/project.git
cd project
```

Self-Guided Learning

In IT, self-guided learning is crucial due to the field's breadth and depth. Professionals often pursue learning new technologies or programming languages independently, using online tutorials and resource guides.

Example:

- **Studying Blockchain Technology**: Self-studying blockchain by using online resources, forums, and practical blockchain development kits.

Conclusion

Continuing Professional Development is essential in the IT field, encompassing a range of structured and informal methods to keep professionals knowledgeable and skilled. From formal courses and certifications to hands-on project work and independent study, the avenues for continuing education in technology are diverse and expansive. By committing to CPD, IT professionals can ensure they remain at the forefront of their field, equipped to handle emerging technologies and complex challenges in their professional careers. This ongoing investment in personal and professional growth is indispensable for those looking to advance and succeed in the ever-evolving tech landscape.